T0275031

DON'T BUY Fruit & Veg WITHOUT ME!

THE FRUIT NERD (THANH TRUONG)

Contents

Introduction

Hi, I'm Thanh, a second-generation fruiterer better known as the 'Fruit Nerd', and I'm here to help everyone have better fruit and vegetable experiences!

The stories, tips, recipes and information in this book are the culmination of my many years as an industry insider, as well as a passionate purchaser and consumer of fresh produce. Many other experts from the world of fruit and veg have also generously shared their knowledge in these pages.

This book is for everyone who buys fresh produce – whether from a supermarket or a farmers' market – and I'm thrilled it's made its way into your life. I live by the mantra that 'good food starts with good produce', and I hope you will too after reading my book!

Why me?

MY CHILDHOOD EXPERIENCES

I grew up in the 90s with my parents as fruiterers, so I enjoyed wonderful fruit and vegetables when I was young. This means I know what good* fruit and veg should taste like, as opposed to anyone born from the 90s onwards, who have generally grown up with the more commoditised produce we know today and – through no fault of their own – accept mediocre flavour and don't expect more.
*'Good' is a subjective term, see page 8.

LUCK OF BEING A SECOND-GENERATION FRUITERER

Fruiterers are the hardest-working people I know. We wake up when everyone is asleep, work the entire day, and then have to do it all over again, seven days a week! As a second-generation fruiterer, I am in a privileged position. I have the industry connections and a sense of belonging, plus all the learnings from my parents' struggles.

MY PROFESSIONAL EXPERIENCE

I grew up in a fruit shop, stacking fruit and learning the tricks of store displays, stock turnover and retail magic. I've worked in the head office at Australia's second-largest supermarket chain, purchasing millions of dollars' worth of fruit, organising promotions, dealing with produce specifications, packaging, pricing and liaising with farmers. I've imported and exported fruit. I've been the agent representing hundreds of Australian farmers selling their fruit. I've been part of fresh produce industry bodies and wholesale market boards and have advised farmers' markets and local councils.

And I am a consumer. My understanding of the industry across the entire supply chain allows me to deduce what and where fruit and vegetables go wrong and what to do to improve it.

MY CONNECTIONS AND NETWORK

Fruiterers have a particular set of skills – they know how to display and handle produce impeccably; they know what their customers want and have good general knowledge about most of the produce they sell. But most can't tell you things like why that nectarine has a rubbery texture, or why mushrooms should be stored in a paper bag.

My broader experience in the industry has given me access to the full range of professionals who live and breathe fresh produce every day. I have almost unlimited access to specialists across the supply chain, making up hundreds of years of experience, who can answer my questions in a technical and matter-of-fact way.

MY FRUIT TRAVELS

I've travelled extensively for work, from fruit shops in Brazil and jungles in Indonesia to industry conferences in Germany and markets all around the world. I don't just see bananas as a snacking fruit with yellow skin; I understand that some communities wait for banana skins to turn black before eating or use green plantain bananas in a savoury dish. Most fruit and vegetables overlap in some way and often the learnings from one can help the other.

MY FOOD VOICE

I've heard so many memorable personal and professional stories from my father over the years in our meetings with farmers and suppliers. His storytelling prowess has always influenced me, but I never thought about it in great detail until I decided to try it for myself. I've always said that I need to distil 40 years of my father's mango knowledge into four minutes, and if I can do that, then the art of fruit and vegetable storytelling might actually be exciting!

Studying a Masters of Food Systems and Gastronomy helped develop my food voice and my ability to distil complex technical information into bite-sized gems. How often have we had delicious fruit but not been able to describe what makes it good? Describing the 'good' is so important because it allows us to communicate our preferences to others.

Ultimately, I would love fruit descriptions to get to the state where we are talking about fruit terroir. This is a wine-industry concept used to explain why the exact same varietal of fruit tastes different when grown in different areas, due to the soil, the weather, the sun and other elements. For now, I'd be happy if the fresh produce industry just focused on labelling the correct varietal and its specific flavour differences! That would go a long way in helping us make good decisions when choosing fruit and vegetables.

WHY THIS BOOK?

In many ways, this book represents my hope, vision and goal for the entire fresh produce industry. For too long, the industry has focused on aesthetics, shelf life, value and convenience, but at what cost? Teaching consumers how to pick good produce will create demand for delicious-tasting fruit and veg, shift the dial for how farmers grow produce, and inevitably lead to greater consumption of fruit and vegetables.

Whether you are a parent purchasing fruit and vegetables for your children's lunchbox, a chef getting the produce ready for service, or a gardener growing produce for home, this book will help you eat more deliciously than ever before. Good food belongs to everybody, and good food starts with good produce.

A history lesson

We need to know about our past to understand how we got to where we are today – and where we are heading into the future. This is evident in the fresh produce industry, where things have changed drastically in the last 50 years. The way we shop now is vastly different from how our grandparents did.

THE POWER TO CHOOSE

A century ago, most people ate whatever fresh produce could be grown locally, and only when it was in season. Most people purchased from local farmers or markets, so the connection to the land, the grower and the produce was very much alive.

About half a century ago, in the 1970s, the exponential development of turning fresh produce into a commodity began. Led by the beginning of the supermarket revolution, consumers were allowed, for the first time, to select their own produce instead of having it chosen for them by the shopkeeper. Produce no longer became a thing someone sold to us and advised us about, but rather it was left on the shelf for us to select without advice or objectivity; in essence, the produce had to sell itself. Most of us, myself included, have never known any other way, so understanding this shift in the way we purchase produce can help explain the changes both supermarkets and farmers have made in the last 50 years.

IT MUST LOOK PERFECT

Produce that needs to sell itself on the shelf has to look beautiful and appeal to the eye. Without the opportunity to ask a trader what to purchase, the first sense we use when engaging with produce is our eyes, and so we begin to over-rely on this mode to make our selection. Over time, our biases led to delicious produce with imperfect shapes and skins becoming undesirable for traders or supermarkets, as they often had to throw out this unsold produce at the end of the day. Our over-reliance on aesthetic appeal is human behaviour which we, the consumer, demand, and the supermarkets, in turn, demand farmers grow and grade produce to supply us with what we demand: perfect-looking fruit and vegetables.

OUR BUSY LIVES

Have you ever wondered why apples and bananas dominate our shopping bags and are always at the front section when we walk into a fruit shop or supermarket? That's because they both suit our modern lives perfectly. The apple, for example, is very convenient; it doesn't require a knife or any preparation, it can be carried easily and eaten on the run, and it can be left in the fridge for weeks. Think about the last time you grabbed a pomegranate over an apple when heading into work – probably never!

CHANGING OUR EXPECTATIONS

Our food system has trained us to expect constant availability and low prices, and changes to this are seen as unacceptable. We have certain vegetables all year round at the same price, so restaurants can charge the same price for the same meal year-round too. We are not immune to the opinions around us, but we can try to think more clearly. We must retrain ourselves to not expect produce whenever we want it because this is unrealistic. Fruit and vegetables are living things, and by seeing them as commodities, we further distance ourselves from the farm.

EFFICIENT GROWING VS FLAVOUR

With rising living costs, the retail price is one of the main reasons consumers decide whether or not to purchase a fruit or vegetable. A few years ago, Jason Cooper, the head of Fresh State, the Australian market representative body that tracks produce prices every week for the industry, showed me the wholesale price of tomatoes in 1990 versus 2020. The prices were almost identical 30 years later, yet according to the Reserve Bank of Australia, the inflation for a basket of goods over the last 30 years has jumped 103 per cent – more than doubled! The costs of producing food – fertiliser, water, power, transport, fuel, machinery and labour – have all increased. As lowering production costs is impossible, today's farmers have to focus all their energies on efficiencies on the farm to keep the supermarket price constant. That means choosing varieties that yield more fruit on the tree and are most resistant to disease, pests and weather. It also means more machinery is used to help grow, pick, grade and pack, which means fruit often needs hardier skin or is picked at a hard, firm stage, so they don't easily bruise with machinery handling. These factors usually mean flavour is not at the forefront of selecting fruit, which is to our detriment.

WHY PACKAGING WILL TAKE OVER

Packaging serves many purposes in the supermarket: think barcodes for correct scanning and pricing, labels for marketing and differentiation, punnets to prevent bruising and net bags for grab-and-go. It also helps increase shelf life for the retail store and for us, the consumer, by preventing food waste, which is always a balancing act.

A downside is that packaging, in some ways, hinders our ability to smell produce; it distorts our view and sometimes doesn't allow us to see if there is damage in the fruit. But it can also help us pick a better product – for example, tight cling wrap on a cut pumpkin or watermelon indicates freshness.

Given how important packaging is for supermarkets, and knowing it is here to stay, makes it even more crucial to develop sustainable packaging in the future.

HOW DOES THIS HISTORY HELP US?

Knowing how the fresh produce industry has changed over the last half a century gives us insight into why fruit and vegetables look, smell and feel the way they do today. It shows us what senses to use, and how to use them, to select the best produce we can. Whether at a fruit shop, a farmers' market or a supermarket, the tips in this book will help when you are confronted with a selection dilemma and need cut-through advice on the best choice for whatever fruit or vegetable you want to purchase. Remember that, deep down, you may no longer be a hunter, but you are still a gatherer ... and good food starts with good produce!

What *is* good produce?

The produce most of us buy has been selected based on aesthetics, shelf life, convenience, availability, price and packaging for multiple reasons. Certainly, all of these things help create 'good' produce, but what is often forgotten is that most important factor – taste.

Think of taste as a multiplier effect. If the fruit or vegetable tastes good, we will have a great experience eating it and want to return for more. 'Good' to me means many things, and 'taste' is very complex and often subjective, so let me break down what I look for in a good-tasting fruit and how I define flavour.

THE TRIFECTA OF POWER = AROMA, TEXTURE, FLAVOUR

We all have our subjective tastes, but in my opinion, the three factors below are the best way to determine whether or not something tastes good. Think about your favourite fruit: does it hit all three?

Aroma – The smell we inhale as we approach the fruit and bring it closer to our nose, the flavour when the fruit is in our mouth and the aftertaste or smell in our mouth after we have swallowed the fruit. Nature has made these aromas and flavours by combining hundreds of volatiles in the fruit. Descriptions are unique as every fruit, even every varietal, has its own unique aroma.

Texture – The feel of the fruit in our hand, the firmness of the initial bite, the density of the fruit that informs its description – creamy, juicy, granular, watery, sticky or firm. The consistency or changing textures of the fruit, from the skin to the core. The mouthfeel includes the sensation of the flesh around your mouth, on your tongue and through your teeth (i.e., stringiness, tannins, oiliness).

Flavour – This is all about intensity and balance. Our tongue sensations are spicy, peppery, sweet, bitter and sour. Intensity refers to its sourness: does it make us cry or does it cut through the sweetness and provide balance? Balance refers to whether or not similar flavours are in harmony and not taking over from each other – for example, if an orange is watery and sweet but isn't sour, and therefore somewhat bland; or conversely, if it's too sour and not sweet enough. We often find things sweet but without much flavour because they lack intensity and balance. The best fruits have what I call 'sweet umami', which is the balance of intense sweet and sour notes (or other notes, such as bitterness and tang). When sweet umami is achieved, I describe the sensation as 'moreishness' – not being able to physically stop eating the fruit because it tastes so good!

Fruit vs vegetable

It's an age-old debate: what produce should be classified as a fruit and what as a vegetable? It's pretty simple, as this quick history lesson shows.

BOTANICAL DESCRIPTION: SEED VS NO SEED

A century ago, we went by the botanical description. Fruit must be produced by a woody stem shrub or tree with a seed or seeds. Vegetables must be a plant with soft stems. In this description, tomatoes and cucumbers are technically fruit.

MODERN DESCRIPTION: SNACKING VS COOKING

Primarily influenced by supermarkets, this is how fruit and vegetables are arranged in store. Supermarkets group sweet, convenient snacking produce as fruit, as opposed to produce we need to process, cut, cook or mix in a salad as vegetables. In this case, tomatoes, which are predominantly cooked in savoury dishes, and cucumbers, commonly used in salads, are classified as vegetables. Remember that most Australians shop for produce in supermarkets, so the way supermarkets categorise fruit and vegetables generally dictates our expectations as to what goes where.

How to store for better taste and less waste

Knowing how and where to store your fruit and vegetables at home is arguably the single most important thing you can do to eat better-tasting produce and prevent food waste. There are plenty of spots for optimal storage: the fridge (with all its different climactic zones), the dining table, the kitchen bench, a dark, cool place or a spot with a stable temperature night and day.

Fruiterers play an important role in making sure our community knows how to handle produce once it's left the shop. Although it's in the best financial interests of the industry sell more fruit and vegetables, regardless of the waste that happens further down the supply chain in our homes, I would argue that a poor eating experience due to over-buying and incorrect storage leads to lost sales. Here are my top tips for getting the most out of your fresh produce!

WHAT GOES WHERE IN THE FRIDGE?

Every part of the fridge has different airflow and every fridge is different! Knowing where the airflow comes out in your fridge is important as this area is generally the coldest part – up to 5°C colder than the fridge door compartments.

My general rule is that any fresh produce in the fridge needs to be eaten within a week, otherwise it will start to deteriorate regardless of the storage method you use. In addition to this, produce should be purchased and consumed fresh – ideally you should buy produce for the next two or three days; I wouldn't purchase produce you will need to keep for more than a week.

Given all of the different ways produce can be stored in the fridge, I almost never place naked produce on a shelf – even a zucchini or cucumber left bare for a day in the fridge can wrinkle and become less texturally appealing. Here is a quick guide to the different fridge zones.

- **The crisper:** This is where the temperature remains more constant, as when the fridge door opens and warm air rushes in, the air inside the crisper remains the same. As such, fruits that can handle and require the coldest temperatures, such as apples, should be kept here.

- **The shelves:** A lot of vegetables and herbs are mostly made up of water. This means that storing them naked in a fridge, which has constantly circulating air, will dry them out, particularly leafy vegetables and fresh herbs. These types of produce should be placed in a container or plastic bag and wrapped in a wet towel to keep humidity high and prevent moisture loss. Some fruits, such as mandarins or strawberries, also need to be shielded from the wind tunnel that is the fridge by being kept in a plastic bag or container, as they can dry out very quickly. The top and bottom shelves in your fridge may vary in temperature – I find the bottom shelf a touch colder than the top, but this might not be the same for your fridge. Find out what's happening in your fridge by storing two of the same fruit on each shelf; see which one holds up better (and maybe test the temperature if you can).

- **The fridge door:** This is the area with the most fluctuating temperatures so I would avoid placing any produce here. The only exception is if you live in an extremely hot climate, in which case I suggest temporarily placing climacteric fruit here to prevent them from ripening too quickly on the bench. Only do this for one or two days, then eat them immediately as all fruit and vegetables dislike constantly changing temperatures.

FRUIT BOWL VS FRUIT PLATES

My first piece of advice? Step away from your fruit bowl! Displaying fruit in an overflowing bowl has been a sign of wealth and abundance since Roman times. As well as being aesthetically pleasing, the continued use of the fruit bowl is linked to the idea that it subconsciously increases fruit consumption by being ever-present as we walk past it. However, the fact that households waste up to 30 per cent of food suggests the fruit bowl isn't having a big impact on fruit and vegetable waste.

Certain fruits – called non-climacteric, meaning they do not continue to ripen after harvesting – should always be stored in the fridge and never in a fruit bowl. For example, cherries will lose their firm bite if stored at room temperature and will shrivel over time, while apples will dehydrate and lose their crispy edge, especially near the skin. Fruits that do need to be stored at room temperature to continue ripening, such as bananas, mangoes and avocados, are called climacteric. I recommend using several fruit plates rather than one fruit bowl to prolong the shelf life of these fruits. Having all your climacteric fruits in the same bowl can lead to them ripening at a quicker speed, which often leads to waste. Fruit ripening is not a linear process, but often exponential. Once the fruit in the bowl is set off, they generally all ripen at the same time, which means you will most likely need to eat a lot of fruit in a short space of time.

As fruits ripen, they emit the gas ethylene at the same time as absorbing the ethylene produced by surrounding fruits. Therefore, the more ripe fruits you have in the bowl, the faster everything else will ripen. Using multiple flat fruit plates rather than one deep fruit bowl can help reduce the speed of ripening by preventing the build-up of ethylene around the fruit. Given that avocados, bananas and mangoes have already begun their ripening process in the supply chain, not in your home, these fruits will ripen very fast on their own on your kitchen bench at room temperature – they certainly don't need help from other fruits in the same bowl. By using two or three fruit plates set away from each other, say on the opposite ends of a kitchen bench, you can slow down the ripening process by one to three days, giving you more time to enjoy each piece of fruit as it reaches its most delicious state.

Separating fruit on multiple plates doesn't just help to slow down fruit ripening, it can also help you better control what fruits you want speed up and ripen. If you want to eat a firm avocado or hard stone fruit within a day or two, you can place it next to a more ripe fruit on the same plate; it will absorb the ethylene the ripe fruit is emitting and start ripening faster. If you want to speed things up further, place these fruits in a paper bag and then back on the plate to trap all the ethylene.

WHAT TO STORE WHERE

Kitchen bench:
- Avocados
- Bananas and plantains
- Guavas
- Jackfruit
- Mangoes
- Mangosteens
- Melons
- Pears (if you like them soft and ripe)
- Pineapple
- Red papaya
- Stone fruit
- Tomatoes

Dark, dry, cool place:
- Garlic (away from onions)
- Onions (away from garlic!)
- Potatoes
- Pumpkin
- Sweet Potatoes
- Watermelon (uncut)

Fridge, anywhere:
- Berries (in punnets)
- Coconuts
- Pomelos

Fridge, fully covered (in plastic bag or container):
- Apples
- Capsicums
- Cherries
- Chokos
- Cut watermelon (plastic wrapped)
- Eggplants
- Ginger
- Grapes
- Jujubes
- Lettuce
- Lychees
- Mandarins
- Nashi
- Oranges
- Pears (if you like them crunchy and firm)
- Pomegranate
- Zucchini

Fridge, covered, with breathing hole or wet towel:
- Asparagus (cover tops of spears)
- Bitter melons
- Broccoli/ broccolini and other brassicas
- Gourds
- Kale
- Leafy greens
- Mushrooms (preferably in a paper bag)
- Snow peas/snow pea tendrils
- Soft-leaf herbs
- Water spinach

FRUIT PLATES GIVE YOU MORE TIME TO ENJOY EACH FRUIT.

From Adam and Eve to keeping the doctor away, the apple is one of the most ubiquitous fruits in the world. Certainly over the last few centuries, the apple reigned as the most popular fruit in Europe, with arguably only the banana joining it as the two most consumed fruit snacks in the world. It's an icon, quite literally. Even the computer I'm writing this on is called an apple and my daughter points to the logo on my mobile phone and says 'apple!'.

Many of us love apples, and the study of why we love them is simple. They're convenient: we can carry them in our bags, they keep for days, and we can eat them whenever we want without any prepping. Modern apples are very sweet and the perfectly designed snack. Even before modern refrigeration technology, apples could be stored in a cool place and still be edible months after harvesting, making them a highly sought-after crop to grow. There's a lot to love about this fruit, but I argue that, today, they are too perfect and this has led to a decline in appeal.

Apples are convenient: we can carry them in our bags, they keep for days, and we can eat them whenever we want without any prepping.

Out with the old, in with the new

Apples are wondrous things, but the sweet snack we know today didn't always taste that way. While we now have between five and ten varietals to commonly choose from, in the past there were many more, but most didn't taste as delightful or as consistent. Tart braeburns that held their texture brilliantly were my favourite apple to use in apple pie, but they are no longer commercially grown, as most of us prefer apples as a snack rather than cooked. The modern granny smith is the last of the so-called 'cooking apple' varieties that are more sour than sweet, and that's because of the granny smith's versatility. For every fuji, golden delicious and royal gala, as well as new varieties such as jazz, pink lady, bravo, cosmic crisp and so on that gets ranged, an older variety is usually discontinued to make way for new apples. Today's apples are a curated list with snacking traits such as crunchy bite, sweet and tangy, and bold skin colours. From a production perspective, most of today's apples are also selected for their high yields and resistance to disease.

Centuries ago, apples were more like a random bunch of varieties, all with different traits and mostly very tart or astringent. Decade by decade this has changed to become the largely snacking range we see today.

Long-life apples

This brings me to arguably the most important aspect of the apple: how are they available 12 months of the year? You might be surprised to know that modern advancement in cold storage has allowed some apple cultivars to be stored for up to 13 months in a 'controlled atmosphere room'. My good friend Chris Fairless from Kyabram Cold Storage has worked in the apple industry for most of his life and his facility stores more than 25 million apples! Chris uses technology whereby apples are stored in rooms with 20 times less oxygen than the outside air. The oxygen is replaced with nitrogen and there's a carbon capture to absorb the carbon dioxide the apples release as they breathe. This process slows the respiration of the apples and prolongs their storage condition for up to 13 months, depending on the variety.

Developed in the 1990s, the most famous technology for prolonging the cold storage of apples and other produce is called SmartFresh. Prior to this, apples were only available three to four months of the year.

What did year-round supply do to apples? Firstly, it led to an increased production and consumption of the fruit, but secondly the romance of a seasonal apple was lost and, in some circumstances, poor apple experiences were had. I want to focus on these poor experiences because I don't want you to have them.

My first tip is to know that apples are harvested in autumn, so the fruit will always taste best around this time. Dr Mala Gamage, a fruit post-harvest scientist at CSIRO, is a good friend who has clarified some of the potential nutrient losses found in apples stored for long periods. Mala says that research shows most apples lose almost no nutrients after nine months of

storage, if stored correctly. While this is great news, it does mean that for the last three months of an apple's storage cycle, it might experience some loss in nutrition. For me, though, it's always about the eating experience.

Do apples still taste good after three, six, nine or 12 months in cold storage? The short answer is yes; the long answer is there are more chances of a poor apple experience the longer it is stored. The texture of the apple tends to get less crispy, and in some cases the apple can sweeten slightly, but that's only because it wasn't picked at its maximum sweetness to begin with. No apple grower will ever argue that an apple stored for 12 months is going to taste the same as one that is just picked, but you could argue there is no difference in the eating experience within the first six months of cold storage, depending on the varietal. Beyond this, I recommend only buying what you need to eat that day or the next, as apples can deteriorate much faster after an extended time in cold storage.

In short, if you're eating an apple in autumn and winter, you're almost guaranteed an abundance of variety and a good eating experience.

Given their incredible consistency, the unquantifiable truth about apples being available year-round is that they aren't always our first-choice fruit. Apples and bananas are steadfast fruit that will always be there; they're often the fruit we see in corporate fruit boxes, being given free to kids at supermarkets, consistently offered on restaurant menus and always in lunchboxes. The unintended consequence of being so consistent is that the romantic notion of 'ephemeral availability' and the urgency to buy when it's in season is lost. If you think about the summertime, when apples are on their last legs in terms of shelf life, they need to compete with summer mangoes, melons, berries and stone fruit. For me, personally, it's not the first fruit I select during this time. I feel that we take it for granted that apples are always there when we want them. It's beauty turned commodity and I challenge you to be appreciative whenever you eat a great apple, and think about why it's the case whenever you have a poor one.

TO GET THE MOST APPLE FLAVOUR AND AROMA WHEN COOKING, MIX GRANNY SMITHS WITH OTHER VARIETALS TO ACHIEVE NATURAL SWEET AND SOUR FLAVOURS. THIS MEANS LESS SUGAR NEEDS TO BE ADDED.

FLAT-BOTTOMED FUJI APPLES HAVE MATURED LATER AND WILL BE SWEETER AND MORE COMPLEX.

PEAK-BOTTOMED FUJIS ARE LESS SWEET AS THEY'RE NOT AS MATURE.

Fuji apple tips

While selecting an apple can be difficult, given its complex post-harvest treatment and varietal nuances, there is one magnificent tip that I received from Mr Ren Jie, a specialist fuji apple grower in Shandong, China. While many countries grow apples, it's interesting to note that China produces more than 50 per cent of the world's crop, with most of their growing methods coming from Japan, mixed with their own experience.

Fuji apples are widely grown throughout the world as they are intensely sweet and sour – their tartness is unique in that it's complementary to the sweet aroma, instead of acidic. Mr Ren explained that whenever he walks through his orchards he can tell when fuji apples are reaching peak maturity by looking at their base. Most apples have a rugged and point-peaked base where the remnants of the flower are – often you might see one or two hairs still hanging out from this spot. When the fuji grows and its flesh expands, it flattens at the base. These flat-bottomed apples taste magnificent and have complex flavours, but are generally higher in sugar content and have a shorter shelf life. So if you're looking for the sweetest fuji apple, look at its bottom. Other varieties of apple have their own traits and some of their bottoms don't flatten, so use this tip exclusively for fuji apples or their variants.

What's next?

The world of apples is fascinating and continues to change. What I am most excited for is smaller snacking apples that are the size of apricots, and new varieties that challenge old-world varietals. My hope is for more fit-for-purpose apples, specifically for cooking. This might be wishful thinking, but I know that trends come and go. Regardless, I hope this inspires you to try different apples as they come along every autumn.

Choose

FUJI APPLES: flat-bottomed fujis show late maturity and can taste 5–20 per cent sweeter than fujis with a peaked base, with a more complex flavour.

BACKYARD APPLES: fully ripe backyard apples should be firm but not too hard. A ripe apple will come off the tree easily when twisted and not pulled off the branch, compared to one that isn't fully ripe.

OTHER VARIETALS: it's hard to tell when most apple varietals will taste good, given their long storage. Generally speaking, you shouldn't have a poor eating experience within the first three months of harvest. Beyond that, good cold storage should have almost no affect on fruit flavour and texture for the next six months. Depending on the varietal, some apples will last even longer. Use your instincts: look at the skin, and feel if the fruit is soft and not firm.

Prep

To get the most apple flavour and aroma when cooking, mix granny smiths with other varietals to achieve natural sweet and sour flavours. This means less sugar needs to be added.

Eat an apple in autumn and winter and you're almost guaranteed an abundance of variety and a good eating experience.

My two favourite apple pies are Willie Smith's apple pie in the Huon Valley, Tasmania, and szarlotka (Polish apple cake), inspired predominantly by Anna Allison's version at The Lion and Buffalo cafe in South Coogee. This recipe is a combination of the two.

This dish is best made at the start of the apple season, around May, when all of the varietals are available. If you're buying apples in January, you'll most likely be using fruit that has been stored for ten months and, according to my information, some apples start to deteriorate in flavour and texture after six months of cold storage. I also suggest using two varieties for this pie: a firm sour apple, such as granny smith or braeburn, for the majority of the filling; and then a sweeter variety, such as red delicious or royal gala, for a different flavour profile.

POLISH APPLE CAKE

SZARLOTKA

SERVES 12

2 kg sour green apples
1 kg sweet red apples
5 teaspoons ground cinnamon
1 teaspoon five-spice powder
1 teaspoon sea salt

PIE BASE
450 g (3 cups) plain flour
250 g cold unsalted butter, roughly chopped
3 teaspoons baking powder
1 teaspoon vanilla essence
5 egg yolks

MERINGUE
5 egg whites
230 g (1 cup) caster sugar

Preheat the oven to 160°C (fan-forced).

Slice the apples in half, then remove the core and 5 mm from the top and base of each half. Cut the apple halves into 3 mm thick slices.

In a large saucepan over medium heat, add the apple, cinnamon, five-spice powder and salt, and cook, stirring occasionally, for 10 minutes, until the apple is slightly softened but still semi-firm. Set aside to cool.

For the pie base, in a bowl, combine the flour, butter, baking powder and vanilla essence and use your fingers to rub the butter into the flour mixture. Add a little cold water, if needed, to help bring the dough together. Set aside 100 g of the mixture in another bowl, then add the egg yolks to the remaining dough and mix to combine.

Press the pie base mixture firmly and evenly into the base and side of a 24 cm springform cake tin. Arrange a layer of the apple slices over the base of the dough without overlapping, then repeat this process, adding more layers, until the apple is used up.

To make the meringue, beat the egg whites using a stand mixer with the whisk attached or with electric beaters for about 4 minutes, until you have soft peaks. Slowly add the caster sugar, a tablespoon at a time, and continue to beat for another 4 minutes, until stiff peaks form. Spoon the meringue on top of the apple to completely cover, then crumble the reserved dough over the meringue. Transfer to the oven and bake for 1 hour or until the crumbs are crispy and golden but the meringue is still creamy underneath.

Set aside to cool, then remove from the tin, cut into slices and serve. Any leftovers will keep in an airtight container in the fridge for 1–2 days.

Growing up in an Asian household, Mum didn't cook much asparagus, although she would occasionally stir-fry it. Asparagus is one of the most convenient vegetables to cook, as it is sold uniformly in shape and size, meaning every spear cooks evenly the whole way through.

I met Mick Motta at the Melbourne Wholesale Fruit Market. His family has been growing produce for decades; they are the largest grower of asparagus in Australia, and each year they grow 140 million individual spears! Mick certainly knows a thing or two about this prized vegetable, and I have visited his farm and packing shed several times to see the family's impressive facilities in action. One of the behind-the-scenes operations that amazed me was the speed at which the asparagus is separated according to size through the machines, and then shipped to different markets, all of which appreciate and use the sizes differently. For instance, XXL asparagus, which is as thick as a fat permanent marker, is often exported and sold to fine-dining restaurants as they are more versatile (can be peeled) and have a slightly longer shelf life. Mini asparagus, which is pencil thin, is sold domestically due to its short shelf life, but is valued for its fibreless and almost stringless texture – it is best eaten raw, if you ask me!

Asparagus is one of the most convenient vegetables to cook. It's sold uniformly in shape, meaning every spear cooks evenly.

Green vs white asparagus

White asparagus is grown and harvested underground, much like digging for potatoes. As the asparagus skin is never exposed to sunlight, photosynthesis never takes place, so the skin remains white. This process of growing vegetables in partial or complete absence of sunlight is called 'etiolation', and it can be achieved with other vegetables, including chives, chicory and kale. These are vegetables that grow in the dark rather than glow in the dark!

Green asparagus tends to have a mild, but delightful, bitter flavour caused by the development of green chlorophyll through the process of photosynthesis, while white asparagus is prized for its more mellow and nutty notes. I have found that white asparagus (grown in tunnels) is juicier, and the skin is more tender as the spears haven't had to grow a thick skin to defend themselves from the harsh elements of the sun, wind and rain.

When I visited Mick's farm, the other thing that blew my mind was learning how white asparagus is grown and harvested in Europe versus Mick's story of innovation to find easier ways to harvest this prized vegetable in Australia. In Europe, white asparagus is grown under triangle-shaped soil rows with dark plastic coverings. The spears are then manually harvested by digging down into the soil.

Two decades ago, to harvest white asparagus, Mick used to walk through his fields looking for any spears with their tips breaking through the soil, then harvest them immediately. It was time-intensive work, and Mick only did it to satisfy his customers and the fine-dining chefs of Melbourne. Mick's frustration with searching for tiny white tips above the soil forced him to think differently. Instead of digging into the soil, he threw a black bucket over a shooting asparagus tip to see if the blocked light would allow the spear to grow tall but still be white. Several days later, he looked under the bucket to find that his experiment had worked.

TRIM THE BASE, THEN PEEL AN INCH OF SKIN OFF THE BOTTOM FOR A BETTER TEXTURAL BITE WITH NO STRINGINESS!

FRUIT AND VEGETABLES ARE LIVING THINGS, NOT SHELF-STABLE LIKE THE FOODS IN OUR PANTRY.

Today, the farm has hundreds of metres of black tunnels that cover the asparagus and keep them white. This makes harvesting much easier, as the spears are exposed above ground and there is no digging into the soil required to retrieve them. The asparagus spears remain much cleaner than their European counterparts, as the vegetable is harvested above the soil instead of 30–40 cm beneath.

When I asked Mick what I should look for in a bunch of asparagus, his words were like music to my ears: 'the spears should look alive, Thanh'. 'Alive' being the key word here. I genuinely see fruit and vegetables as living things, and I believe any fruiterer would say the same. While a more logical idea of 'alive' would be something with a conscience and/or being able to move, I would argue that vegetables, like flowers, move towards the sun; they grow and react to their surrounding environment.

To this day, I appreciate both green and white asparagus even more, knowing that each spear needs to be hand-harvested and that both have their unique characteristics. Mick gave me some excellent tips on picking a good bunch, and now you have them too!

THANH'S TIPS

Choose

1. Look for vibrant, green and 'alive' stems, especially towards the top of the spears.

2. Tightly clustered scales (leaves) at the top should look plump and full. Avoid scales that look brown, shrivelled or separated.

3. Choose firm stems; a wobbly stem won't be crunchy and crisp.

Store

You can store asparagus in an airtight container or plastic bag in the fridge to prevent airflow, which will dehydrate the spears, but the best method is to store the spears in the fridge in a glass of water, with the top half covered with wet paper towel or a plastic bag.

WHY? Asparagus spears have water channels similar to a flower stem, so popping them in a glass of water allows the spears to drink the water and stay hydrated. After a day or two, the cut area closes up and can mould, so cut off the bases every one to two days to keep the asparagus fresh and able to drink the water!

Prep

Trim the dry base of the asparagus spears, then peel an extra inch off the bottom for a better textural bite with no stringiness. Cook the asparagus whole or peel into long strips and toss through a salad for lots of texture, or, my favourite, enjoy it raw for its nutty and earthy notes.

In 2020, Matt Preston asked me to contribute a few recipes to his @lockdownkitchen.com.au Instagram page, to inspire home cooks to create delicious, nourishing and simple food. It was asparagus season, so I added my own twist to asparagus grower Mick's dip recipe to give it more depth and umami, while still allowing the asparagus to shine ... Shine asparagus, shine! Simplicity and good-quality produce will always result in clean and moreish flavours, like this delicious dip.

ASPARAGUS DIP

MAKES about 400 g

75 ml extra-virgin olive oil
3 Thai red shallots, finely diced
1 garlic clove, finely diced
300 g asparagus spears (about 2 bunches), woody ends trimmed, spears cut into 1 cm lengths
½ teaspoon sea salt
2 teaspoons fermented chilli bean curd, or to taste
extra asparagus spears or rice crackers, to serve

Heat the olive oil in a frying pan over medium–high heat. When the pan starts to smoke, add the shallot and sauté for 1 minute, then add the garlic, asparagus and salt and sauté for 2–3 minutes, until bright green and tender.

Transfer the asparagus mixture, along with the oil in the pan, to the bowl of a food processor and pulse until you have your preferred dip consistency. Spoon into a serving bowl, add the fermented chilli bean curd and break it up with a fork. Stir the bean curd into the dip.

Serve the asparagus dip with raw asparagus spears or rice crackers for dipping.

AVOCADOS

We hate and love avocados. In that order. We hate it when the flesh is bruised and black; we love it when the flesh is oily and creamy, and has the potential to transform any salad, toast or dip into umami heaven. I can remove any hate and ensure you only love avocados forever.

I have purchased tens of millions of dollars' worth of avocados in my career. I may have cut open and analysed more avocados than anyone in the world. In 2013, as a national buyer for Coles, it was my job to purchase approximately one-third of all the avocados in Australia. I'd forecast demand, work with ripeners to ensure ready-to-eat supply, negotiate prices with growers and work with the quality-control (QC) teams to improve fruit-eating quality. I pretty much ate avocados every day for the good of all Australians!

On most days, the avocados would randomly arrive from the distribution centre for us to QC. We'd inspect the fruit to ensure it was good enough quality for the customer, then distribute the avocados among the fruit team for taste-testing, who would report back if any weren't up to scratch. Remember, this was a decade ago when avocados were all the rage and the price of this oily fruit was, on average, $4.50 a pop!

I may have cut open and analysed more avocados than anyone in the world.

While most of the team would happily take and eat the avocados with toast, crackers, a spread of vegemite or a sprinkle of salt, I vigorously taste-tested every piece from every grower. I admit, at first I had no idea what I was looking for. But when I ate avocados every day, my palate became extremely sensitive to any slight changes in flavour, and as the weeks went by, I could identify differences so vast I noticed them like chalk and cheese.

A good avocado should have a smooth, creamy, oily-like texture with minimal or no strings, and have a nutty and earthy flavour, as opposed to a 'green skin' flavour. I discovered that large, oval avocados always ate better, and that I never cut open a bruised avocado. Nearly all shoppers have experienced a bruised avocado, but the avocados I ate every day came straight from the distribution centre, where no human had touched the fruit since it was packed. At store level, an avocado might be squeezed up to ten times by other shoppers until it is ultimately purchased. Industry body Avocados Australia did significant testing, which showed that consumers were mishandling avocados in store, trying to pick a soft avocado to eat that day, but squeezing and unintentionally bruising all the semi-firm avocados when making their selection. The supermarkets went to extreme lengths to discourage shoppers from touching avocados by packaging them in plastic with labels saying 'RIPE', but no one would listen. Consumer data and research showed that most consumers wanted to purchase and eat avocados within 24 hours, but I always questioned what was more important: the consumer's convenience or a bad eating experience? Surely the edibility of a bad avocado is much worse than waiting another 24 hours to eat a perfectly ripe and unblemished avocado?

Given how hot and new avocados were to the mainstream fruit and veg scene at the time, and that the industry is now worth half a billion dollars in Australia, I never understood why more energy wasn't put into creating fun, engaging and educational content to ensure a better avocado eating experience.

Why large, oval-shaped avocados are best

First, some vital information: avocados are graded in size by machines that take thousands of photos of the fruit per minute and then guide them to the appropriate conveyor belts, where they are packed and sent to different markets or customers. Most single-purchase avocados are medium-to-large and fit nicely in the palm of your hand, while smaller fruit is often netted in a bag and sold for less. Whenever I ate the smaller-sized fruit I noticed that it would taste very 'green', even if it was soft and had reached maturity. I always preferred small avocados because they were the perfect size for a single meal, and more convenient than using only half a large avocado and storing the other half in plastic wrap. However, I could never find a small avocado with the oils and complexity that a larger-sized hass avocado has. After tasting hundreds of avocados, and looking at the insides and anatomy of the two sizes, I realised that small avocados have much less flesh, so there is significantly more contact with the skin, giving it that raw and earthy green-skin flavour ... an undesirable flavour, if you ask me. It can be seen as the green ring close to the skin when the avocado is cut, as opposed to the yellow-coloured flesh closer to the nut.

Why flesh contact with the nut is key

My manager always told me that nutty flavours are desirable in an avocado, but no one could tell me why or how to achieve them, so I had to discover this for myself.

Nutty flavours are desirable in avocados because of their culinary diversity. Avocados tend to be used as a replacement for spreads on toast, as the rich ingredient in a dip, or as an oily condiment that binds dishes, such as salads. The nutty flavour comes from the amount of oil in an avocado's flesh, which is measured by dry-matter testing. Industry tests revealed that the closer you are to the nut (techincally a seed), the lower the percentage of dry matter and, hence, the higher the amount of oils and waters. As you look at the anatomy of a cut avocado, you can see that the colour closest to the nut is more yellow (oily), whereas towards the skin it's more green (fewer oils). I also noticed that when the size of the nut was larger, it imparted more flavour to the avocado; this is my personal experience, but it also makes sense as there is more surface area of the flesh touching the nut.

Whenever I ate small and elongated avocados, I noticed that they didn't have an oily texture or nutty flavour, and as I ate closer to the stem area, the flavours became less and less pronounced. This supports my theory and the industry tests, as elongated avocados have more flesh further away from the nut and, therefore, fewer oils.

I'm very confident in saying that whenever you select a hass avocado, a large, oval-shaped avocado will generally have the best flavour.

It's not 'buttery'!

Avocados are often described as 'buttery', but I think this description is misleading. They may have a buttery or margarine-like texture, but in terms of flavour, it is nothing like butter. I describe it as a 'nutty flavour' that is unique to avocados. Describing and defining what you like in a fruit is important, so you can easily identify what is good, or in this case, a good-flavoured avocado!

Hass avocados

Hass avocados make up most of the avocados grown commercially in the Western world. This is because they have a high oil content, making them desirable from a flavour perspective, in addition to being visually easy for a customer to select as their skin turns purple when ripe. Technically, however, the firmness rating of an avocado is more important than the colour, as it is the key marker that the fruit is mature, ripe and ready for sale. The industry uses a firmometer, penetrometer or densimeter, which punctures the fruit, measures resistance and pressure, and gives a firmness rating from 0–100, with 0 being inedibly soft and 100 being rock hard.

Why have avocados taken the world by storm?

It's not just because avocados have been marketed as a superfood and a healthy substitute for oils that make them so popular; it's also because they're irreplicable. Think about it: if there are no pears, you might eat an apple; if there are no limes, you might opt for a lemon; spinach might be substituted for rocket; but what do you choose to replace an avocado? The answer is you can't. It's called an non-substitutable product, and that's also why it has huge fluctuations in price, unlike other fruit and vegetables.

Choose

1. Look for firm avocados that you will eat in a few days. After one to two days the fruit will be perfect, without internal bruising.

2. Larger is better.

3. Oval is better than elongated.

Store

Store avocados at room temperature. If only using half the avocado, wrap the side with the nut intact in plastic wrap and store in the fridge for one to two days – any longer and the avocado will have oxidised too much.

Why is this recipe awesome? It's the ultimate food-waste saver. If you ever have leftover avocado, freeze the flesh in ice-cube trays and use them in this recipe whenever you feel like a smoothie! You won't find avo on toast in Vietnam, but you will find sinh tố bơ (avocado smoothies) on the streets, served chilled. The smoothie can be thick or thin, depending on your preference. In Vietnam, they are very particular about which part of the avocado is added, and avoid using a spoon to scrape the flesh as inevitably you also scrape part of the shell, which has bitter notes. Many people use a knife to remove the skin and green part of the flesh, before slicing into cubes and blending.

AVOCADO SMOOTHIE

SINH TỐ BƠ

**SERVES
2**

2 avocados, halved and peeled,
   seed removed
2 cups ice cubes
250 ml (1 cup) milk
2 tablespoons sweetened
   condensed milk, plus extra
   if needed
1 teaspoon sugar
½ teaspoon sea salt

Place the avocado halves, cut-side down, on a chopping board and use a paring knife to remove the thin layer of green flesh on the outer edge of the avocado. Discard. Cut the avocado into cubes, then transfer to a blender, along with 1 cup of the ice, the milk, condensed milk, sugar and salt.

Blend for 1–2 minutes, until smooth or to your desired texture. Taste and add more condensed milk if you prefer a sweeter smoothie.

Divide the remaining ice between two tall glasses, pour over the avocado smoothie and serve.

BANANAS & PLANTAINS

I'm not going to lie, I don't have any tips for picking a good cavendish banana. Not yet, anyway. For most of you reading this who don't live in a tropical climate, where bananas are easily grown, it's highly likely that the banana sold at your nearest store is a cavendish banana. This monocrop fruit is grown on such a mass scale that entire growing regions are not just dedicated to growing one fruit, but one specific variety. In the case of bananas, the cavendish rules supreme. Not only does it grow uniformly, its skin can handle the rigours of transport and it is such a hardy specimen that it can keep for weeks without going bad. Most importantly, it has been resistant to Panama disease, which wiped out the cavendish's predecessor, the gros michel.

The gros michel banana was a richer and sweeter variety than the cavendish banana we eat today, but this monocrop fell victim to the disease, a soil fungus that spread throughout banana plantations, wiping out entire banana industries until the resistant cavendish was planted. Now a new variant of Panama disease known as TR4 threatens to cripple the cavendish banana.

If you're unaware of the profound scale of the cavendish banana industry, let me give you a glimpse.

I almost can't tell the difference between two cavendish bananas. They are near perfect clones in so many ways.

A decade ago I walked through the ripening rooms of Costa Farm's banana facility in Derrimut, which supplies a large percentage of the bananas in Victoria. Tens of thousands of banana boxes, all stored in cool temperatures, were waiting to be moved to ripening chambers, where they would be heated and force-ripened with natural ethylene before being distributed to customers. This equates to millions of hard, green cavendish bananas waiting to be ripened for you and me to eat. Fast forward to today and there are many facilities all filled with green bananas waiting to be ripened. The reason I say I still can't pick a good cavendish banana is that they are grown, processed and sold with such clinical consistency that I almost can't tell the difference between two bananas. They are a near perfect clone in so many ways.

As a fruiterer, I have discovered that all of us enjoy bananas at different stages of their ripening maturity. Some prefer very ripe and soft bananas, while others prefer a firmer and less sweet fruit. Each to their own, I say.

Cool bananas!

I enjoy bananas and still marvel at how convenient they are as a snacking fruit. I buy smaller cavendish bananas as I find them to be less starchy, although this is my personal opinion without any scientific evidence. I like to eat bananas at a semi-late ripe stage, when the skin is no longer stiff but starting to stretch and soften. When black dots start forming on the skin I know it's time to eat.

I also enjoy other banana cultivars and varieties, such as monkey and ducasse, but, ironically, my best ever banana experience was a locally grown banana at Melbourne University's horticulture campus in Burnley. There, my old lecturer and good friend Chris Williams grows an unidentified species of 'cool bananas' that literally taste like banana candy. It's been one of my personal goals to find out which fruit cultivars commercial candy fruit flavours are based on and, for me, banana candy has to have been inspired by a 'cool banana', likely the gros michel or a variant of the one grown at Melbourne University.

Plantains

When I first started working with my dad at the market I saw some hard green bananas and I wondered what variety they were. My cousin explained to me that they were plantains and that the Pacific Islander communities who lived near him cooked them like potatoes. It's always intriguing when you find out there is another world to an ingredient or fruit you think you've known your whole life. Of course, I've learned throughout the years that plantains aren't just eaten by Islander communities, but also African, Central and South American and even some Asian communities. What is fascinating is that plantains are cooked both as a starchy vegetable and as a ripened sweet fruit in a multitude of ways. I asked two friends, who come from different sides of the globe and both of whom I met on cultural cooking show *Plate of Origin*, to share with me a Venezuelan and Cameroonian plantain dish for this book. Both dishes taste delicious, yet both are so different. The tostones on page 40 literally taste like potato cakes, or potato scallops, while the plantain banana in the Born House planti on page 42 tastes like a boiled potato that has absorbed a tremendous amount of smoked fish flavour and spices.

My newfound knowledge drove me to ask my growers in Queensland to plant more horn plantains to service the African community in Melbourne. Providing different communities in Melbourne with culturally relevant produce is a goal my father achieved in his lifetime as a fruiterer and distributor, and it is a goal I hope to achieve in my lifetime, too. If you've never tried plantain bananas before, there's no better time to start! They're tasty and a great textural alternative to potatoes.

Choose

CAVENDISH BANANAS: no tips ... yet!

PLANTAINS: the fruit starts off green (firm and starchy), then turns yellow (sweet and non-starchy), before turning black. Green, starchy plantains should be firm to touch but not hard – if they have some 'give' it shows they were picked at the right moment. If you're after riper, sweeter plantains for deep-frying, either buy them green and wait for them to ripen (about 1 week) or purchase later-ripened yellow fruit.

Store

Store bananas and plantains in a cool place (ideally 13–18°C), but not in the fridge. Eat or cook when they reach your desired ripeness.

THANH'S TIPS

A BEAUTIFUL BANANA FLOWER, SOMETIMES CALLED A BANANA BELL.

My good friend Alejandra Utrera is a dynamo of Venezuelan cooking. She is one of the most, if not the most, passionate cooks I have met. Aly has taught me so much about Latin cuisine, and I am so excited to have her insight on plantain bananas and what they mean to Venezuelans. I couldn't possibly write about this dish as well as Aly, so she has kindly written the following story of what plantain bananas mean to her.

'There is always a basket full of plantains in my mother's house. Not only are they striking to look at, but these big, starchy bananas are one of the most popular vegetables in Venezuela. You can buy plantains everywhere, but the best are sold directly from old farm trucks that gather along the roadside every morning.

'Venezuela is not a rich country, and plantains are a staple that we eat almost every day. They thrive in the tropical climate and are part of our culture, making an affordable and filling meal that's enjoyed by all. Plantains can be baked or boiled, but I think they are best deep-fried. For Venezuelans, eating tostones (fried plaintains) on the beach is a must.

'This recipe is one of my mum's treasures, and she shared it with me the first time she visited me in Australia. I hadn't realised how much I missed the traditional flavours of home. That day she taught me the secret tricks to make crispy and delicious tostones at home, just like the amazing ones sold on the beaches in Venezuela. We enjoyed them with a traditional ensalada rallada (coleslaw), salsa rosada (seafood cocktail sauce) and queso fresco (fresh cheese), and, of course, a couple of ice-cold cervezas (beers)!

'Tostones are crispy, savoury and salty golden coins of pure deliciousness. They will make you feel like you're walking on sunshine. Here is my recipe (with a bit of help from my mum).'

ALEJANDRA UTRERA'S VENEZUELAN TOSTONES

SERVES 2

750 ml (3 cups) vegetable or canola oil, for deep-frying
2 large green plantains, peeled (see Tips) and cut into 1.5–2 cm thick discs
2 garlic cloves, crushed
2 teaspoons sea salt, plus extra to serve

TO SERVE (OPTIONAL)
coleslaw
seafood cocktail sauce
queso fresco (see Tips)

Heat the oil in a deep frying pan over medium heat to 180°C on a kitchen thermometer. Working in batches, deep-fry the plantain for 3–5 minutes, turning once, until lightly browned and slightly soft. Remove using a slotted spoon and drain on paper towels.

Place the fried plantain on a chopping board in a single layer and cover with a clean wet tea towel or Chux cloth. Using a plantain press, a small plate or another chopping board, gently press the fried plantain, until lightly smashed and flattened (don't make them too thin, or they will fall apart).

Combine the garlic and salt in a bowl, then brush the mixture over one side of the flattened plantain.

Return the oil to 180°C and fry the garlicky plantain, in batches, for about 1 minute, until golden and crisp. Drain on paper towels and sprinkle with extra salt.

Serve the tostones with coleslaw, seafood cocktail sauce and queso fresco on the side.

TIPS Plantains and queso fresco can be purchased from Latin American grocers. To peel a plantain, trim the ends, then slice in half lengthways and use a sharp knife to cut away the peel.

My wonderful friend Ashley Vola is a champion of Cameroonian cuisine. I asked Ash to tell me the most culturally significant plantain dish in Cameroon, and she didn't hesitate: Born House planti. Ash's mum, Justine, explained to me that 'Born House' is a celebration to welcome a new baby into the world and 'planti' is short for plantains.

This is Ash's recipe, which she has cooked for many friends and family in Australia to celebrate this special occasion. Traditionally, bitterleaf is added to the dish, which is hard to source in Australia, although it may be available dried. If you can't find it, simply substitute with baby spinach. Ash also tells me that she likes to add a little chilli, preferably habanero.

Justine and Ash stress that you must eat this dish with your fingers, not with a fork!

ASHLEY VOLA'S CAMEROONIAN BORN HOUSE PLANTI

SERVES 4–6

1 kg goat meat, bone-in, roughly chopped into chunks
2 small Maggi veggie stock cubes
¼ onion, diced
5 green plantains, peeled and cut in half
200–300 g smoked fish, such as sawai
30 g (½ cup) dried baby shrimp/crayfish
3 cm piece of ginger, peeled and grated
5 large garlic cloves, grated
1 habanero chilli, finely chopped
250 ml (1 cup) red palm oil (see Note)
1 teaspoon country onion powder (optional; see Tip)
sea salt and cracked black pepper, to taste
4–5 handfuls of baby spinach

Bring a large saucepan of water to the boil, add the goat, stock cubes and onion, reduce the heat to a simmer and cook for 20 minutes, until the goat is almost cooked.

Add the plantain, smoked fish, dried baby shrimp, ginger, garlic, habanero, palm oil, country onion powder (if using) and salt and pepper to the pan, then reduce the heat to low, cover and cook, stirring every 30 minutes, for about 3 hours, until the plantain is soft and the goat is falling off the bone. Stir through the spinach, then taste and season with more salt and pepper if needed.

Divide the Born House planti among bowls and serve.

NOTE: Red palm oil is used widely in West African cooking. It is a culturally important ingredient, sourced from small-crop farms, and known for its natural health benefits. It is not the same as mass-produced refined palm oil. Red palm oil can be purchased from African grocery stores.

TIP Country onion powder can be purchased from African grocery stores. If you can't find it, simply omit from the recipe.

Every Lunar New Year, Mum spends an entire day making bánh tét cakes for our family.
I have four siblings, which means Mum bakes and wraps around 20 cakes! Once steamed,
the banana bánh tét is a vibrant pink, almost purple colour, and it's incredibly tasty.

Ripe bananas are key to balancing the sweet and savoury flavours in bánh tét. You need
to use ducasse bananas – called 'chuối xiêm' in Vietnamese – which are available at most
South-East Asian fruit shops. Mum usually buys them a week in advance and waits for
a whole hand of bananas to turn yellow, with some black. If you can't find ducasse bananas,
then you can substitute ladyfingers. You need to start this recipe a day ahead.

MUM'S STEAMED BANANA GLUTINOUS RICE CAKES

BÁNH TÉT

MAKES 8

3 cups (750 g) glutinous rice, rinsed and soaked in cold water overnight
100 g dried black-eyed peas, rinsed and soaked in cold water overnight
400 ml can coconut milk
2½ teaspoons sea salt
8 fully ripe ducasse bananas, preferably wide in shape, peeled
2 teaspoons sugar

Drain the rice and black-eyed peas and set aside.

Warm the coconut milk in a large saucepan over medium-low heat. Add the rice, black-eyed peas and 2 teaspoons of the salt, then cook, stirring constantly, for 4 minutes, until slightly thickened.

Pour the sticky rice mixture into a large bowl and set aside to cool for 10 minutes (you want to wrap the sticky rice while it is still warm but not hot, as it is easier to mould).

Place the bananas in a large bowl, add the remaining ½ teaspoon of salt and the sugar and toss to combine.

To wrap the bánh tét cakes, tear two 30 cm squares of foil and one 10 cm square of foil. Place the 30 cm squares of foil on a work surface, overlapping by 5 cm. Place the 10 cm square of foil on top, where the foil overlaps. Mould 100 g of the sticky rice mixture into a fat rectangle on the top square of foil, large enough to fit the length and width of one banana. Place a banana on top, add enough sticky rice mixture to cover the banana, then, using wet hands, mould the rice mixture around the banana to completely enclose.

Starting with the side of foil closest to you, wrap the foil over and around the sticky rice mixture and roll away from you, then fold in the two ends to form a secure rectangular parcel. Cut a piece of kitchen string more than twice the length of the parcel and wrap it lengthways around the parcel, then tie in a knot to secure. Next, cut three shorter pieces of kitchen string and wrap them, equally spaced apart, around the body of the parcel and tie to secure. Repeat with the remaining ingredients to make eight bánh tét.

Bring a large saucepan of water to the boil and add the bánh tét, making sure they are completely submerged. Reduce the heat to medium and cook the bánh tét for 4 hours, topping up with more water if necessary (check the pan every 15 minutes).

Transfer the bánh tét to a wire rack and allow them to cool to room temperature.

To serve, cut the string and unwrap the foil. Cut the bánh tét into 1 cm thick slices and serve at room temperature, or warmed in the microwave for 20 seconds. Leftovers will keep in an airtight container in the fridge for up to 1 week.

TIP If you would like to use traditional banana leaves to wrap your bánh tét, wash and dry eight large banana leaves and cut each into two 30 cm squares (you don't need the extra 10 cm square). Dunk them into just-boiled water to soften and make them easier to work with.

BITTER
MELON

y favourite dish cooked by my mum is stuffed bitter melon soup (see page 52). It's a wholesome home-style dish that you won't find in Vietnamese restaurants. The dish itself is meaningful, nourishing and polarising. Why polarising? Unless cooked well, the unsurprising bitter flavours can put many children off, and most kids grow up disliking it, especially if their parents enjoy the bitter flavours. There is even a meme among the Vietnamese community about growing up 'being forced to eat bitter melon', with some hating it and others loving it. It takes skill to cook it well so the flavours are balanced – the bitter flavours in Mum's bitter melon soup are balanced with rice and pork, and served with an abundance of fresh herbs.

In the Western world, bitter melon is still seen as a vegetable oddity, an 'exotic vegetable' not as readily accepted as, say, bok choy. In Eastern dietetics, however, bitter melon is prized as one of the most 'cooling' vegetables available. Eating too many 'heating' foods or produce creates an imbalance of yin and yang in the body, resulting in negative bodily reactions. A simple example would be eating too many lychees or candy in one sitting; you might feel unwell or break out in pimples! The idea is to always eat in balance: a diet of cooling foods, such as cucumbers, lettuce and other vegetables, is vital to balance heating foods. Given bitter melon's ranking as the coolest of vegetables, Vietnamese parents always tell their kids to eat it to counteract all the junk they consume daily!

Although the concept of yin and yang may be unfamiliar if you've grown up in the Western world, its principles are very similar to ancient Greek dietetics. Around 200 AD, the Greek physician Galen believed that an imbalanced diet filled with 'excess' could lead to changes in mood, health and the four humours: blood, yellow bile, black bile and phlegm. Galen's theory influenced Western medicine for the next 1000 years, and a balanced diet was considered the best way to maintain and restore health for the better part of the last 2000 years. Only the advancement of modern science in the last two centuries has changed the idea of food as medicine. I'm sharing this because I have always tried to find the commonality between Eastern and Western food philosophies, but the bitter melon remained an anomaly my whole life until recently when studying food history. The moral of this story is to eat in balance and if you've had lots of junk food, eat bitter melon!

The future of bitter melon is, ironically, less bitter. My work travels to find new seeds for my growers in Australia brought me to the East-West Seed company in Chiang Mai, Thailand, where I discovered that they're developing bitter melon species that aren't as bitter! Although this may sound counterintuitive – nutritionally, bitter usually means better – the hope is that the bitter melon will become more attractive to more consumers, especially the next generation of bitter melon eaters!

Having travelled Asia extensively for work, I have eaten many varietals of bitter melon cooked in myriad ways: in Kyoto, Japan, I ate fried white spiky bitter melon, called 'goya', from a street stall; in Shenzhen, China, I was served finely sliced 'ku gua' bitter melon pickled in sugar, served on a bed of ice and tossed with peanuts and carrots; and at my

Bitter flavours are odd; we detest overly bitter flavours but love subtle bitter flavours. Take coffee, for example: it's predominantly bitter, yet we love it for this flavour.

local Indian takeaway, I've enjoyed 'karela', a deep-fried mini green bitter melon, served with biryani.

My favourite variety of bitter melon is the small, spiky, dark bitter melon native to India that has a sharp, bitter kick. Even so, the bitterness soon dissipates, meaning you get a new bitter kick with every bite. In Vietnamese hotels, chefs working the breakfast buffet will make a bitter melon omelette on request, another favourite of mine. However, in all my travels, my favourite way to enjoy bitter melon is still my mum's stuffed bitter melon soup.

I am optimistic that bitter melon will continue to become more popular and mainstream, as Western audiences seek punchier flavours.

Bitter melon is a fruit, not a vegetable!

I found this out in the most multicultural fruit industry way possible. A Lebanese fruiterer named Ahmed, whose fruit shop has predominantly Indian and Vietnamese customers, was at my store and looking through a box of bitter melon. He dug deep and pulled out a very yellow-skinned and ripe bitter melon – the stuff of nightmares for a wholesaler; ripe fruit means discounted produce. He held up the fruit, snapped it in half, dug out the bright-red jewel seeds and ate them, then said, 'My Indian customers love this, Thanh!'. I was flabbergasted. I thought Ahmed was completely mad ... surely a raw bitter melon was even more bitter than a cooked one, but he explained that it's super sweet and told me to try some. I hesitantly agreed, given his facial expression was filled with delight, and to my surprise it was sweeter than candy! I couldn't believe that something so bitter could turn into something so sweet. After further research, I also discovered that eating the bitter melon flesh around the seeds is considered beneficial for those suffering from diabetes within the Indian community. You see, vegetables can become fruits too, especially climacteric fruits that ripen up!

Choose

1. Firm to touch, with plump skin.

2. Bright-green uniform colour.

3. Avoid shrivelled, dehydrated or yellowing skin.

Store

Store bitter melon in a plastic bag in the fridge. The cool temperature and high humidity (above 80 per cent) will help keep the vegetable firm and bitter, rather than soft, mushy and bland. Leaving the bitter melon uncovered in the fridge will cause the skin to dehydrate.

Prep

Cut the bitter melon in half and scoop out the seeds with a spoon. Soak the bitter melon in iced or salted water for about 20 minutes, to mellow out the flavour.

One of my favourite stir-fried egg dishes that my mum makes is eggs with bitter melon. Mum's recipe is not only a quick and easy way to enjoy bitter melon, but the eggs' richness cuts through the strong taste of the fruit. As with most recipes, balance and technique is key. You need to slice the bitter melon finely and refrain from adding too much. The classic Vietnamese method fries the bitter melon first with onion, then the lightly beaten egg, which is scrambled quickly to ensure the egg remains somewhat creamy.

During the pandemic, I became obsessed with mastering the classic French omelette, inspired by Jacques Pépin. I discovered that cooking the perfect omelette is a skill learned by 1000 eggs, but don't worry, as long as it's not overcooked, this dish will still be delicious. You only need a small amount of bitter melon for this recipe, so seek out baby Indian bitter melons if you can, which are less sharp than the regular fruit.

BITTER MELON OMELETTE

SERVES 1–2

¼ bitter melon, washed and ends trimmed
3 eggs
1 teaspoon sea salt
2 teaspoons vegetable oil
1 Thai red shallot, finely diced

TO SERVE
chopped red chilli
coriander leaves
soy sauce
steamed jasmine rice or bánh mì (optional)

Cut the bitter melon in half lengthways, use a spoon to scrape out the seeds and white pith, then cut the flesh into 2 mm thick slices. Add the bitter melon to a large bowl of well-salted water and leave to soak for 10 minutes, then drain and rinse under cold running water. Set aside to dry on a clean tea towel (or use a salad spinner).

Meanwhile, crack the eggs into a small bowl, add the salt and lightly whisk.

Heat the oil in a 20–24 cm non-stick frying pan over medium heat to 130°C (or until the end of a wooden chopstick sizzles when placed in the oil). Add the bitter melon and cook for 1 minute, then add the shallot and cook for a further 30 seconds or until golden. Reduce the heat to medium–low, then remove the pan from the heat for 1–2 minutes to cool slightly. Return the pan to the heat, add the beaten egg and swirl to coat the base of the pan. Cook for 30 seconds or until the base of the egg is just set but not coloured. Using chopsticks or a wooden fork, stir the egg in a figure-eight motion to break the curd while moving the pan up and down for about 5 seconds. Cook for another 30 seconds, then tilt the pan on a 45-degree angle and force the egg to slide to one side. Using a spatula, wooden fork or chopsticks, flip the outer edge of the omelette onto itself, then flip the other side over the top. Cook for a further 30 seconds, then grab a plate, place it on top of the frying pan and invert the omelette onto the plate.

Scatter the omelette with a little chilli, coriander and soy sauce, and serve with steamed jasmine rice, in a bánh mì or enjoy on its own!

If you've never tried bitter melon, I hope you'll give this welcoming recipe a go. It's one of the dishes I cooked in the final of the TV show *Plate of Origin,* which my team received 10/10 for, and I'm very proud of it. I've amended my mum's bitter melon soup by intensifying the other flavours, so my kids would be more likely to eat it, and they love it!

PORK-STUFFED BITTER MELON SOUP

CANH KHỔ QUA

SERVES
4

20 g vermicelli glass noodles
30 g dried sliced wood ear
    mushrooms
boiling water
3 light-coloured bitter melons
300 g pork neck (minced twice)
100 g pork jowl (minced twice)
2 garlic cloves, grated
5 cm piece of ginger, peeled
    and finely diced
2 teaspoons sugar
1 teaspoon sea salt
1 teaspoon white pepper
1 tablespoon fish sauce

PORK NECK BROTH
2 kg pork neck bones
8 x 10 cm long pork baby
    spare ribs
2 tablespoons sea salt,
    plus extra if needed
2 tablespoons fish sauce,
    plus extra if needed
2 tablespoons sugar,
    plus extra if needed

DIPPING SAUCE
2 red bullet chillies, finely sliced
1½ tablespoons 'dipping' soy
    sauce (see Tips)

TO SERVE
bunch of coriander, leaves and
    stems roughly chopped
bunch of spring onions,
    finely sliced

Preheat the oven to 220°C (fan-forced).

To make the pork neck broth, place the pork neck bones and baby spare ribs in a large roasting tin and roast for 20 minutes, until browned. Transfer the roasted bones to a large stockpot, cover with 8 litres of water and bring to the boil. Reduce the heat to a simmer and cook for 1 hour or until the liquid is reduced to about 6 litres (no need to skim the surface of impurities). Season with the salt, fish sauce and sugar, then keep warm on the very lowest heat.

Meanwhile, place the vermicelli noodles and dried wood ear mushrooms in separate heatproof bowls. Cover both ingredients with just-boiled water and leave the noodles for 7 minutes and mushrooms for 15 minutes. Drain. Snip the noodles into 7 cm lengths, and chop the mushrooms.

Cut the bitter melon into 4 cm long cylinders, then use a spoon or knife to remove and discard the spongy internal flesh, leaving the surrounding firmer green flesh and sides intact. Transfer the hollowed-out bitter melon to a large bowl of salted water and set aside for 15 minutes. Drain.

Place the minced pork in a large bowl, add the noodles, wood ear mushrooms, garlic, ginger, sugar, salt, white pepper and fish sauce and use your hands to thoroughly combine the ingredients. Using a spoon or your fingers, stuff the pork neck mixture into the hollowed-out bitter melon cylinders, pressing the mixture into both ends to prevent any air pockets from forming. Roll any leftover mixture into small balls and add to the soup.

Add the stuffed bitter melon to the broth, increase the heat to a simmer and cook for 30 minutes or until the bitter melon is soft and the filling is cooked through. Taste and season the soup with more salt, fish sauce and/ or sugar, if needed, then cook for a further 5 minutes.

To make the dipping sauce, combine the ingredients in a small bowl, then divide among dipping bowls.

Divide the soup and stuffed bitter melon among bowls, top with the coriander and spring onion and serve with the dipping sauce on the side for dipping the stuffed bitter melon.

TIPS Dipping soy sauce is less concentrated than cooking soy sauce. Find it at Asian grocery stores. Ask your butcher to mince the pork neck and jowl mince twice for you. If you're in a hurry, you can use a premade pork broth.

Chinese takeaways worldwide have a version of beef in black bean sauce. What you may not know is that there is an even better rendition of this dish, and it includes bitter melon. Bitter melon's sharp and bitter taste cuts through the salty and rich flavours and cools you down – a match made in heaven. The vermicelli noodles used here are Vietnamese bún made with rice flour, not vermicelli made with tapioca starch, which are called glass noodles.

BEEF, BLACK BEAN & BITTER MELON ON FRIED VERMICELLI

豆豉苦瓜牛肉

SERVES 2

1 bitter melon, washed and ends trimmed
400 g dried bún (rice vermicelli noodles)
140 ml vegetable oil
2 tablespoons light soy sauce, plus extra if needed
1 tablespoon cracked black pepper
1 teaspoon potato starch mixed with 2 tablespoons cold water
200 g stir-fry or sirloin beef (or lean pork), finely sliced

BLACK BEAN SAUCE
3 tablespoons fermented black beans, roughly chopped
4 garlic cloves, roughly chopped
2 tablespoons light soy sauce
1 tablespoon oyster sauce
1 tablespoon Shaoxing rice wine
1 tablespoon brown sugar
1 tablespoon sesame oil

Cut the bitter melon in half lengthways and use a spoon to scrape out the seeds and all the white pith. Diagonally cut the bitter melon into 5 mm thick slices. Transfer to a large bowl of well-salted water and leave to soak for 10 minutes. Drain and rinse under cold running water, then set aside to dry on a clean tea towel (or use a salad spinner).

Cook the bún as per the packet instructions, then drain and leave in the colander to dry for at least 10 minutes.

Heat 2½ tablespoons of the vegetable oil in a heavy-based frying pan over high heat until smoking. Add half the bún noodles and use a spatula or chopsticks to evenly spread the noodles across the base of the pan, ensuring there are no gaps, adding more noodles if necessary. Cook for 3–4 minutes, until the base of the noodles is crispy and browned. Carefully flip the noodle cake over and cook for another 1–2 minutes, until crispy. Remove the noodle cake from the pan and drain on paper towel, then cut into quarters (if very large). Repeat with the remaining noodles and another 2½ tablespoons of oil.

Combine the soy sauce, pepper and potato starch slurry in a bowl. Add the beef and mix well to evenly coat the beef in the sauce, then set aside for 15 minutes to tenderise, or velvet, the beef.

Meanwhile, to make the black bean sauce, combine all the ingredients in a small bowl.

Heat the remaining 2 tablespoons of vegetable oil in a wok over high heat, until smoking. Add the tenderised beef and stir-fry for about 1 minute, until sealed. Remove the beef from the wok.

Add the bitter melon to the wok and cook over high heat, tossing frequently, for 2 minutes. Add the black bean sauce and stir-fry for 1 minute, then return the beef to the pan, along with its juices. Stir thoroughly for 1 minute, until the sauce is thickened, then taste and season with more soy sauce if needed.

Spoon the stir-fried beef and bitter melon over the fried bún vermicelli noodle cake and serve!

BROCCOLI

Is there a more humble green vegetable than broccoli? I would argue not. Broccoli is so easy to eat that it is the hero vegetable for fruiterers and parents alike. Nearly everyone is comfortable cooking broccoli, and nearly everyone enjoys its flavour. Only the pickiest eaters despise broccoli. Most of us boil it for a few minutes and have it on our plates for dinner, but how often do you see broccoli served in a fine-dining restaurant? Probably rarely, maybe never. Think about it. I rest my case – broccoli is the most humble of all vegetables in the Western world.

Broccoli is a universally loved vegetable. It even has its own emoji – that's when you know you've hit peak vegetable love.

Amazing broccoli

There are moments in every industry when your sector hits the news, and for all the wrong reasons. In the winter of 2022, Australian vegetable prices hit peak inflation, with lettuce creeping above $10 a piece. I filmed an ABC News explainer about why produce was so expensive and I pleaded with Aussies to look at other good-value produce that was in season, specifically brassicas.

Vegetables aren't the most glamorous subject to make the news, and so when 'veg' hit the headlines it gave the industry a chance to champion other vegetables, such as broccoli. That year the Melbourne winter was cold, wet, foggy and frosty. Local vegetable growers were saying that the cold snap had helped certain vegetables and that they were 'eating well', but none spoke about the technical reasons why. If freezing air temperatures last long enough, most vegetables growing in the ground are damaged or perish, but not brassicas and especially not broccoli.

You see, produce is amazing and creates all sorts of natural adaptions and defences against the elements, namely frost, which is when the temperature drops below freezing, or 0°C. Broccoli plants respond to frost by releasing enzymes called amalyse, which break down the starches in broccoli and turn them into sugars, and this lowers the freezing point of the plant. Broccoli can survive if the temperature doesn't drop below -3°C. Not only is this an incredible defence mechanism, but it also makes the broccoli sweeter. This magical mechanism can be found in many crucifers or brassicas, including cauliflower, kale and brussels sprouts. Why would we worry about the price of lettuce when broccoli and other brassicas weren't only good value, but arguably the best-tasting they could be?

I detest the term 'in season' because it's somewhat meaningless in the modern food system that ensures year-round supply of vegetables such as broccoli. If growers and fruiterers say winter vegetables are in season, we need to prove it; they need to taste better than when they're out of season. Furthermore, we need to celebrate these reasons and not be fearful of giving buyers a minute-long explainer instead of using the vague term 'in season'.

Broccoli is the most humble of all vegetables in the Western world.

THE PERFECT BROCCOLI.

THIS BROCCOLI HAS A FLOWERING BUD MEANING IT'S NOT AS TENDER.

AVOID YELLOW OR PALE-GREEN BROCCOLI, AS THIS SUGGESTS AGED STOCK

A scientific explanation

While visiting Agriculture Victoria's horticulture production science team at the AgriBio Centre at La Trobe University, I asked crop physiologist and research scientist Christine Frisina some of the burning questions I've always had about broccoli. Agriculture Victoria has performed research on all types of crops grown in the state for the benefit of growers, from examining production all the way to post-harvest management and storing the produce. Researchers like Christine are my heroes and the true fruit nerds of the world! I may be a communicator, but they are the real scientists who figure out the tips and technical reasons why produce tastes good or bad.

Broccoli can last for weeks in the fridge and is transported from farms to markets packed in ice. Christine says that a good broccoli should be dark green in colour; pale florets can suggest the produce has aged or been mismanaged on the farm. Christine also gave me her hack for storing broccoli in the fridge. She explained that broccoli shouldn't be suffocated in a plastic bag, although it does need a humid environment so the florets don't dehydrate. In order to achieve this without a commercial breathing bag, Christine places the broccoli in a plastic bag, ties it up and pokes her finger where the knot is to create a small air hole for the broccoli to breathe. Christine explains that if the broccoli can't breathe, after several days it will start to generate an anaerobic response, where it uses carbon dioxide rather than oxygen to breathe, and develops strange flavours in order to survive. While temporary storage of broccoli for a day may not need a breathing hole, creating a hole is a far more conscious way to store and treat this 'still-alive' brassica with the respect it deserves, so it tastes as great as it can!

Embracing stalks

I love broccoli stalks, but I know why many people don't. A lot of people are put off by the thick skin that develops at the base of a broccoli, which is often stringy and hard. Depending on the age of a broccoli, sometimes I remove the skin and cut the stalk into crunchy sticks to boil with the florets. I suggest generously cutting off the skin and only eating the internal part of the stalk if you're not usually a fan. You can freeze the broccoli skin offcuts and use them in your next soup stock!

Ironically, broccolini is loved because of its crunchy and tender stalks. What you may not know is that broccolini is a trademarked seed, also known as a PBR (Plant Breeder's Rights), where a company exclusively owns the rights to sell and market the vegetable. It is a variety bred from Chinese broccoli with regular broccoli traits. I recently discovered that before broccolini existed, local Italian vegetable growers used to cut the side shoots off a broccoli plant and fry them up. Anatomically, these side shoots didn't have a thick skin and were loved because of their tender crunch. Broccolini almost exactly replicates this without being a side shoot of a plant and curly in shape; instead its stalks are straight and uniform. Choosing broccolini is easy because they are grown and harvested to be tender, hence they don't have a long shelf life like broccoli.

On an interesting note, one of the first produce videos I ever created – which, funnily enough, was never watched – was out in Werribee, a key broccoli-growing region for Australia. I was told to pick the broccoli out of the ground and eat it raw, and it was arguably the sweetest broccoli I have ever eaten. There is something very primal about eating raw broccoli straight from the ground. Growers have told me that the natural raw sweetness disappears hours after picking broccoli from the field, yet they have never been able to explain why. So if you do grow broccoli in your backyard, pick it out of the ground on a cold winter's morning and go for a bite – you'll be sweetly surprised.

Choose

1. Look for dark-green produce with a firm stalk. Avoid yellow or pale-green broccoli, as this suggests it is aged stock.

2. Small beads on the broccoli head are best; large beads can be a sign that the broccoli was picked at a mature stage and close to flowering (meaning the broccoli won't be as tender).

3. A cracked base won't affect flavour, but it will affect shelf life (most fruiterers report dehydration and mould developing faster with cracked stalk bases).

Store

Store broccoli and broccolini in a plastic bag with a small hole, to allow the vegetable to breathe while keeping humidity high, in the coldest part of the fridge.

THANH'S TIPS

When I first made this broccoli pasta dish for my kids, they devoured it. As a parent, it was a meal that ticked multiple boxes: it was a quick dish for hungry kids, it included plenty of veg, and it was also food that I wanted to eat. There are many variations of broccoli pasta in Southern Italy, from Puglia to Sicily. While you can find broccoli pasta recipes online, I think this version is more efficient and flavourful, and I have my good friend and food editor Camellia Aebischer to thank for it. Camellia first tasted broccoli pasta when her vegetarian friend ordered it at Feliciano, a small Italian restaurant in Adelaide. The dish inspired Cam to reinvent it at home, and the result was a spaghetti aglio e olio crossed with a pesto pasta that is healthy, moreish and convenient. Cooking the broccoli florets until they start to break down and cling to the pasta makes for a tastier meal than one where the broccoli is cooked separately. I've taken Cam's method but changed the ingredients and removed the chilli, but feel free to add some if you don't have small children – hah! Look for broccoli with large florets for this recipe, but the stalk is also fabulous, so any broccoli will do!

PASTA WITH BROCCOLI

SERVES 4

2 tablespoons sea salt
500 g orecchiette (see Tip)
2 heads of broccoli, florets separated, stalks diagonally sliced into matchsticks
3 tablespoons olive oil, plus extra for drizzling
4 garlic cloves, finely sliced
¼ cup pine nuts or macadamia nuts, roughly chopped
finely grated zest and juice of ½ lemon
50 g grana padano, shaved
½ teaspoon cracked black pepper

Bring a large saucepan of water to the boil and season with the salt. Add the orecchiette and cook for 3 minutes, then add the broccoli and cook for 8 minutes or until the broccoli is soft and the orecchiette is al dente. Drain and return the broccoli and orecchiette to the pan.

Meanwhile, heat the olive oil in a small frying pan over low heat, add the garlic and nuts and cook for 2–3 minutes, until fragrant. Add the lemon zest and stir, then pour the mixture over the broccoli and orecchiette. Squeeze in the lemon juice and scatter over the grana padano, then season with the pepper and drizzle with a little extra olive oil. Toss well to combine, then divide among bowls and serve.

TIP If using another pasta shape, such as spaghetti, check the pasta's cooking time and add the broccoli 8 minutes before the end.

CHERRIES

Cherries deserve their own entry, not only because they're my favourite fruit, but because their flavour can reach a level of intensity beyond their stone-fruit siblings. As a Melbournian, there is nothing quite like the taste of cherries at Christmas. Local cherries peak at this time and so, for me, cherries mean celebration. While the cherry season extends for three months in Australia, when I was a kid you only saw cherries on the shelves for a few weeks of the year. Dad would always bring home a box just before Christmas, gifted to him by one of his best mates, Jamie, who had a cherry farm in Shepparton. Jamie grew a few old varietals of cherries, but I always remember the merchants. Merchant cherries have a dark-purple skin and their flesh is sweet, dripping with juice when you bite into them. Stained fingers are inevitable when enjoying a box of these beautiful cherries.

> **Why are good cherries so hard to find? Cherries are hyper-seasonal and cannot be kept in cold storage for weeks or months like other fruit.**

Annual cherry hunt

Why are good cherries so hard to find? For a start, cherries are hyper-seasonal and cannot be kept in cold storage for weeks or months like other fruit.

Every December, you'll find me running round the wholesale market hunting for the best-tasting cherries, or what I call the finest 'produce of the moment'. Every day a new batch arrives from a different state, with varieties all competing with one another. You could say it's the most exciting time of the year for me, because when I do find a memorable box of cherries, I savour it as I don't know when another amazing box will appear again. The hunt for a wonderful cherry is, in a way, the antithesis of the eternally available cavendish banana and the commoditisation of the fruit industry. A good cherry is not available year-round; it's momentary, ephemeral!

As cherries don't ripen post-harvesting, farmers have to pick the fruit when it's already very sweet and mature, meaning the fruit breaks down relatively quickly and has a short shelf life. Once picked, cherries only last a week before their optimal eating period ends and they start to lose flavour. Each variety must be completely harvested within a two-week window, and then a new variety begins. This means that every two weeks, cherries will likely taste completely different.

Cherries are also very susceptible to weather. A big storm might knock the fruit off, or too much rain may cause the fruit to absorb excessive nutrients through the tree, which can cause the fruit to 'split'. All of these reasons explain why you can have a good cherry one week and a bad one the next. But that is also why the thrill of finding a good cherry excites me: because it is so hard, and when you find a good one, the experience is unbeatable.

WHEN BOTH 'INTENSITY' AND 'BALANCE' OF SWEETNESS AND SOURNESS IS ACHIEVED, I DESCRIBE THIS EATING EXPERIENCE AS 'SWEET UMAMI'.

Q: Why are cherries my favourite fruit? A: Sweet umami

What is sweet umami? A cherry can be intensely sour and intensely sweet at the same time, which makes for a deliciously moreish experience. Balance is also important: being too sweet often means the fruit has lost too much acid and flavour; and too sour often means inedibility as a snacking fruit. When both 'intensity' and 'balance' of sweetness and sourness is achieved, I describe this eating experience as 'sweet umami', which is defined by 'not being able to stop eating the cherries' – aka 'moreishness'. It is my criteria for a good fruit and the model I use for critiquing produce when customers ask me if a fruit is good or not.

For me, the best cherries I have had in my lifetime reach an intensity and balance of sourness and sweetness greater than all other fruit! Why is balance important? Over the last 30 years, fruits have been grown and selected to be sweet without sourness, tartness or funk, and this leads them to be tasty but one dimensional. For instance, producing sweet watermelons is an obvious flavour profile, but watermelons don't have an intense flavour or aroma; they are neutral, without strong aromas, sour notes or tang. Conversely, eating pineapple that is too sour often isn't a great eating experience; even though most of us love the acid in pineapple, too much can be unpleasant. That is why balance is key to achieving sweet umami.

Why mouthfeel is so important

An amazing cherry, or any fruit for that matter, must have a pleasing first bite and mouthfeel experience. This idea may seem foreign, but it's a sought-after element in Eastern food culture. The Chinese describe this idea as 'kou gan' (口感), which quite literally translates to 'mouth-feeling', but more accurately describes the textural character of a fruit.

Some varieties of cherries have a very crunchy bite, with juicy flesh that's consistently firm and pleasant to bite through. Due to their smaller size, cherries have more skin contact than other stone fruits, and chewing the skin brings out lots of tart notes, which I love. Conveniently, there is no skin to peel, in addition to the whole fruit being small enough to enjoy in one bite. If I compare a cherry to a lychee, both have great flavours, but I don't need to peel the cherry and the edible skin gives it extra mouthfeel points.

When it comes to the stone, the cherry will make you work for it, but not in a laboursome way like removing the seeds from a papaya. All the work is completed in the mouth during the eating process and, for me, this only adds to the overall mouthfeel and textural experience.

Visuals and aromas

Cherries are visually stunning. The contrast of the long green stem against the bright-purple, red or white skin makes them eye-catching and alluring. One area that does let cherries down in the points department is their lack of aroma. Despite this downside, the cherry's visual appeal and intense flavours put it in a league above many other fruits.

Cherries also have a special power: melatonin. I've usually got multiple things on my mind and a stressful schedule, making it difficult for me to sleep. However, whenever I eat a bunch of cherries before bed I find it easy to fall into a deep, relaxing sleep, and it's definitely the melatonin from the cherries. Many people consume tableted melatonin, but why not try nature's fresh option instead?!

Choose

1. Green stems are a great indicator of freshness, suggesting the cherries have been recently picked and maintained at an appropriate cool temperature. Stemless cherries can be a sign that the cherry trees were weak, either due to insufficient nutrients or disease.

2. Look for shiny skin and a plump shape with high shoulders (like a heart shape).

3. Avoid cherries with splits, brown rot (identified by small brown spots) and mould.

Remember that all varieties have different flavours. Cherries can be purple, red or white; some have naturally soft skin, while others have firm flesh. These differences are important – you don't compare granny smiths with fuji apples and say that one is sweeter than the other, when the granny smith is naturally a sour varietal. The same goes for cherries!

Store

I recommend only purchasing enough cherries to eat that week, or else share them! Store cherries in a closed, preferably breathable, bag in the fridge.

CHILLIES

I once made up a game where the loser had to eat a very spicy white-fleshed bush chilli. My dad and I were visiting our herb growers up in Townsville and we invited my cousins, who are also fruiterers. My cousin Raymond Truong lost the bet and he ate the chilli straight like a champion, as confident as those YouTubers who mukbang anything and everything. Raymond's face and forehead started to sweat, then his cheeks turned numb and, scrambling for water, he looked like he was going to faint.

While most people enjoy the tingling sensation of chilli, why do some people crave the thrill of intense spice, while others don't enjoy any heat at all?

Flavour vs spice

I have always sought to understand the chilli, for there are a few things going on when eating this interesting fruit. There is the heat, and then there is the flavour, which often gets forgotten in the craze for spice, but is equally important.

> " While most people enjoy the tingling sensation of chilli, why do some people crave the thrill of intense spice, while others don't enjoy any heat at all?

Understanding spice is not easy, so I was beyond excited when I had the chance to chat about it with chilli grower, entrepreneur and expert David De Paoli, founder of AustChilli Group, Australia's largest distributor of fresh chillies. David explained to me that capsaicin – the compound that makes chillies spicy – comes from the middle thread of the chilli, also known as the placenta, and spreads to the seeds. If the thread and seeds contain the spice, then the flesh and skin are where the flavour lies, but this often fades into the background because the spice is so overwhelming in terms of a sensory experience.

In Australia, we differentiate non-spicy chillies as 'capsicum' and spicy chillies as 'chillies', while in the United States they are grouped together as 'peppers', which is technically more accurate as they are part of the same family. Red and green capsicums are picked at different stages of maturity for the different flavours the skin and flesh give. While we may not think there is much flavour in chillies due to the overwhelming spice, there certainly is, and this is why certain varieties of chillies are so culturally significant for different cuisines.

Cultural chillies

The importance of chillies in Mexican cuisine, as well as Mexican identity, is unmistakable. From habaneros and jalapeños to poblanos, whether dried, fresh or blended into a hot sauce, the flavour of chillies is a defining characteristic of Mexican food and culture. I often visit one of my neighbouring produce wholesalers who specialises in and only sells chillies. Ross Ferrinda and Vince Brancatisano dedicate their days to the chilli trade and explained to me how immigration has expanded the chilli market, largely due to the demand for different varieties, which are culturally significant to those cuisines. Why culturally significant? Because the combination of spice and flavour of different chillies characterises the individual dishes those cuisines are made up from. In my time in the market, I've seen the introduction of shishito peppers for Japanese restaurants, padrón peppers for Spanish restaurants and jinda chillies for Indian restaurants, and so much can be said about the flavour each chilli imparts. The next time you eat a chilli, think about its flavour as much as its spice.

For the Vietnamese, the bullet chilli, commonly called the bird's eye chilli, is culturally significant; however, at times, it's too spicy for my liking. Depending on my mood, sometimes I will remove the thread and seeds to decrease the spiciness of my mum's nước chấm (dipping sauce; see page 74), but I will still always use the bullet chilli for its sweet flavour and aroma, as this is what defines nước chấm in Vietnam.

Quality control

David shared some great insights with me, including that chillies get spicier as they mature, and this is largely due to photosynthesis. This backs up what I already thought: red chillies are much hotter than green chillies of the same variety, and the amount of capsaicin is largely determined by the amount of sunlight hours the plant receives. This is why chillies grow well in desert-like environments and in the summer in temperate climates.

The Scoville scale, which is the measure of how much capsaicin a chilli variety contains, is not always precise, due to constantly changing growing conditions that can affect the levels of spice. If it rains for a week before picking or there is little sunlight, a super-hot chilli might be far less spicy than the Scoville rating it's given, which is why most chillies are given a 'range'. This is why quality control of spice is important. To be the best fruiterer, I believe you should quality control as much produce as possible. Even today, I often see fruiterers snap a chilli in half and lick the exposed seeds to check the capsaicin levels before purchasing the box. Although this might seem old-fashioned and perhaps extreme, it shows the dedication of fruiterers to ensure their produce is the best. I cherish these moments, which numbers and commoditisation can't quantify, in the unique trade of fresh produce.

Choose

1. Ross says that a green stem is a great indicator of the freshness of a chilli. Soft, dehydrated or brown stems suggest that a chilli is well past its pick date and may have black seeds inside and taste bitter.

2. Look for chillies with firm skin. As a chilli ages, its skin becomes soft as a result of dehydration.

Store

David taught me that chillies are sensitive to changing temperatures and environments, so the best place to store them is in a zip-lock bag, with the air pushed out to prevent mould, in the crisper drawer of the fridge. That way the temperature won't change when the fridge door opens and closes.

If you can't finish all your chillies and want to prolong their life, store them in the freezer, infuse in an oil or dry them out. If you decide to dry them out, David says to leave them in the sunlight but be wary of the mould aflatoxin, which can grow in humid environments. A spot with full sunlight is best.

Prep

If you would like your chillies to be less spicy, remove the internal thread and seeds, noting that the core thread is more spicy than the seeds. This is where the oil, which contains the capsaicin, is located.

THANH'S TIPS

Every Vietnamese household has their own version of nước chấm (dipping sauce), which is colloquially called nước mắm (fish sauce). Nearly all families use bullet chillies, as they're sweet and not too spicy, although red cassette chillies are also used by those who prefer more heat, as they have about double the quantity of capsaicin on the Scoville scale. Mum's secret is to deseed the chillies to make the sauce less spicy. She also adds a little grated carrot for sweetness.

If you're making a large batch of nước chấm to keep in the fridge, omit the grated carrot until serving; otherwise, you'll end up with soggy carrot in your dip, which is not exactly a desirable texture. If fresh bullet or cassette chillies aren't available in your area, you can always purchase them frozen from Asian grocery stores. Substituting a different varietal of chilli will change the flavour of this nước chấm because the bullet chillies add a distinctly sweet taste, which is synonymous with the sauce. The biggest unknown is the fish sauce – some are saltier than others, so depending on the brand you may need to scale back or add more. If you're not familiar with the salt intensity of your fish sauce, add it slowly at the end and taste as you go; if you need more, then continue to add. Remember, you can't take it out once you've added it!

MUM'S NUOC CHAM

NƯỚC CHẤM

MAKES about 80 ml (⅓ cup)

30 g brown sugar
1½ tablespoons hot water
1 garlic clove, finely chopped
1 red bullet chilli, deseeded and finely chopped
1½ tablespoons fish sauce
3 teaspoons freshly squeezed lime juice
¼ carrot, grated

Combine the brown sugar and hot water in a bowl and stir quickly to dissolve. Add the garlic, chilli, fish sauce and lime juice and mix well. Add half the grated carrot and stir – it will bleed its sweet juices into the sauce, completely changing the flavour. Taste the nước chấm – it should taste sweet, spicy, salty and sour. Divide the nước chấm among dipping bowls, adding the remaining carrot when ready to serve.

Leftover nước chấm will keep in a jar in the fridge for up to 3 days.

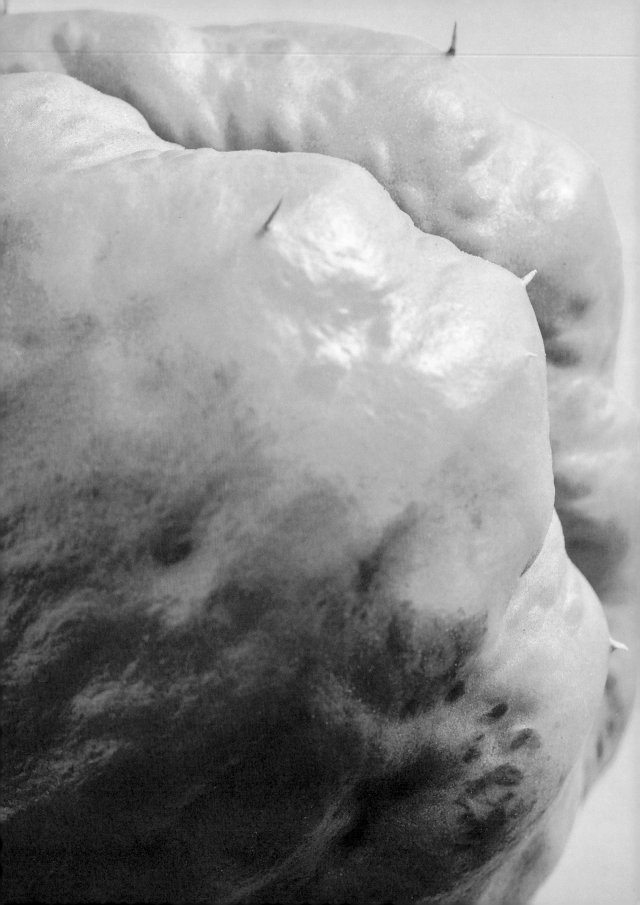

CHOKOS

The humble choko is often seen as nothing more than a creeping wild vine across Australian backyards, sheds and neighbourhoods, but this fruit has a long and travelled history. Originating in Mexico, where it was a staple food for the Aztecs and other indigenous societies, the choko travelled from Central America to Europe during the Columbian exchange in the 16th century. From there, it traversed Asia and, finally, came to Australia. While its more common name is 'chayote', with Spanish roots, Australians were first introduced to this fruit by Chinese immigrants who most likely brought it over during the Gold Rush. In Cantonese, the word for chayote is 'chai yuet' (菜芋), which gradually became 'choko' in Australia.

The choko is most often cooked as a vegetable, and it is a polarising ingredient for many Australians. While it's better known in Chinese cuisine as a staple vegetable with various cooking methods, the history of its culinary use in Australia is far different. Chokos in Australia were known as a 'filler' for low-income families during the Great Depression. Given the choko's ability to grow wild and yield plenty of crops, it was seen as a free backyard source of fibre and nutrition. I can understand why some people can't touch choko if they ate it a lot in their younger years and got sick of it – I'm not sure I would want to eat it a couple of times a week.

The choko is most often cooked as a vegetable, and it is a polarising ingredient for many Australians.

Choko versatility

Many Aussies have shared with me on social media that the most common way they prepare choko is to boil it or bake it with butter, salt and pepper. Whenever I bake choko, it gives me potato-crossed-with-broccoli feels, but there are so many other ways to prepare it. Variety is the spice of life and the culinary world of chokos is vast, from choko gratin and choko in curry, to pickled choko and cheese-stuffed choko served in a soup – the possibilities are endless. Trust me, give this underappreciated vegetable a chance and you'll be pleasantly surprised.

While wild-vine chokos are often very spiky, the commercial cultivars you see at the shops are selected because they don't have spikes. They have smooth skin and are much easier to harvest, handle and peel. Generally speaking, as the fruit ripens, it will expand and look plumper. My fruiterer cousin, Raymond Chau, says most customers will pick the plump chokos because they are easier to peel, although it means the seed will be bigger. Darker-skinned fruit is also a sign of maturity.

In Australia, as in Asia, chokos are grown to full maturity and then they are cooked or preserved; however, in South America, they pick the fruit when it is very young and eat it raw. These tender baby chokos have not developed thick sap in the skin and are crispy and fluffy, instead of dense and with a seed.

The tendrils, young leaves and shoots of the choko plant are also edible. They have slight bitter notes and can be used in stir-fries, soups and even dumplings. Although not widely available, you can find them in speciality Asian fruit shops in summertime.

THANH'S TIPS

Choose

MATURE CHOKOS

1. Look for chokos that are firm, heavy and plump, with few grooves or channels.

2. Darker-coloured chokos suggest maturity.

3. Avoid chokos that show signs of shrinking or the seed bulging at the base.

YOUNG CHOKOS

1. Look for chokos that are small and light in colour.

2. They should be skinny in shape and have a thin skin.

Store

Store chokos in a plastic bag or airtight container in the crisper drawer of your fridge – the cool and constant temperature will help slow the maturity of the fruit, while the plastic bag or container will keep the humidity high and prevent moisture loss.

Prep

1. Wear kitchen gloves to prevent the sap from irritating your skin.

2. Cut the choko in half and remove the seed by slicing at a 45-degree angle either side of the seed.

3. Peel and bake whole or slice and add to stir-fried dishes.

Growing up, I loved it when Mum cooked su su xào. I never saw choko in the supermarket, only in Asian fruit shops, so it was always known as 'su su' to me, which is the Vietnamese word for choko. To this day, I can't stir-fry choko as well as my mum, but I still try! When stir-fried, it has a distinct flavour and a firm but soft texture that I love. Make sure you thoroughly cook the choko until it starts to turn translucent, otherwise it will have a very green taste.

STIR-FRIED CHOKO

SU SU XÀO

SERVES 1–2

1 choko
1½ tablespoons vegetable oil
1 small Thai red shallot, diced
2 garlic cloves, diced
1 teaspoon fish sauce
sea salt
steamed jasmine rice, to serve

Peel the choko, then cut it in half and use a knife to slice a diamond shape around the seed to remove it. Cut the flesh into 3 mm thick slices on the diagonal.

Heat the vegetable oil in a large frying pan with a lid over medium heat. Add the shallot and garlic and sauté for 2 minutes, until fragrant. Add the choko, toss the pan to coat it in the shallot and garlic, then add the fish sauce and 2½ tablespoons of water. Stir to combine, then cover with a lid and cook for 5 minutes or until the choko is translucent and tender. Season with salt, to taste.

Serve immediately with steamed jasmine rice.

There's nothing like enjoying a clear broth soup at the dinner table in a Vietnamese household. As a kid, most nights Mum would cook a soup, stir-fry and condiment dishes to pair with jasmine rice. The soups were almost always a variation of pork or chicken, with different vegetables adding flavour, nutrition and fibre. Mum loves to stir-fry choko, so it was rare for her to add it to soups, but that was not the case for my good friend and champion of Vietnamese home cooking, Duncan Lu, who grew up eating choko soup. Given he still eats it regularly, I asked Duncan for his recipe and thoughts on choko in clear bone broth. He replied: 'The natural sweetness and texture of choko when simmered until tender, but still firm, is what makes it the perfect fruit for this soup. My variation of choko soup combines chokos and carrots to create a sweet and savoury umami flavour.'

DUNCAN LU'S VIETNAMESE CHOKO SOUP

CANH SU SU

SERVES
2–4

2 chokos, peeled and seeds
    removed, chopped into
    2–3 cm chunks
1 carrot, peeled and chopped
    into 1–2 cm chunks
sea salt, to taste
sugar, to taste
bunch of coriander, leaves
    picked
cracked black pepper
steamed jasmine rice, to serve

PORK BONE BROTH
1.5 kg pork neck bones
1 onion, base removed, skin
    left on
2.5 cm piece of ginger, crushed
5 g dried shrimp
2 tablespoons fish sauce
⅓ teaspoon anchovy salt or
    MSG (see Note)
1 tablespoon sea salt
30 g rock sugar or
    1 tablespoon sugar
bunch of coriander roots,
    scraped clean and rinsed

To make the pork bone broth, place the pork neck bones in a large stockpot and cover with plenty of water. Bring to the boil, then drain immediately and rinse under running water to remove any impurities.

Return the pork neck bones to the pot, along with the remaining pork bone broth ingredients. Cover with 5 litres of water and bring to the boil, then reduce the heat to low and simmer for 2 hours.

Add the choko and carrot to the pot and simmer for a further 10 minutes or until the choko is tender but still firm. Season to taste with salt and sugar.

Divide the choko soup among bowls, top with the coriander leaves and a pinch of pepper, and serve with steamed jasmine rice and other Vietnamese savoury dishes, such as braised lemongrass chicken or thịt kho (see page 90).

NOTE: Monosodium glutamate (MSG) has been treated unfairly over the years by Western media, not unlike the durian! MSG occurs naturally in many foods and is added as a delicious umami flavour enhancer to many Chinese and other East-Asian dishes. MSG can be bought from Asian supermarkets.

COCONUT

my love for coconuts started when I was nine years old. As a child, I tagged along with my parents to visit one of the first coconut farms in Samut Sakhorn, Thailand. Back then, you couldn't buy young coconuts in Australia and my father, a pioneer in specialty Asian produce, wanted to change that. He became the first importer of young coconuts to the country, and while he struggled to sell the produce at first, fast forward two decades and the world's appetite for what is considered the 'fruit of the gods' has grown dramatically.

While walking through the packing shed, I remember the intensely uncomfortable humidity, the guillotining sounds of sliced coconut husks and the unusual blending of nature going through a human-yet-mechanical process of uniformity, to create perfectly cut diamond-shaped young coconuts ready for retail, ready to drink. I remember being awestruck at the workers' speed, ease and skill, and wanting to cut one myself, but my mother refused to let me hold such a sharp knife!

A few years later, when my mum started to develop mild arthritis, I offered to cut our coconuts for her; she begrudgingly said yes, guiding me so I wouldn't cut my fingers off! One of Mum's most cooked dishes is thịt kho (see page 90), a Vietnamese braised pork stew that requires the water of a young coconut to give it a fragrant, sweet aroma. After I learned to cut coconuts confidently, Mum always asked me to do it for her when she cooked this dish, which was usually every week or fortnight.

Young vs old coconuts

While the industry differentiates young and old coconuts as 'immature' and 'mature' respectively, technically they can be the same variety or species. Young coconuts are harvested 20–35 days after flowering; the liquid inside is clear and aromatic, and the meat is thin, tender and soft. Old coconuts will have hung on the palm tree for more than 11 months; their liquid will be oily and the meat thick and creamy. They have different uses and purposes. At a retail level, young coconuts are white-husked diamond-shaped fruits, while old coconuts are circular brown nuts with fibres attached to their skin.

Young coconut is most commonly consumed as a drink, while old coconut is used to make coconut cream and added to desserts or savoury dishes like curries.

Fresh young coconut water vs bottled coconut water

The most commoditised young coconut in the world is the nam hom (aromatic) coconut, and this is the variety that created the young coconut boom we see in the West today. However, if you are in Sri Lanka, you'll find that the king coconut, with its yellow skin, is very popular and sweet but has less aroma, while the Vietnamese dua xiem coconut is intensely sweet and rich, but not as aromatic.

What makes things confusing is that the young coconut water sold in cartons and bottles is a mix of different cultivars, as well as old and young coconuts, which compromises flavour. This is why a fresh young coconut still in its husk is incomparable to bottled coconut water. Think a single vineyard wine versus cask wine. I've tasted coconut water from India to Brazil, but none has the balance of aromas and sweetness as the water from a nam hom coconut. Other coconuts usually have mild neutral flavours of sour tang, mild salts and rich and oily nutty notes. The common flavour profile of a coconut hanging from a palm tree on a beach is not very sweet. They are satiating from a thirst point of view, but not satisfying in terms of flavour. This is because these cultivars aren't grown for flavour, compared to coconut palms grown on a plantation, which are. Needless to say, each market prefers different types of young coconut water.

Coconuts and culture

There are many cultural associations with coconuts in coastal communities and it's not surprising that a lot of them are to do with 'purity'. Thailand's largest exporter of fresh young coconut is my dad's good friend Kai. Kai once explained to me that coconut water is so clean and pure that it's said to be the only fruit that the gods consume, because no other fruit in the world contains 'clear water'. All other fruits are consumed with fibre and flesh.

My dad always retells stories of the Vietnam War (which he lived through), where he saw soldiers on stretchers with coconuts above them, dripping the water into their veins. To find the purest coconuts, locals were asked to climb palm trees and harvest the fruits at the very top, as they were considered clean, pure and suitable for IV fluid. These stories only add to the mystical 'purity' of this liquid fruit gold, and whenever I drink coconut water I always think about these rich cultural and historical meanings.

Arguably every country consumes and celebrates coconuts differently, but perhaps none more so than the Hindu community. The coconut is considered a 'spiritual' food or 'satvik' in Hinduism, and it is important not only from a culinary point of view, but also from a religious and cultural perspective. I know this because our family business sources old coconuts with the three 'eyes' covered for the Hindu community. My Hindu customers have told me that in their religion, mature coconut is considered a sacred offering to the gods and goddesses. In many rituals and ceremonies, a coconut (or many coconuts) is broken open as a symbol of breaking the ego; the water and meat inside are offered as prasad (a spiritual offering). The breaking and offering of the coconut is an act of devotion and is believed to bring blessings, protection and prosperity. The three eyes of the coconut, also called 'chakras', are considered to represent the three Hindu deities Brahma, Vishnu and Shiva. In Hindu rituals, it is customary to break open a coconut by hitting it on one of these three marks.

YOUNG COCONUT

OLD COCONUT

Choose

YOUNG COCONUT

1. Look for heavy coconuts. Light coconuts may only be 70–80 per cent full of water. Hold the coconut, diamond-side down, in the palm of your non-dominant hand and tap the base of the coconut with your other hand. The more vibrations you feel in your non-dominant hand, the more the water is sloshing about in the coconut, meaning it contains some air and less water. Full coconuts will not vibrate much and will deflect, rather than absorb, your tap.

2. Avoid coconuts with mould on the base, as the water inside may be sour. Holes or gaps in the husk are natural and not defects.

3. The best-before date on a coconut is not a good indication of whether or not it is fresh, as producers dictate their own dates and the best-before date is not regulated.

MATURE COCONUT

1. Look for a heavy coconut – the heavier it is, the more water it will have inside.

2. Check the surface and 'eyes' for white mould. The area where the shell is thinnest will show mould first. If this looks fine, then you're good to go.

3. Any white to blue mould on the skin is a no go, as the flesh inside is most likely off.

Prep (young coconut)

As the years went on after I first cut open a coconut for my mum, I began to use less and less power to do so. I gradually began to understand the anatomy of the coconut husk and shell, as well as its weak points.

Every fruit has its unique pros and cons, and for coconuts, so much of our enjoyment of this fruit is dependent on how difficult it is to open. You'll need some confidence with a knife or a cleaver, but armed with the following instructions, cutting open a coconut will be a breeze.

Young coconuts have been shaved into a uniform diamond-shaped, white-husked fruit, usually wrapped in plastic to prevent the husk from shrinking as a result of dehydration. They are cut in this way to make it easy for the consumer to open, as the internal shell of the coconut is within 1 cm of the diamond top. The flat base of the young coconut is actually the top of the coconut, where the eyes are located. This is where the coconut was connected to the palm and where the nutrients came from.

EASY-PEASEY METHOD

This is the easiest way to access the water of a young coconut. Using a cleaver, cut the top (diamond) husk off so the nut sits flat on a surface and doesn't roll over. Now slice the bottom husk off, find the weak eye and poke a hole in it. This eye is where the nutrients from the palm flowed into the coconut, and it is the thinnest part of the coconut shell (the very top). It can be broken with a metal fork or knife once the husk is removed. Insert a straw and enjoy.

PENTAGON METHOD

This is the most common method and one I hope you all learn, as it allows you to easily drink the water *and* scoop the flesh. The diamond top has deliberately been cut this way so you can use a cleaver and literally chop the top off. The most common methods are the triangle cut or square cut, but over time I've realised that it's actually easiest to make a pentagon cut, as it's closer to the shape of the circle that surrounds the diamond-shaped top. Cutting in the triangle or square method requires you to use more power to cut deeper into the husk, while the pentagon method means your cuts will be closer to the thinnest part of the diamond-shaped top and hence less power is required. The opening that you cut is also usually bigger, making it easier to insert a spoon and scoop out the flesh. I had been cutting coconuts for 20 years before I learned this!

BUTTER KNIFE METHOD

If there are no sharp knives available, you can use a butter knife to remove the light white husk and access the coconut. Slice through the top of the coconut horizontally in a sawing action until you reach the shell circle or ring. Keep slicing to remove all of the white husk around this circle. You will notice three prominent ridges – these are the strongest points of the shell – but between the ridges is a smooth round surface, which is weaker. Using the back of the butter knife, whack this smooth area until a crack starts to form. Now you just need to stick the knife into the crack, give it a wiggle and remove the broken shell lid. Voila!

ONLY HAVE A POCKET KNIFE?

Use the butter knife method, but use a rock or anything sharp to make the cracks.

Prep (mature coconut)

An old coconut has had its husk removed and may or may not have its three eyes exposed. Remember, the covering of the eyes is purely for praying purposes, although in my experience I have found that exposed eyes also result in a coconut with a shorter shelf life. This is important when selecting a good coconut.

Understanding a coconut's anatomy will allow you to exploit its weakness:

1. Holding the coconut with the three eyes at the top, you will see three ridges that run from the top of the coconut to the base. The 'waist' of the coconut, on the other hand, is its weakest point – specifically, the midpoint between each ridge.

2. Use the back of a cleaver or a hammer (with a bowl underneath to catch the coconut liquid) to whack this area. Move to the next midpoint and whack again, and keep going until a crack forms along the coconut's waist and the liquid gushes out.

3. Stick the cleaver into the coconut and prise it open. To remove the meat, slide a knife between the coconut meat and the shell and prise the meat away. You can peel the brown skin off the meat if you like – this will remove some of the nutty flavour, but if you're making coconut milk it yields a cleaner and richer taste. Alternatively, use a peeler to make coconut chips and gently toast in a low oven until dry.

As a teenager, I can't recall how many times I came home to a big pot of thịt kho simmering away on the stove. Mum always made food in large quantities as there were seven of us to feed, and we all loved and devoured thịt kho. Back in Vietnam, before refrigeration, thịt kho was a dish my parents ate regularly too, as the pork would be preserved in the salty and sugary liquid. While the backbone of the dish requires a good darkened caramel with smoky flavours, the aroma is transformed by the addition of young coconut water for the braising liquid. The heaviness of the meat is lifted, and the natural sweetness of the young coconut water adds extra vibrancy and a delicate sodium-like sour tang that makes the stew seem richer, as though a layer of coconut fat and nutty palm aroma has been added naturally. On the days when Mum made thịt kho without young coconut water, I would know immediately as the dish, although delicious, felt flat. This dish takes me back to sitting with my mum and cutting coconuts on the floor a the chopping board on top of old newspapers!

VIETNAMESE BRAISED PORK BELLY IN YOUNG COCONUT WATER

THỊT KHO

SERVES 4

1 kg boneless, skin-on pork belly, cut into 2 cm pieces
1½ tablespoons fish sauce, plus extra to taste
2 tablespoons Vietnamese caramel sauce
2½ tablespoons peanut oil
30 g piece of ginger, peeled and finely chopped
5 garlic cloves, finely chopped
5 Thai red shallots, sliced
water from 2 young coconuts (see page 88 for how to open a young coconut)
500 ml (2 cups) chicken stock
4 eggs
1 tablespoon sugar
3 teaspoons sea salt
steamed jasmine rice, to serve
5 red bullet chillies, finely sliced, to serve (optional)

Place the pork belly in a large non-reactive (not metal) dish, add the fish sauce and caramel sauce and rub it into the pork. Set aside to marinate for 10 minutes at room temperature.

Heat the peanut oil in a large saucepan over medium–high heat. Add the pork belly and cook, stirring, for 3–5 minutes, until just starting to colour. Add the ginger, garlic and shallot and stir for 1 minute.

Add the young coconut water and chicken stock, bring to the boil, then reduce the heat to a simmer.

Meanwhile, cook the eggs in a saucepan of boiling water for 5 minutes. Drain and carefully peel the eggs, then add them to the pork mixture. Reduce the heat to low and cook, slightly covered, for 1½ hours or until the pork is tender and the sauce is rich (it will still be quite runny). Season with the sugar, salt and more fish sauce, if needed.

Serve with steamed jasmine rice on the side and chilli scattered over the thịt kho, if desired.

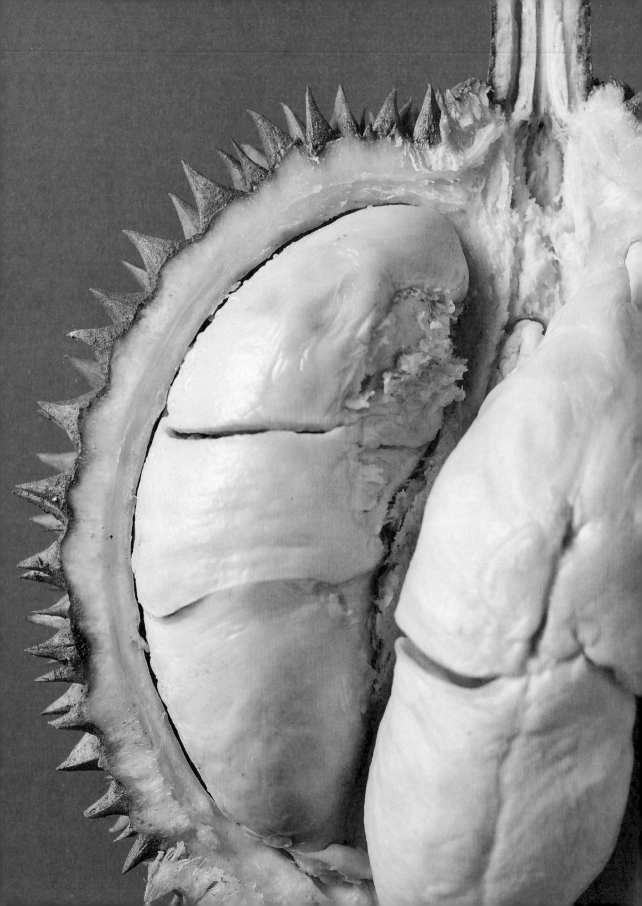

The 'King of Fruits' earns its title just by the sheer sight of its magnificent and imposing figure. It has a powerful smell which, unfortunately, many don't perceive as a pleasant perfume, instead describing it as an off-putting odour. Those who do see its beauty consider durian to be one of the most delicious fruits in the world. Having grown up eating it, and as a tropical fruit specialist, I am in the latter camp and will talk about durian from the perspective of someone who adores it.

The smell

Let's get the facts straight! Where does the durian's aroma come from, and why is it so strong and divisive? The fruit's unique aroma is caused by the combination of sulphur-containing compounds, not gases. Some of these compounds smell like caramel or bitter chocolate, while others smell like garlic, onion, leek and blue cheese. They combine to create a concoction of smells, and it's this combination that we sensorially experience. For me, I smell the beauty of all the volatile compounds, while others cannot get past the less appealing ones. These volatile organic compounds evaporate easily at room temperature, can be smelled from a distance and can linger in the surrounding air. This is why frozen durian does not have a strong smell, but once it has defrosted the aroma comes alive and is released into the environment.

Odour to aroma

Often I see Western food media describe the smell of durian as an odour, not an aroma. I am hurt by this idea, as it has continued to trickle down and create a rift between Eastern and Western views of what fruit is good and what fruit is bad, without considering perspective. As a comparison, let's think about blue cheese. The food media rarely has any negative rhetoric about blue cheese being horrible. It's more often described as punchy, pungent, gourmet, strong, flavourful and complex. At its very worst it is described as challenging or not to everyone's taste. Durian, on the other hand, has only very recently, in 2020, been described in a *New York Times* article as 'the most infamous fruit which stinks of death', and as having a 'whiff of skunk'. Those who have not tried durian but have read that article might never want to try durian in their life. I believe this rhetoric, which plays out constantly, is unfair, and it is up to those who love durian and can describe its beauty to change this perception.

Experience, not sustenance

Given its hefty price tag, its size and the skill it takes to open, durian should be seen as an experience, not sustenance. Much like going to a Michelin-star restaurant, it's the experience you are paying for. When my parents brought home a durian, we would smell it as soon as we walked through the door, then after dinner we would all sit around the table and Dad would slowly cut it open. No one knew if it was going to be good or bad; there's always that gamble with durian. Once the arils had been successfully removed from the Bowser-like shell, we would all have one piece, and maybe an extra one if there was a spare. We would slowly suck the flesh off the seed and enjoy it like ice cream.

Durian is my third favourite fruit behind cherries and mangosteens, but in terms of flavour, it is arguably the most intense fruit. It is beautifully creamy, sulphuric, bitter, sweet and caramelly all at the same time, but it is also heavy and too rich to eat a lot of in one sitting. There comes a point where it is no longer moreish. Trust me, I've eaten more durian in one sitting than nearly anyone I know; I do it for educational purposes, of course!

Fresh vs frozen

When I was young, only imported frozen durian was available and, in fact, that's still the case for many countries today. Depending on how fast the fruit is frozen and the cold-storage conditions in transit, the texture and quality of frozen durian can be pretty close to fresh. Unfortunately, there are many opportunities for temperatures to fluctuate on a frozen durian's journey, leading the fruit to deteriorate, and it's pot luck whether the retailer and consumer purchase a good or bad durian. Besides freezing considerations, there are other factors to consider, such as inconsistency in grading and choice of varietal. Packing sheds often gather durians from many farms and grade them based on size, shape and imperfections. There is even a grading system in Malaysia that ranges from BB to AA, almost like the diamond trade. However, because grading is based on aesthetics, the quality of the flesh inside is not often considered; instead, buyers are reliant on the reputation of the exporter and the varietal.

> **When selecting a whole fresh durian at the market, look for fruit with a scaley stem. This will likely be fully developed inside, with favourable sweet and textural traits.**

In my lifetime importing durian from Thailand, the Philippines, Vietnam and Malaysia, I have found that some varietals hold better texture when defrosted than others. Musang king, or cat mountain king, is arguably one of the most famous varietals in the world, and one 2 kg piece of it can cost $80 in Australia. Musang king is a great example of a cultivar that performs well when frozen, as when it thaws, its texture is still relatively consistent with fresh durian. Conversely, one of my favourite durians, gan yao or 'tall stem' – known for its long stem – is famous in Thailand for its cheesecake-like texture. I love the mouthfeel of fresh gan yao, but frozen gan yao does not defrost well, as the water splits from the fibre and the cheesecake-like texture is lost. It's hard to know which varietals will perform well frozen, but if you eat durian for its favourable textural experience, rather than pure flavour profile, there is a higher chance of being disappointed. The difficulty of finding good durian in the Western world only adds to the appetite of those who love it, and further fuels their desire for a good durian experience.

The last decade, hastened by Covid-19, has transformed the frozen durian industry. Firstly, more fruit and vegetables are being purchased from online stores, particularly from niche premium produce distributors. These companies are better able to control the cold chain and deliver superior frozen durian, given their direct links with importers and customers. If you haven't purchased premium fruits from the internet before, give it a go – it will change your life. In my opinion, fresh produce internet shopping has saved the frozen durian market and made it better.

The second development is the changing durian palate. Prior to 2010, the frozen durian game was dominated by Thai durian, predominantly the monthong, or golden pillow, varietal, known for its big shape, large flesh, small seed and sweet flavour. However, the coming of age of the Chinese market, as well as durian lovers' desire for stronger-flavoured fruit, has given rise to bitter notes. Those who have always loved durian mainly sought sweet varietals, but as with any seasoned eater, over time we desire more intense flavours as we become accustomed to the norm. Customer palates are changing, and the sulphuric bitter notes seen in some varieties are gaining popularity, disrupting traditional markets and changing the selection you see at Asian grocery stores.

While travelling to Chanthaburi to visit durian farms with my father's good friend and fruit exporter Mr Theerachai, who I also consider my uncle, he taught me how to pick durian and how Thai people like it. In Thailand, consumers prefer durian to be 90 per cent ripe, meaning it is right on the edge of maturity. While walking through the market, Mr Theerachai would ask the fruit-stall holders to tap their durians and ask for 'breaking maturity'. The trader would tap between ten and 20 durians with a bamboo stick, with the durian held up to their ear. Every vibration or thud relays the millimetre gap between the flesh and shell wall of the fruit. As a durian matures and ripens, the flesh becomes soft and detaches itself from the shell wall. This gap is then exploited and used as the marker of maturity. A thud would mean no gap and, therefore, an immature fruit; a hollow sound would mean a big gap, indicating a certain level of ripeness. Identifying the sound where the flesh is still attached to the shell wall but starting to move as the outer shell is knocked is an art form. Like someone who has perfect pitch, it's a truly wonderful experience to watch in action.

My tip for selecting ripe, fresh durian is to use the tapping method – if you can hear a hollow sound, you know that it is mature and probably good to eat.

I have been selling fresh Australian durians for more than a decade. I've found that, due to changing palates, consumers now prefer 100 per cent ripe durian or 'tree-dropped' fruit for maximum flavour over interesting texture. I am often left with an oversupply of a box or two, most often the fruits with awkward shapes – I call them gnarly and interesting. I often bring them home to eat and they are even more delicious and complex than the more perfectly shaped durians. Good friend and durian tour guide and authority Lindsay Gasik agrees. In her years of travelling to hundreds of durian farms across multiple continents, her experiences with awkwardly shaped fruits have always yielded 'flavourable' returns. Yes, I just made that word up! Lindsay says that younger trees often yield more favourable round-shaped durians; however, the trees don't deliver the complex flavours that a 20–100-year-old durian tree will. Older trees more often yield gnarly fruits with awkward shapes, and their flavour is often more intense.

Lindsay also taught me how the state of the stem can indicate the age of the fruit. Durian, when less than 90 per cent mature, will be hard and almost starch-like, not sweet. A durian must almost fall off the tree to be edible, sweet and delicious. As durian reaches its final maturity phase on a tree, the stem will turn from green and smooth to brown and scaly, and from firm to slightly soft. This is because the tree is preparing to drop the fruit, so it must loosen its stem to allow it to fall (hence the term 'tree-dropped' durian).

Richard Koivusalo, Lindsay's husband and experienced durian epicure, once told me of other physiological changes in a durian as it reaches full maturity. As with most fruits, a whole ripe durian gets drier and lighter as the starches turn to sugars. In addition, the thorns, especially those around the stem, dry out and break easily when fully mature. Richard describes these thorns as though one 'blew hot air over them and they melted together like plastic'. You may also see cracks in between the thorns. So look for blackish and weak thorns when next selecting a fresh durian!

Choose

FRESH

1. When selecting a whole fresh durian at the market, look for fruit with a scaley stem. This is a sign the durian has reached full maturity and will likely be fully developed inside, with favourable sweet and textural traits. Hold the durian up to your ear (wear a glove if it's very spiky) and tap the durian with a stick or utensil a few times. An unripe durian will sound like you're hitting a wall; it's basically the sound of the stick hitting the skin. At 85 per cent ripe, the fruit will vibrate on the inside. At 100 per cent ripe, the durian will sound hollow when tapped, like there is an air pocket in the fruit.

2. A crack at the base of the fruit suggests it is 'tree-dropped' and will be ripe. There may be rubber bands holding the durian to prevent it from breaking any further. Check that no insects have found their way in; if not, the fruit will be good.

3. A scaley and brown stem indicates the durian is fully mature and will eat well. A green and smooth stem suggests the fruit was been picked too early and is unripe.

4. Black and brittle thorns show that the fruit was picked at late maturity and is a sign the fruit will be tasty inside.

FROZEN: make sure there isn't any ice forming on the skin of the durian. If you see icicles, it's likely the durian has been stored in inconsistent freezing temperatures and the fruit has been thawing and re-freezing constantly. This has an extremely detrimental effect on the quality of the durian.

Store

FRESH: store uncut fresh durian at room temperature for a few days, and consume on the day you open it.

FROZEN: consume thawed frozen durian straight away.

Prep

Cutting durian is really a matter of practice and becoming comfortable with the fruit. If this is the part of the durian experience that scares you, well, I have a great method for any first-timer. As far as I know, Dad invented this technique, or at least he's the only person I know who cuts durian this way, and it stemmed from his desire to not be pricked constantly. At first, I was unimpressed because it requires little skill and anyone can do it. It also removes a portion of the base and I prefer the aesthetic of an intact durian. However, if you're not after a photo moment, or if your durian-opening skills are less than polished, this is the cutting method for you! I call it the 'star hack' method because once you remove the base of the durian you expose its crack lines (which look like a star), allowing you to then easily remove the skin. This method is perfect for most durian varietals with thin-to-medium skin. For very thick-skinned durians, such as duyaya, it's a little more difficult, but it's still a great technique.

DAD'S 'STAR HACK' TECHNIQUE FOR FRESH AND THAWED FROZEN DURIAN

1. Using a large sharp knife or cleaver and a sawing action, cut 1 cm off the base of the durian. This will reveal the crack lines, which look similar to a star.

2. Insert your knife or cleaver midway into one crack line on a 45-degree angle. Twist the knife or cleaver to break the skin away from the flesh. If the skin doesn't crack, run the knife or cleaver along the ridge line to create an opening, taking care not to cut into the flesh. Repeat with the remaining crack lines, if necessary.

3. Once enough of an opening has formed, use both hands to slowly pull the durian apart.

4. To remove the segments from the core, place your palm on the outer edge of the inside rind and push away from the internal core thread. The durian segment shell will split and reveal the arils in each pocket.

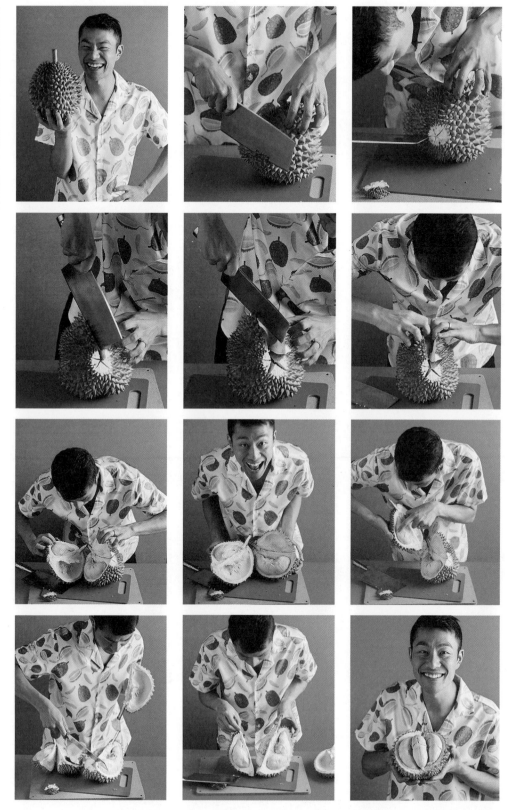

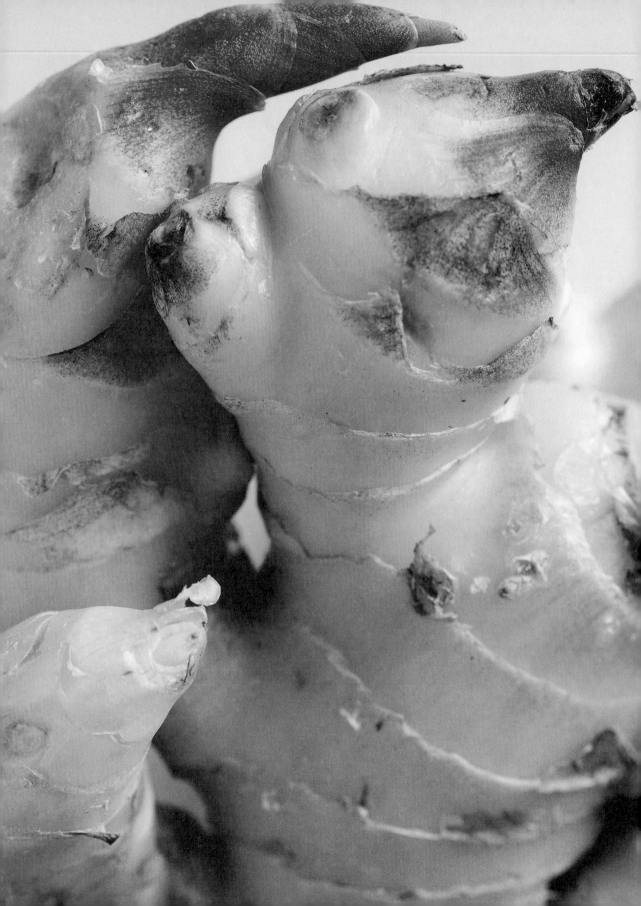

GINGER

um tells me to drink lemon–honey tea with a chunk of ginger whenever I'm sick. It's the warming motivation I need to get better, but what does the ginger do, and what healing abilities does it have?

For most of us, our first interaction with ginger is probably medicinal rather than culinary. Even today, whenever I eat ginger for its taste I always feel better, even though it's subconscious. In Eastern medicine, ginger is known for its 'heating' properties; in Western medicine, studies into its compounds have revealed a range of benefits, from boosting our immune systems to being anti-inflammatory.

As a fruiterer, my focus has always been on the freshness of ginger, as this means more robust flavour and nutritional benefits. Having sold ginger for more than a decade now, I find that few people can recognise the difference between young and old ginger, as they usually only buy a small thumb-sized knob each time; however, there is a big difference in texture, flavour and price.

In Eastern medicine, ginger is known for its 'heating' properties.

Young vs old ginger

Although they are the same plant and root, young and old ginger are harvested at different stages of maturity. Old ginger is grown three to four months longer than young ginger, during which time the underground stem, better known as the rhizome of the ginger plant, grows larger, develops a thick brown skin, and becomes more fibrous with spicy oils. By comparison, young ginger is pale white with almost no skin.

Since spice is the primary flavour we seek in ginger, old ginger is generally more popular, but young ginger definitely has its place, with its gentle heat, fewer 'strings' and crisp, light texture. The most common use of young ginger I see is the pink pickled ginger that's served with sushi.

As young ginger is picked very early in the growth cycle, it has a much higher water content, meaning its shelf life is very poor, often only lasting one to two weeks after harvest. Old ginger, with its thick brown skin, less water and more fibrous body, means its shelf life can be two to four weeks, depending on storage conditions. Given young ginger's short shelf life and reduced oil content, it is has a much cheaper price point than old ginger.

Know what you're paying for

Although supermarkets and fruit shops may simply state 'ginger' on their labels, it's worth knowing what you are paying for. Young ginger can contain less than half the amount of oils as old ginger, so you'll need to buy double the amount to obtain the same level of spice and flavour. Most recipes call for old ginger, which is the grade of ginger mainly sold at retail level. Generally speaking, young ginger is often only sold when old ginger is scarce or unavailable, or when discount ginger is required.

Ginger is graded by its size, and this usually determines the price. The main part of ginger is the rhizome, and it's the flesh inside that we seek. Rhizomes should not be confused

IF THE SPICE OF OLD GINGER IS TOO MUCH FOR YOU,

TRY YOUNG GINGER. IT HAS A LIGHTER FLORAL SPICE, WHICH DISSIPATES ONCE IT HITS YOUR BACK PALATE.

with bulbs, which are the gnarly protrusions attached to the rhizome. Bulbs have more skin-to-flesh ratio, so there is more to peel, leaving you with less flesh. That's why, for value, it's better to pick large rhizomes with few bulbs attached.

If the spice of old ginger is too much for you, try young ginger, as it has a lighter floral spice, which dissipates once it hits the back of your palate. Biting into raw old ginger will leave a lingering heat in your mouth.

Although there are many varieties of ginger, most growers select cultivars that grow large rhizomes. Even though some smaller cultivars may be more spicy and oily, they tend to return lower prices to the farmer. A classic example of this is Queensland ginger, which is generally 30 per cent smaller than Hawaiian ginger, but is spicier. In the last decade, I've seen the Queensland varietal go from representing a sizeable percentage of the ginger market to barely none at all being grown commercially in Australia. Instead, the growers I represent in Queensland have opted to grow only a small percentage of Queensland ginger as it is more resistant to disease.

The last time I went to their farm, I visited the cleaning shed to see where all the dirt is brushed off the ginger. I found the processing work fascinating. We see the pruned roots in stores, which are cleaned of nearly all of their dirt, but this dirt is completely normal and, just like brushed potatoes, it's likely to preserve the ginger for longer. It's another reminder not to be focused on aesthetics, especially as we remove the skin anyway.

Choose

THANH'S TIPS

1. Select large rhizomes with few bulbs attached to make peeling easier.

2. Understand the differences between young and old ginger, their levels of spice and culinary benefits.

3. Avoid shrivelled (dehydrated or shrinking) pieces of ginger.

4. Don't be put off by dirt on ginger – this is completely natural as the rhizomes grow in the ground. However, wet dirt isn't good as it will cause mould.

Store

Store ginger, uncovered, in the fridge to ensure moisture doesn't build up and result in mould development. If you've bought too much, freeze it before it starts to shrivel, lose moisture and sink into itself.

Prep

Remove any dehydrated ends from the ginger, then use either a spoon to peel the skin or I prefer to use a knife, which removes more of the fibres and yields less flesh. Keep the skins in a zip-lock bag in the freezer. I then infuse them in neutral oil over low heat and use the oil to spoon over fish or to sear meat (see opposite page).

Don't throw away your ginger skins! Whether you use a spoon or a knife to peel your ginger, there are always small pieces of flesh attached to the skin, which is where the delicious spicy oils are found. My friend, chef Dan Hong, taught me how to infuse oil with ginger skins when I was a contestant on SBS's *The Chefs' Line*. The oil is super versatile, but is most effective in stir-fries – it adds spice and fragrance to any protein. Normally, when I'm cooking stir-fried beef or pork, I add a few slices of ginger as an aromat, but the ginger oil replaces the need for fresh ginger. It's also a wonderful way to cook fish, as the oil helps remove any fishy aromas and infuses the fish skin. With Cantonese-style steamed fish, sliced ginger and spring onions are usually scattered over the skin before hot oil is poured over the top. Ginger-infused oil makes this process very convenient, as you don't need to add any fresh ginger.

Note that this recipe only works with old ginger, as young ginger has barely developed a skin with any oils. Often, I don't have time to infuse ginger skins immediately after peeling, so I freeze the skins in a zip-lock bag to make at a later date. If you freeze your ginger skins, don't thaw the ginger before adding to the oil, as this will remove the precious ginger spice oils. Instead, place the frozen trimmings straight into the cold oil before heating.

GINGER-SKIN INFUSED OIL

Place the ginger skins in a small saucepan and add enough oil to cover the skins by 1 cm. Place the pan over low heat and gently warm until the ginger starts to sizzle. Allow the ginger to sizzle for 10 minutes, reducing the temperature to the lowest heat possible if the oil starts to bubble too vigorously.

Very carefully strain the oil into a glass jar and discard the ginger skins. Allow to cool, then store away from direct sunlight for 1–2 months.

ginger skins
neutral oil, such as grapeseed
    or vegetable oil

MAKES
1 jar

When I lived in Fukushima, my host family would sometimes take me to a sushi train restaurant. My host mum, Okāsan, would eat huge servings of tsukemono (Japanese pickles) between each sushi dish, the two most common being radish pickles and young ginger pickles. You've probably come across the bright pink and spicy young ginger pickles in little rectangular packets when ordering sushi. They're specifically eaten for their crunchy, spicy and sour traits, which cut through each serving of raw fish as a palate cleanser.

You need young ginger for this pickle recipe, as old ginger is too fibrous and spicy. Pick the largest ginger root you can find so you can cut long slices. Young ginger rhizomes have a pink blush where the new bulbs start to grow; if you retain this pink-tinged skin, it will turn your ginger pale pink after pickling for a day.

JAPANESE PICKLED YOUNG GINGER

新生姜の甘酢漬け

MAKES
500 ml

1 piece of dried kombu
300 g piece of young ginger
1–2 tablespoons table salt
150 ml Japanese rice vinegar
½ teaspoon Korean solar salt or sea salt flakes
70 g caster sugar

Rehydrate the kombu in 200 ml of water for 1 hour.

Peel the ginger using a spoon or a knife, keeping any pink skins attached to bulb. Wash the peeled bulb to remove any residual skin or dirt. Diagonally slice the ginger into long 5 mm thick pieces.

Bring a small saucepan of water to the boil, add the ginger and flash boil for 1 minute, then immediately drain. Using a spoon, press out the excess water, then spread the ginger over a plate or tray in a single layer. Sprinkle the table salt over the ginger and set aside for 5 minutes – this helps to remove excess moisture. Once the ginger is cool, squeeze the pieces to remove any remaining liquid.

Pour the rehydrated kombu and its soaking water into a saucepan and bring to the boil.

Meanwhile, combine the rice vinegar, salt and sugar in a 500 ml sterilised glass jar (see Tip; page 275). Strain the kombu-infused water into the jar and stir until the salt and sugar are dissolved. Add the ginger to the liquid and use chopsticks to stir and separate the ginger slices. Secure with the lid and place in the fridge.

The ginger pickles will be ready to eat in 12 hours, but leave for 24 hours to fully develop the flavours. Store the pickles in the fridge for 2–3 weeks.

GRAPES

In our ever-changing, fast-paced world, we often forget what things used to be like, and table grapes are an excellent example of a changed fruit. When I was young, every grape contained seeds, and it was the norm to spit the pips out. It was so long ago that you may have forgotten! Red grapes ruled the world, especially the red globe varietal, a large spherical grape with translucent green flesh and seeds that would be annoying, not that we knew any better. Then, year by year, the seeds started to disappear and the more expensive, but far more popular, seedless red grape started to take over the shelves in fruit shops. It may not have changed overnight, but in my lifetime I have witnessed the evolution of the grape. Out with the old; here cometh the New World grapes!

When one considers New World versus Old World grapes, you could be forgiven for thinking of wine grapes. Old World table grapes refer to grapes you typically see in Renaissance paintings; varieties such as concord, muscat and sultana, grown in Europe, Asia and Africa. New World grapes, on the other hand, refer to new varieties developed predominantly in the United States; nonchalant table grapes that lack the terroir notes of their wine counterparts, but can be devoured without thinking. Their evolutionary traits have been ground-breaking, yet their social status is far more humble.

What's so good about New World table grapes?

Seedless table grapes, with a larger berry size and thicker skin, are one of the ultimate convenient fruit snacks. The way we eat grapes today is very different from three decades ago when I was a boy, and the choice of varietals will be even more diverse by the time my children are my age. The race among botanical geneticists to develop exciting new varietals and market them has been driven by several large companies in California. Their worldwide influence on the grape industry has been monumental. They have developed varietals, such as crimson seedless and sapphire, via traditional cross-breeding and sturdy agricultural practices, and in the last five years I have seen the advancement of flavours including 'candy cane' and 'fairy floss'. Owning the PBR (Plant Breeder's Rights), or intellectual property, to a varietal is very financially rewarding. Given royalties can come in the form of 'per boxes sold' or 'kilograms harvested', it can be like printing money if you hit the jackpot with the right traits.

Have you ever eaten a very soft grape with very thin skin? I'm tipping not in the last two decades. It's like going through a time machine, and I certainly felt this way during my grape-eating travels. The last time I travelled to Xinjiang, known as the table grape capital of China, I was left feeling disappointed after travelling the market

> " Never turn down the opportunity to taste a high-quality kyoho grape. You'll think it's fake and some kind of candy, but it's a natural fruit.

stores and eating the local grapes. It was fascinating travelling to a non-Western country and almost receiving a culture shock that Old World grapes still existed! Fast forward to today, seven years after that trip, and I've heard that every table grape farm in Turpan City in Xinjiang is now growing American grapes.

Grape flavour

As part of my work, I travel abroad seeking new produce for Australians. My international fruit trade travels led me to Cheonan in South Korea, where they grow Japanese-style kyoho grapes, known as 'kobon' in Korean. These grapes are on another level! When we think of lollies, especially grape-coloured lollies like purple snakes, or grape-flavoured drinks, such as Gatorade, we feel that the flavour is artificial. However, this flavouring actually replicates the authentic flavour of kyoho grapes, and eating them is like tasting grape-flavoured lollies or drinks! While the lollies are intensely sweet because of their sugar content, kyoho grapes are incredibly moreish. Kyoho grapes are a cross-breed variety of the concord grape, which is a cultivar of Vitis labrusca, a wild grape variety native to North America, and purple-grape candy flavour is based on the concord grape. The first time I figured this out, I was lost for words. I wish someone had told me this when I ate my first grape candy.

Never turn down the opportunity to taste a high-quality kyoho grape. You'll think it's fake and some kind of candy, but it's a natural fruit.

Procuring fruit for purpose

Kyoho grapes are known not only for their fantastic flavour but for their aesthetic appeal. Grape growers struggle through the seasons, managing pests, diseases and animals, as well as consumer demands. Growers need to constantly prune the number of berries on each bunch in such a way as to make a perfect downward conical-shaped bunch and to ensure that each berry is the same extra-large size. Once the cluster, or bunch, of grapes is at full maturity, it will be wrapped and packaged to be sold as a gift. It is tireless, back-breaking work under the vines, and the artistic skill required to forecast where and how fast each peduncle will grow and which berry to cut is mastery of the epic kind.

This kind of presentation and gifting culture in fruit selling did not exist in Australia ... well, not until I brought it to Australia! Like my father before me, having a positive impact on the Asian communities we serve, by making available the fruit and vegetables significant to them, has been one of my greatest achievements as a fruiterer.

In my shelf-life testing of kyoho grapes, I have noticed that thicker stems translate to healthier vines, giving each berry more nutrients, meaning they will keep longer and taste better.

Fruit-gifting culture

In Asian cultures, 'gifting fruit', often for special occasions, such as weddings or during festivals such as Lunar New Year and Autumn Moon Festival, shows you are giving health, wealth and respect to others.

The desire for perfect kyoho grapes is driven by the culture of fruit gifting in Japan, started by samurai Benzo Ohshima in the 19th century. Ohshima was a skilled fruit grower whose orchards yielded excellent-quality fruits. He would gift these fruits to lords and other high-ranking officials of the shogunate to gain their favour and support. This practice of gifting eventually caught on among the upper classes, becoming a symbol of status and wealth. Although the fruit-gifting culture in Japan is the most extreme example, Ohshima's influence spans Asia. The more perfect looking the fruit, the more respect one is showing the giftee. Imperfections on fruit are also admired, such as the pattern on a musk melon. It's fascinating and otherworldly if you haven't grown up in this culture.

Travelling to the famous Sembikiya store in Tokyo was a pilgrimage for me. With attendants wearing soft fabric gloves treating fruit like diamonds, and a dizzying amount of spotlights shining on each fruit, nothing you can imagine will prepare you for the prestige of entering one of these Tiffany & Co. fruit shops. While fruit-gifting culture is still in its infancy in Australia among the Asian community, the Sembikiya store and its owner have undoubtedly influenced it.

Never did I think exporting Australian grapes for gifting would be so difficult. On the surface, it's about collecting fruit and organising transport, but it's actually far more about knowing what you have, the expectations of the culture you're exporting to, and what is happening in world markets. When exporting grapes to China, for example, I was constantly being asked about the colour of the skin or, more specifically, the bloom. The bloom on grapes is the white powdery substance that covers the grape's skin. It is naturally occurring and seen as a positive because it is an indicator of the grape's maturity, quality and flavour. Additionally, the bloom can protect the grapes from sun damage, pests and diseases. My Chinese clients were adamant that if the grapes did not have a certain percentage of bloom, they couldn't accept the fruit. The level of technical knowledge in their purchasing was off the charts, and their dedication to procuring the best grapes, although seemingly based on aesthetics at first, was purely related to purchasing flavourful fruit.

Choose

THANH'S TIPS

1. Look for strong, bright-green stems – a thick stem and peduncle is a sign that the bunch has more nutrients to draw from.

2. Berries should be firmly attached to the stem.

3. For many grape varietals, such as crimson, a strong bloom can show maturity and indicates flavour and freshness.

4. Avoid stems that are dry, dehydrated and shrivelled, or bunches with lots of fallen berries at the bottom of the bag – this is called 'shatter' and is a sign of poor fruit quality or aged produce.

Store

Store grapes in a plastic bag or airtight container in the crisper drawer. Grapes must be kept as cold as possible to keep them firm and crispy. Any moisture loss will affect the stem first. After the stem shrivels, the grapes will start to break down very fast.

WHITE POWDERY 'BLOOM' ON THE SKIN OF A GRAPE IS A SIGN OF GOOD FRUIT.

GUAVAS

If only the texture and flavour of a guava was as amazing as the aroma. I mean this in the most earnest and positive way, as the aroma of both the white and pink guava is incredible. White guava has a mild and zingy aroma, while pink guava has a to-die-for aroma and a tangy punch. Where guava can be polarising is its texture and mouthfeel. Some guava varieties have hundreds of small yellow seeds, which can be a little uncomfortable to bite through. Eating around the seeds is not an option, as this is where you find the sweetest flesh. In many ways, it's best for consumers to first try guava juice before eating the actual fruit. The flavour of the guava fruit is why its juice is a popular drink in the parts of the world where it is grown.

I first drank guava juice in a can, when my parents owned their fruit shop, before I ate the fresh fruit. My first interaction with the fruit was during a trip to Vietnam when I was a kid. I remember the guava being cut up in one of those mini mobile glass-box kitchens on the back of a motorbike on the street, and then dipped in salt and chilli, just like my pineapple street snack recipe on page 212.

As a wholesale fruiterer, I sell both white and pink guava; each fruit has their own customer base and they are eaten in very different ways. I love this, especially considering they are two cultivars of the same fruit, but loved and grown by different cultures and communities. White guava isn't the sweetest fruit, but it does have a crunchy and grainy texture which is unique and that some people love. I don't mind it but, depending on the guava, I need to be in the mood to crunch through those seeds or just swallow them whole like my kids. Pink guavas are the opposite and ripen to be very soft and sweet. They're rare in Australia, but should you be in the mood, and if you are patient enough for the guava to ripen and become aromatically its best, it can be an exciting fruit. The fruit itself tastes great, but the aroma is mind-blowing. It's my favourite fruit smell!

While many Asian cultures peel guava, the skin is edible and can offer a lot of flavour. It also mellows out the flavour of the flesh.

Choose

1. Look for guavas with light-green skin – all guava start off dark green on the tree and become lighter in colour as they mature.

2. Pink guavas give off an aroma during late maturity and when ripe, even when firm. If it doesn't have an aroma, the fruit has been picked too early.

3. As pink guavas mature, they plump up and become rounder and smoother, with a thinner skin. Avoid fruit with ridges, bumps, lines and cavities on the skin, as these show the fruit is less mature. The fruit should look full-bodied around the waist.

THANH'S TIPS

> **While many Asian cultures peel guava, the skin is edible and can offer a lot of flavour. It also mellows out the flavour of the flesh.**

GREEN SKIN SHOWS IT'S NOT AS RIPE AS IT COULD BE.

YELLOW SKIN IS A SIGN OF RIPENESS.

YELLOW FLESH IS A SIGN OF RIPENESS.

When I stayed in Sydney while filming the TV show *Plate of Origin*, I met Alejandra Utrera who was a contestant representing Venezuelan cuisine. She is a beautiful, positive spirit whose energy can fill any room. On the days we weren't shooting, the contestants would cook for each other, and on one occasion, I was lucky enough to sit in Aly's kitchen and watch her make tequeños – crunchy fried pastry sticks filled with cheese and/or pink guava. They make a great finger food and snack – where cervezas (beers) are served, tequeños must be nearby!

Finding fresh pink guava isn't easy in Australia. There are only two commercial growers and both are relatively small outfits; however, you can purchase shelf-stable or frozen pink guava paste if you can't find any fresh. This recipe doesn't work with white guava, as it doesn't have a strong tropical fruit aroma. Aly uses haloumi in Australia, but in Venezuela she uses a particular type of cream cheese, which melts after frying. This is a great snack to bring to your next party, because is it even a party if there aren't any tequeños?!

ALY UTRERA'S GUAVA & CHEESE STICKS

TEQUEÑOS VENEZOLANOS DE GUAYABA Y QUESO

MAKES about 20

500 g (3⅓ cups) plain flour
1 tablespoon brown sugar
½ teaspoon sea salt
¼ teaspoon baking powder
125 ml (½ cup) milk
125 ml (½ cup) vegetable oil
200 g haloumi, cut into 8 cm x 7 mm batons
4 pink guavas, cut into 8 cm x 7 mm batons (or use pink guava paste)
vegetable oil, for deep-frying

Combine the flour, sugar, salt and baking powder in the bowl of a stand mixer with the dough hook attached and mix for 20 seconds. Add 125 ml (½ cup) of water, the milk and vegetable oil and mix on medium speed for 4 minutes or until the dough comes together.

Transfer the dough to a clean work surface and knead for 1–3 minutes, until the dough no longer sticks to the surface. Shape the dough into a disc, cover in plastic wrap and rest in the fridge for 30 minutes.

Roll the dough out until it is 2–3 mm thick, then cut into long 2 cm wide strips.

Place one stick of haloumi on top of one stick of pink guava and lightly press together. Wrap a strip of dough around the cheese and fruit, from end to end, then continue to wind the dough around the filling, on the diagonal and slightly overlapping, and slightly stretching the dough as you go, until completely enclosed. Roll the dough back and forth between your hands, so the warmth of your hands softens the dough and transforms it into a smooth stick.

Heat enough oil for deep-frying in a saucepan over medium heat to 180°C on a kitchen thermometer. Working in batches, fry the tequeños for 2–3 minutes, until golden brown. Drain on paper towel and serve hot.

JACKFRUIT

When I was a kid, Mum would lay a whole bunch of newspaper on the floor in the kitchen, place a chopping board down and roll a jackfruit over it. A huge cleaver came out and, cut by cut, she would remove the skin, core, strands, seeds and seed skins of the jackfruit. An intense aroma of bubble gum would fill the air and the fruit's sap would spread all over the newspaper. Mum put the seeds in a bowl to be later boiled and shared between us, and my siblings and I would ravage the jackfruit flesh, but for some reason no one ever loved it as much as I did.

I enjoyed watching Mum skilfully break down the fruit – she was always so efficient – and I absorbed her knowledge, as well as the therapeutic joy of processing the jackfruit. For the unacquainted, breaking down a jackfruit might seem more challenging than filleting and removing the bones from a fish at first. My brothers and sisters would wander off and do their own thing while Mum cut the fruit, but I would stay back in the kitchen and wait for the seeds to boil, then eat them with her. It would be way past my bedtime, but I loved staying up and watching Mum cook in the kitchen. The seeds always tasted nutty, with a pasty texture similar to a boiled chestnut.

> **One jackfruit can grow to weigh more than 50 kg. To put this in perspective, that's 12,000 times heavier than a blueberry!**

While my family has always enjoyed jackfruit, it's not commonly eaten in Australia or elsewhere in the Western world. In Australia, jackfruit is mostly associated with vegan food – green (unripe) jackfruit can be cooked to yield a similar texture to pulled pork – but the sweet ripe fruit can smell like bubble gum and is incredibly delicious. Its flesh can have both soft and crunchy textures and the aroma is intoxicating, with an intensely sweet and unique tropical perfume. While not as strong as durian, jackfruit is certainly noticeable within close proximity and some varietals exude an aroma that can be as pervasive as durian – notably the cempedak.

The world's largest fruit, one jackfruit can grow to weigh more than 50 kg. To put this in perspective, that's 12,000 times heavier than a blueberry! One jackfruit tree can produce more than 10,000 kg of fruit – there isn't a fruit tree in the world that's more productive.

A versatile fruit

There are many varietals of ripe jackfruit, but there are generally two types enjoyed by West Asian and South-East Asian countries. One has a hard, crunchy flesh, and the other is soft and juicy. Some communities prefer one over the other and to use in certain dishes. For example, the Filipino dessert halo halo often contains strips of crunchy jackfruit, called 'langka' in the Tagalog language. In Vietnam, softer jackfruit is often enjoyed by the older population as it's easier to digest, while green jackfruit is used similarly to a potato, except with the texture of pulled jackfruit combined with water chestnuts, if you cook the unripe seeds too. Green jackfruits are also commonly cooked in curries throughout India. As you can see, jackfruit is extremely versatile, so why isn't it grown more? Why don't we see it in the shops?

A weighty problem

I've been supporting a research project in Australia looking at whether jackfruit production should increase and how farmers can expand the market here. If the project is a success, its findings could contribute to 'saving the world' in terms of food security, given how prolific one jackfruit tree can be.

While the jackfruit has the potential to be a truly great fruit, it is also one of, if not the most, inconvenient fruits to process. Experience and mastery with a knife are key in cutting a jackfruit, as is an understanding of the fruit's anatomy. I like to think of it as an art, but sadly it is an art that is fading, and without this skill processing jackfruit can be one of the most demoralising and time-consuming tasks. The main culprit is the sap that's excreted as soon as you cut into the fruit. It's so thick and viscous that it will bind to your knife and render it useless unless you lather it with oil. Secondly, a ripe jackfruit can easily weigh more than 10–20 kg, and some up to 50 kg or more. It's no easy task getting around a fruit so large without experience and flow. Being so heavy also means that there is a tremendous amount of fruit to cut around. Often you may see jackfruit sold in quarters or even eighths in the fruit shop, as the regular shopper and their family couldn't eat a whole jackfruit in one sitting.

For the consumer, it's a huge barrier to commit to the time and skill needed to break down a whole fruit. For fruit shops, it's the availability and cost of skilled labour that's preventing jackfruit from being a big hit at a retail level. Growers also typically struggle to find workers happy to harvest jackfruit, given how heavy and back-breaking the processing can be. The jackfruit's unique size and shape also makes it difficult to transport them, adding further to its woes. These barriers shouldn't stop you purchasing a ripe or green jackfruit, nor should they be a reason not to try it. Its flavour is unique and incredible. If you're lucky enough to be travelling through Asia and find jackfruit already processed and in packaging, definitely take the chance to eat it. I hope it will give you the jackfruit bug and entice you to buy a segment, if not a whole fruit, at home!

Selecting jackfruit

Picking a good jackfruit can also be tricky. My family has been distributing Australian-grown jackfruits for more than 20 years and my father is a master of the fruit. In my teens I travelled to the Northern Territory with Dad to visit our grower, Tropical Primary Products, who grow the jackfruit we sell. I remember Han Shiong, whose family runs the farm, driving me around in his golf buggy and us climbing trees and cutting jackfruits that were so heavy we could barely lift them. A lot of what I know about selecting jackfruit has come from Han and my father, but I'm proud to say that my colleague Long Ngoc To has also added to my knowledge of selecting jackfruit in his years working with me.

Long Ngoc To sold our jackfruits for more than five years and he would always watch as buyers selected the fruit and ask what they were looking for. Some looked at the shape of the fruit; others pressed the skin; some inspected how spaced out the spikes were; and others would be wary of bruises and water damage. To be sure of how ripe the fruit was, one buyer taught us to make a tiny incision in the jackfruit using a paring knife and bend the skin slightly to inspect the colour of the revealed aril and note the ripeness of the flesh. If the cut was minimal the jackfruit would close up on itself without damaging the fruit. Long became a master of jackfruit in his own right and a fruit nerd himself, and some of my tips for selecting a tasty fruit come from his learned experiences.

Selecting a whole ripe jackfruit can be difficult; selecting a cut and wrapped segment of ripe jackfruit is much easier. As you feel the firmness of the flesh, check if it's leaking juice, as well as the colour and maturity of the aril itself. Selecting green jackfruit is even easier, as it hasn't ripened and should be firm to touch, although not rock hard.

Whether ripe or green, jackfruits have so much potential if we only take the time as consumers to appreciate the process of breaking them down.

Choose

GREEN: look for bright-coloured skin; as the jackfruit ages its skin will turn brown, which is fine, but it may also mould, resulting in a shortened shelf life.

RIPE: feel the fruit, it should 'give' a little when squeezed. Check for water damage, which will show as a bruise or brown blotches sunken on the skin, most often seen on the shoulder, as well as any mould growth, which suggests age and a shortened shelf life. Very awkward-shaped jackfruit can yield less edible arils.

CULTIVAR: jackfruit textures and aromas differ among cultivars, so ask the fruiterer what type of jackfruit they are selling.

Prep

GREEN JACKFRUIT

1. Wear kitchen gloves and oil your knife with neutral oil to prevent sap sticking to the knife. If you don't have gloves, then oil your hands.

2. Place paper towel, cardboard or newspaper on a chopping board.

3. Remove the top stem area, then cut the jackfruit into 4 cm thick rounds.

4. Cut the rounds in half to make semi-circles.

5. Cut the skin off. If the jackfruit is semi mature, you can remove the stalk too.

6. Cut the jackfruit flesh into 3 cm x 2 cm rectangles.

7. Place the jackfruit in a bowl of water with a teaspoon of salt until cooking to prevent oxidisation. You can also freeze the chopped cubes in a vacuum-sealed bag for later use.

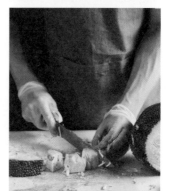

RIPE JACKFRUIT

1. Wear kitchen gloves and oil your knife with neutral oil to prevent sap sticking to the knife. If you don't have gloves, then oil your hands.

2. Place paper towel, cardboard or newspaper on a chopping board.

3. Remove the top stem area. Slice down through the stalk and cut each half into quarters.

4. Cut away the internal stalk and core, to reveal the yellow-orange arils.

5. Using both hands, hold one segment at either end and bend backwards, as if reading a book – the fibres and arils should break apart. Remove the arils by hand, ensuring any threads are removed and put aside.

6. Use a paring knife to make a slit from the top to bottom of each aril, then remove the seed, including the surrounding membrane. Keep the seeds for boiling and to eat like a nut (see page 127). Enjoy the yellow-orange arils.

When my father brought home a whole jackfruit for the family to eat, Mum would process the fruit, removing all the seeds and threads around the arils. I usually helped with some kitchen gloves on to protect myself from the jackfruit sap. After we'd eaten the jackfruit, Mum would boil the seeds and we would sit, peel and eat them in the evening. Boiled ripe jackfruit seeds taste like boiled chestnuts, but with cashew flavours. They're abundant in ripe jackfruit, and it is a waste to throw them out after eating the sweet, ripe arils. I've heard from friends that boiled jackfruit seeds are sometimes seasoned with spices, such as chilli powder or ground cumin, in Indian cuisine. Jackfruit seeds are creamier and richer than any nut; you get full just by eating a small bowl. Although they do make you gassy, so be careful of eating too many!

BOILED JACKFRUIT SEEDS — EAT THEM LIKE A NUT!

After taking apart the ripe jackfruit and eating all the arils (see page 125), reserve the seeds.

Rinse the seeds to remove the outer slippery membrane, then transfer to a saucepan of cold water, add the salt and bring to the boil. Reduce the heat to low and simmer for 45 minutes or until a knife slips through the seeds easily.

Drain the seeds and set aside to cool. Remove the shells with a knife and enjoy immediately!

1 ripe jackfruit
2–3 teaspoons salt

MAKES about 1 kg

For my 30th birthday, my mates bought me a cooking class voucher. I chose Sri Lankan cuisine because I love how it uses similar produce to Vietnamese food but in different ways. In the cooking class I learned how to make Sri Lankan cutlets – deep-fried balls of herbs and vegetables dusted in flour – and I've loved them since. If you purchase a whole green jackfruit, you'll find you have more than the 300 g of fruit needed for this recipe, although you can buy green jackfruit cut and portioned, if you're lucky. Otherwise, canned jackfruit also works, but you'll need to wash out the brine thoroughly and dry the jackfruit chunks before mixing and frying. Enjoy!

SRI LANKAN JACKFRUIT CUTLETS

MAKES 15

250 g potatoes, peeled
600 ml coconut oil, plus 2 tablespoons extra
12 curry leaves, left whole
2 Thai red shallots, finely chopped
2.5 cm piece of ginger, peeled and finely chopped
4 garlic cloves, finely chopped
½ teaspoon ground white pepper
300 g green jackfruit, skin and seeds removed, flesh cut into 2 cm chunks
2 teaspoons sea salt
2 teaspoons tamarind paste
75 g (½ cup) plain flour
150 g panko breadcrumbs

TAMARIND MAYO
120 g (½ cup) good-quality mayonnaise
2 teaspoons tamarind paste

Place the potatoes in a saucepan of salted water, bring to the boil and cook until a knife slips through the potato easily. Drain and mash the potatoes, then set aside.

Melt the 2 tablespoons of coconut oil in a frying pan over medium heat, add the curry leaves, shallot, ginger, garlic and white pepper and sauté for 2–3 minutes, until fragrant. Stir through the jackfruit and 100 ml of water, then cover with a lid and cook for 30–35 minutes, until soft.

Add the mashed potato, 1 teaspoon of the salt and the tamarind paste, and cook for 5 minutes or until the mixture is very thick. Transfer the mixture to a bowl and set aside to cool.

Mix the flour, the remaining 1 teaspoon of salt and 150 ml of water in a bowl until you have a pancake batter consistency. Place the panko breadcrumbs on a plate.

Shape the cooled green jackfruit mixture into 2 cm balls. Working in batches, dunk the jackfruit balls in the batter to coat, then roll in the panko breadcrumbs until completely covered. Place the cutlets on a plate, ensuring that they aren't touching, and refrigerate for 30 minutes.

Meanwhile, to make the tamarind mayo, combine the ingredients in a small bowl and set aside in the fridge.

Heat the 600 ml of coconut oil in a deep saucepan to 180°C on a kitchen thermometer – the oil needs to be high enough to cover the cutlets. Working in batches, fry the cutlets for 3–4 minutes, until golden (don't let the oil temperature drop below 160°C), then drain on paper towel. Serve hot, with the tamarind mayo for dipping.

TIP I suggest cooking a big batch of these cutlets and freezing them, then simply bringing them back to life in an air-fryer when you're hungry. They're great as an appetiser or served at house parties when you have many guests.

The fibrous strands surrounding the arils in green jackfruit are very similar in size and texture to pulled pork. I once blindfolded two friends and made a video of them eating a pulled green jackfruit burger, and they genuinely couldn't tell it wasn't pork! I made my own version of the burger from the video, and I noticed that although green jackfruit has the same texture as pulled pork, it has a neutral aroma and is almost flavourless in its immature state. When you barbecue meat, 50 per cent of the flavour comes from the sauce used to marinate the meat, and the remainder comes from the actual protein. To achieve this smoky flavour in green jackfruit, and to make it convenient for the home kitchen, I decided to add liquid smoke. I guarantee that you'll love this recipe even if you're a meat eater, and that you'll also understand the exact flavour meat gives, once you try green jackfruit instead.

If you can't find fresh green jackfruit, you can use canned or frozen but if the canned jackfruit has been preserved in brine rather than water, you need to wash away any brine thoroughly. It will also cook in about one third of the time and you may not need all of the stock.

SMOKY PULLED GREEN JACKFRUIT BURGERS

SERVES 4

1 tablespoon olive oil
1 onion, chopped
3 garlic cloves, chopped
1 teaspoon sweet paprika
1 teaspoon ground cumin
1 teaspoon liquid smoke
1 tablespoon brown sugar
1 teaspoon sea salt
500 g green jackfruit, skin and
    seeds removed, flesh cut
    into 2 cm dice
300 ml vegetable stock
50 g salted macadamias, crushed

SMASHED AVOCADO
1 avocado, halved and peeled,
    seed removed
½ Thai red shallot, finely chopped
1 coriander stem with leaves,
    finely chopped
juice of ¼ lime
½ teaspoon sea salt
½ teaspoon cracked black pepper

TO SERVE
4 sesame or brioche buns, cut
    in half and lightly toasted
1 carrot, shredded
¼ red cabbage, shredded

Heat the olive oil in a large frying pan with a lid over low heat, add the onion and sauté for 6–8 minutes, until browned.

Meanwhile, in a bowl, combine the garlic, paprika, cumin, liquid smoke, sugar and salt.

Add the spice mixture to the frying pan and stir for 30–50 seconds, until fragrant, then add the jackfruit and stir to combine. Add half the vegetable stock, cover with a lid and cook, stirring occasionally, for 45 minutes, adding more stock if the mixture starts to dry out, until softened and easy to shred.

Meanwhile, roughly mash the avocado in a small bowl. Add the shallot, coriander, lime juice, salt and pepper and mix to form a chunky paste.

Shred the jackfruit chunks in the pan using two forks (if the jackfruit is still too firm, cook for a few more minutes, then try again). Add the crushed macadamias and cook for a further 3 minutes, until the mixture thickens.

Smear the smashed avocado over the base and lids of the toasted buns, then top with the carrot, cabbage and pulled green jackfruit mixture. Finish with the bun lids and serve.

JUJUBES

When I ask people if they've eaten a jujube before, the most common response is 'what's that?', followed by 'do you mean the herb?'. While jujubes are native to China, they are better known globally for their use in traditional Chinese medicine than as a fresh snacking fruit. In China's Xin Jiang province, I have seen millions of jujubes being sundried on the ground to make this medicinal herb. Dried jujube is often added to Chinese soups and is known as a super food, given its high levels of antioxidants. But things are changing, and the fresh jujube is gaining momentum simply because it tastes like an exceptional apple.

A great jujube has crunch and an intense tartness mellowed out by intense sweetness. Depending on the varietal, jujubes are a very conveniently shaped fruit. They are slightly bigger than a cherry, with a tiny seed and a predominantly aerated apple texture and flavourful flesh.

When I first started working in the family business, we had a handful of boxes of fresh jujubes and they fetched big money among the Chinese community. Fast forward a decade and the volume we sell has multiplied several times over. I've found that fresh jujubes, also known as 'fresh dates', are also loved by Middle-Eastern cultures as well as other Eastern communities. While superfood-marketing concepts, such as 'antioxidants', sometimes go a long way to promoting produce, I find that 'good-tasting produce' always wins in the long run. Consumers keep coming back for more and so the industry grows. That's the case with fresh jujubes – I'm almost certain I've never met anyone who has tried one and didn't like it.

Fresh jujube has one big downfall: its shelf life. With more than a decade's experience selling this fruit, I can't stress how exponential its ripening curve is. Jujubes are often picked at least 50 per cent green and within five days they're usually 100 per cent red. While you may enjoy a mango or banana that is at 100 per cent colour, a 100 per cent red jujube is no longer at its optimal eating moment. It tends to lose acidity, becomes slightly soft and its overt sweetness turns to a fermented alcohol flavour. I have received lots of negative feedback when the fruit is sold overripe, so I always suggest that you purchase and eat fresh jujubes before they turn completely red. My personal opinion is to eat the fruit at 80 per cent colour, which offers the best balance between a crunchy texture, good acidity and developing sweetness. I prefer to buy my jujubes around 60 per cent red and give myself one to two days to eat them. Once you get onto the fresh jujube train you'll be waiting for them every season. Beware, they are little pockets of addictiveness!

A great jujube has crunch and an intense tartness mellowed out by intense sweetness.

Choose

1. Look for fresh jujubes that are green with some blush – 70 to 80 per cent red is optimal for fruit that has good levels of acidity, sweetness, crunch and moreishness.

2. Remember the ripening process is exponential, so it might take two days to get from 60 to 80 per cent colour, but only one day to get from 80 to 100 per cent colour.

3. Avoid soft or wrinkly jujubes, as they're likely to be overripe, with flavour loss and sour notes developing. Aged fruit will lose acid and turn alcoholic in flavour.

4. There are many varieties of jujubes, so size and shape are not good indicators of quality or freshness. The most common and popular variety, li, is around 3 cm tall, while chico jujubes are around 1.5 cm tall, and shaman jujubes are 2 cm tall but rectangular in shape rather than oval.

Store

Store fresh jujubes in a permeable bag or a plastic bag with a hole poked in it, so they don't lose moisture, anywhere in the fridge. They'll ripen quickly, so check the colour of the skin daily. Eat within one to two days.

THANH'S TIPS

IT TAKES ONLY FIVE TO SEVEN DAYS TO RIPEN FROM GREEN/YELLOW TO FULLY RED!

UNDERRIPE

PERFECT TO BUY

PERFECT TO EAT

OVERRIPE

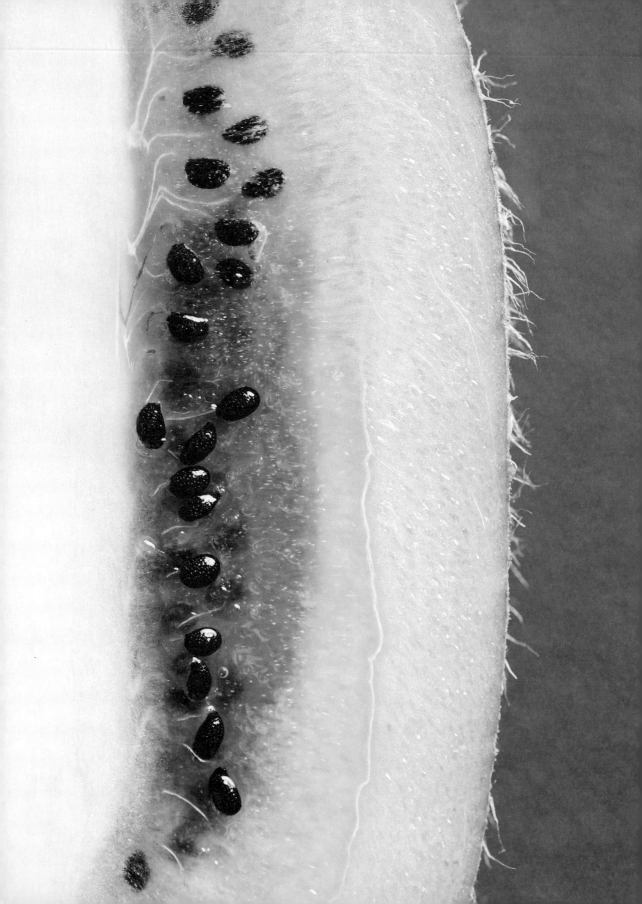

KIWIFRUIT

When I joined the fresh produce team at Coles, I was given the portfolios for kiwifruit, avocados and organic produce. The first thing I remember is one of the managers eating a kiwifruit whole, skin on. This turned out to be the most surprising moment I'd have while managing the kiwifruit portfolio, simply because it's such a nonchalant fruit that shows up every day and doesn't give you much trouble. Having said that, I've had both amazing and terrible eating experiences with kiwifruit.

As a climacteric fruit that ripens after being harvested, kiwifruit can survive for up to five months in cold storage – an amazing feat. When they're left on the shelf, they are sturdy and don't perish as fast as most other fruits. And while you shouldn't compare kiwifruit to other climacteric fruits, such as apples, you should compare them to, say, mangoes, which barely last a day after you purchase them. Kiwifruit, on the other hand, can last a week in the fridge and then several days more once you put them on a fruit plate. Consistency is the kiwifruit's most marketable asset, although in the East it's selected and marketed as a fruit that's high in vitamins. Regardless of which attribute you think markets kiwifruit well, its growth internationally has been largely due to New Zealanders, even though the kiwifruit vine – míhóutáo (猕猴桃) – originated in China.

"

A bad kiwifruit I ate in Shanghai had a fake kiwifruit sticker on it. Counterfeiting exists not just with fake luxury handbags but also in the fruit world!

A game changer

So what has New Zealand done to change the kiwifruit game? Nearly everything, but for the most part it has to do with quality consistency. I'll explain. I've had both my best and worst experience of kiwifruit in China. I once purchased a green kiwifruit from a street trader; it was completely unripe and stayed hard as a rock, even after three days facing the sun in my dorm room. The eating experience was so tart it put me off kiwifruit for the rest of my trip. On a different trip to China, I purchased a red heart with green flesh kiwifruit, originating from Shaanxi, at a hypermarket in Ürümqi. When I bit into the fruit it was the most tangy and sweet kiwifruit I'd ever had in my life. The aroma was incredible, and although the texture wasn't as firm as I like my kiwifruit to be, it was, you could say, at peak ripeness.

These two polar-opposite experiences are akin to kiwifruit Russian roulette when it comes to our enjoyment of the fruit, and New Zealanders have reduced this risk by mastering the art of kiwifruit harvesting, post-harvest management, distribution and sales. Kiwifruit aren't just a fruit that a grower picks off the vine and sends to the fruit shop. The entire season is planned out, even down to how many units are forecasted to be sold every week, based on historical data.

At Coles, one of my roles was to promotionally plan an entire kiwifruit season so that growers could harvest and store the fruit, shipping lines could book containers, ripeners could clear out rooms and the catalogue could reserve space for specials. In the detail of all of this is how New Zealand's planning of kiwifruit enables you to have a consistent eating experience, and it all comes down to exactly how ripe the fruit will be when you purchase it.

All kiwifruit is picked hard off the vine and stored in large cold-room chambers. The fruit is then warmed to a certain temperature before natural ethylene is pushed into the room, kickstarting the fruits' amylase enzymes that break down the starches and turn them into sugars, making the kiwifruit softer and sweet. This phase is tightly scheduled so kiwifruits perform consistently well in terms of their ripening timeline. The kiwifruit leave New Zealand in shipping containers, spend about three days at sea, and are then distributed to shops in Australia. At times there will be highs and lows in demand and supply, but this is all managed carefully by operations teams both in Australia and New Zealand, and with the quality of the fruit being at the forefront of everyone's minds. A ripening manager may need to manage the condition of millions and millions of kiwifruit for today, tomorrow, next week and the following weeks.

From Chinese gooseberry to kiwifruit

You might be thinking, why has New Zealand played such an important role in the world of kiwifruit? Well, the kiwifruit was originally known as the Chinese gooseberry before being rebranded as 'kiwifruit' in the United States due to quarantine reasons. In 1959, a man named Jack Turner from a New Zealand export company renamed his Chinese gooseberries 'kiwifruit' at the request of US importer Norman Sondag and legendary exotic fruit distributor Frieda Caplan. While Caplan was given the title 'kiwi queen' due to her passion and success in championing the fruit in the United States, she has been mistakenly attributed by many news articles as the one who named the fruit. The term 'kiwifruit' was created as it was synonymous with the word 'passionfruit', with the emblem of New Zealand also being the kiwi. The growth and success of kiwifruit exports out of New Zealand eventually led to growers all around the world growing the crop. Prior to the 1950s the fruit could be barely found anywhere in the world, besides China.

Collective management

Beyond creating the name 'kiwifruit', it was New Zealand's desire to improve and save their industry which changed the kiwifruit from good to great. Although New Zealand was the dominant kiwifruit exporter in the world in the 1990s, the industry had to reform

due to its imminent collapse as farmers competed against each other year on year, often selling their fruit at a loss. In 2013, as national buyer of kiwifruit for Coles, I couldn't figure out why every company was quoting me the same price every week. I found out that in 1999 the Kiwifruit Export Regulations in New Zealand stipulated that exporters were allowed to discuss and align pricing on export kiwifruit to ensure stable returns to farmers as part of the national interest.

In addition, the kiwifruit company Zespri was formed in the 1990s and became New Zealand's only allowed export company of Class 1 kiwifruit. This was to ensure the continual financial viability and demand for their produce, so the growers wouldn't go bankrupt as they almost did. To Zespri's credit, they've successfully controlled the quality of every piece of kiwifruit leaving New Zealand ever since, ensuring that customers have good eating experiences. Quality control has been done in a variety of ways, from planning, grading and ripening to packaging and marketing. As far as I'm aware, there isn't another company in the world that not only represents a nation in its fruit name, but also champions the quality of that fruit around the world.

As a result, Zespri has become the most globally recognised fruit brand in the world. When you drive into Shanghai's import fruit market, the first thing you see is a giant wall with a huge Zespri Kiwifruit banner. Over the last three decades, Zespri and other exporters have continually worked to improve the cultivars and the science behind kiwifruit management to ensure good-quality eating, but perhaps their biggest influence is in kiwifruit marketing. No other co-op of farmers has been able to work so effectively to improve the sales of a single fruit in the world. These historical events inadvertently allowed the kiwifruit to become the fruit powerhouse that it is today.

I find the history of the kiwifruit over the last 100 years utterly fascinating, not just because New Zealanders adopted the fruit and sent it back to where it first originated, but because the fruit itself has been so improved from a century ago that, in a way, it deserves to be called by a new name. So what's in a fruit's name? A lot more than we can sometimes imagine! Did I mention that a bad kiwifruit I ate in Shanghai had a fake kiwifruit sticker on it? Counterfeiting exists not just with fake luxury handbags but also in the fruit world! If you are abroad, look out for counterfeit kiwifruit posing as New Zealand Zespri.

Besides being the most consistent of fruits, kiwifruits have a burst of flavour, which predominantly comes from the acid in the fruit. They also have enzymes that are powerful enough to break down the fibres in meat, such as lamb. I like to use kiwifruit to tenderise meats for barbecuing before putting them over coals (see opposite page).

In the future, keep your eyes out for new varieties of kiwifruit that may even stretch your imagination beyond the gold kiwifruit, which has become a sweet favourite, largely due to you know who – the New Zealanders!

Choose

1. Look for heavy and plump-looking kiwifruit with tight, shiny skin.

2. The fruit should 'give' a little when gently pressed; avoid rock-hard fruit.

3. Avoid wrinkly or shrivelled fruit, as this suggests the kiwifruit is past its best.

Store

Store kiwifruit in a plastic bag in the coldest part of the fridge (0–2°C). If you plan to eat the fruit in the next one to seven days, then store on a fruit plate at room temperature.

THANH'S TIPS

CHOOSE KIWIS THAT ARE PLUMP AND FULL.

AVOID ANYTHING SOFT OR WRINKLY.

In 2017 I went through a phase of cooking a lot of barbecued meats, specifically Xinjiang-style lamb skewers (新疆烤串). The recipe requires significant preparation and marination of the meat before finally cooking it over coals. The one thing that elevates skewered meat from good to great is how tender it is once cooked over extremely high heat. Herein lies the fruit hack – use kiwifruit to tenderise the meat just before placing it over coals!

Kiwifruit has enzymes that tenderise meat by helping break down the connective tissue, which makes meat tough. The fruit also has a neutral flavour – unlike pineapple and papaya which contain similar, stronger enzymes – which doesn't affect the taste of the protein. Be careful though, as kiwifruit enzymes are potent and I have ruined entire batches of skewered lamb chunks by over-tenderising the meat and turning everything to mush. Through trial and error I established that one kiwifruit can tenderise a 4 kg lamb leg, with a marination period of 15 minutes. Do not allow kiwifruit to tenderise meat for more than 30 minutes, as the meat fibres will start to fall apart. So if you want to cook a tough cut of meat, but don't have time to slow cook, marinate the meat with slices of kiwifruit for 15 minutes before you begin cooking and ensure you remove the kiwifruit afterwards.

This method of tenderising meat is such a game changer. Of course, I laughed with Dan Hong one day about how using fruits to tenderise meats is more expensive than velveting meat with potato starch and deep-frying. However, velveting doesn't work when you cook over flames or coals and doesn't break down the meat at the speed of kiwifruit. So the next time you're having a barbecue, think kiwifruit!

KIWIFRUIT TO TENDERISE MEAT

Slice the kiwifruit horizontally into seven slices, then cut the slices in half to make 14 half moons.

If cooking over a coal barbecue, light the barbecue and allow the coals to burn until they're coated in a fine layer of ash.

Place the lamb in a large non-reactive (not metal) bowl and add the kiwifruit, tossing well. Set aside to marinate for 15 minutes, then remove the kiwifruit and immediately cook the lamb over the coal barbecue, or using your preferred method.

1 kiwifruit, peeled
4 kg boneless leg of lamb,
   cut into chunks

SERVES
8–10

Matt Preston is a gentle giant with a never-satiated desire for more flavour. Whether on TV, radio, social media or in print, I've been blessed to be a fruitful part of his food journey. We often discuss our love and hate for different fruits, and one time Matt asked if I had ever roasted a kiwifruit. Of course I had not and I became intrigued immediately. No doubt the flavour would change, but why and how? Following Matt's guidance I roasted the kiwifruit to perfection, waited for them to cool and went straight in. Soft and gelatinous, tart and full on – these are the words that describe oven-roasted kiwifruit. Eating roasted kiwifruit on its own is unbearable, but pairing it with something sweet is what Matt always intended, so I've added vanilla ice cream for sweetness and honeycomb for bitterness. What you get is a textural feast of gelatinous and juicy, soft and cold, crunchy and chewy. Only someone as audacious as Matt would try roasting a kiwifruit and I'm glad he has, because now I see kiwifruit in a different light and you might too!

MATT PRESTON'S ROASTED KIWIFRUIT WITH HOKEY POKEY ICE CREAM

SERVES 4

4 large kiwifruit, topped and tailed to make a barrel shape
vanilla ice cream, to serve
icing sugar, to serve

HOKEY POKEY
¼ cup honey
425 g caster sugar
125 ml (½ cup) liquid glucose syrup
1 tablespoon bicarbonate of soda

To make the hokey pokey, grease a deep heatproof tray and line the base and sides with baking paper. Place the honey, sugar, glucose and 80 ml (⅓ cup) of water in a large deep saucepan and bring to the boil. Cook until the syrup reaches 160°C on a sugar thermometer, then remove from the heat and immediately whisk through the bicarbonate of soda. Pour the mixture into the prepared tray and allow it to set for 20 minutes or until it cools to room temperature, then break into shards.

Preheat the oven to 160°C fan-forced. Grease a small baking tray and line the base with baking paper.

Place the kiwifruit on the prepared tray, standing upright, and roast for 20 minutes. Reduce the oven temperature to 120°C and continue to roast the kiwifruit for a further 20–30 minutes, until just soft but still holding their shape – they should be juicy, sticky and chewy (but not burnt). Remove from the oven and cool completely.

Divide some ice cream among four bowls, top with roasted kiwifruit and hokey pokey shards, dust with icing sugar and serve.

LEMONS & LIMES

nlike most fruit, which is consumed for snacking, lemons and limes are mainly used in cooking for the flavourful zesty taste and sharp sourness they add to a variety of dishes, from cakes and salads to cocktails and sauces. My most typical use for lemons and limes is as an essential topping for pho; the acidity cuts beautifully through the rich and flavoursome broth. Although many of us appreciate and use lemons and limes interchangeably, it's worth noting that my parents only ever ate limes, as lemons weren't available in Vietnam when they were growing up.

Given that the trait we prize most in lemons and limes is their acidity, the need to search for a 'good' fruit seems meaningless, since we pick these fruits early so they are sourer. Unlike snacking fruits, where we need to wait for their maturity to peak so we can obtain the optimal sugars and sweetness, lemons and limes don't require this level of maturity. Or do they?

Although the industry picks lemons and limes early, any fruit that stays on the tree for longer generally becomes more 'plump' and full of juice. As lemons and limes plump up, the juice inside expands and the skin stretches, making the peel thinner. A thinner peel and more juice means that the fruit will feel tender rather than firm when pressed. Unfortunately, the majority of lemons grown and sold in Australia – the eureka and lisbon varieties – are quite thick-skinned, making it harder to tell how juicy they might be inside. That's why homegrown lemons and limes are nearly always juicy and have a higher water content than store-bought ones. In addition to the extra juice, the fruit tends to have more sugars and taste slightly sweeter, albeit not significantly.

The industry defines the maturity stages of lemons in colours, from green to silver to yellow. Green is hard and unripe; silver is halfway between unripe and mature; and yellow is fully ripe. Most growers will pick lemons at the green–silver stage, knowing they will continue to gain a bit of colour once they're packed and distributed. Essentially, lemons can be stored commercially for two to three months and retain an acceptable level of juice, while still being able to offer us the main trait we seek: acidity. Gently squeeze a lemon or lime; if it gives a little, it's likely to be a mature fruit.

The cultural significance of lemon and lime varietals

Different cultures love the unique aroma and taste of specific lemon and lime varietals that are grown in their own part of the world. Mexican and Vietnamese cuisines, for example, prefer limes with a slight extra bitterness; while the French prefer the more linear sourness of lemons in their patisserie. These flavours are very prominent in the peel, which is often used in dishes, either zested or pounded using a mortar and pestle.

Although less aromatic, the juice also holds unique aromas and flavours. Think of why the famous 'key lime pie' isn't just called 'lime pie'. It's because of the unique scent in the yellow juice that key limes impart on the creamy, eggy filling. Although I've travelled to Keys West in Florida, my first experience of key lime pie was in Hawaii, and its lime flavour was undoubtedly different from the more common Tahitian lime. Over in Thailand, makrut lime skins and leaves are used in myriad dishes, including the famous green curry, while in the Philippines, the juice of calamansi limes is used in the sour seafood broth, sinigang. Ultimately, the aroma and flavour of these specific varietals contribute to culturally important dishes that wouldn't taste the same if different lemons or limes were substituted.

Another important fact to know is that while makrut limes are known as 'kaffir' limes in South-East Asia, the word is a highly offensive racial slur in South Africa. Given our global world, it's important to understand such cultural sensitivities, to make sure we are respectful and not offensive. In Thailand, I would still use the term 'kaffir' when talking about limes (as this is their language word), but perhaps if I was travelling in other parts of the world, I would be more careful.

The main difference between lemons and limes is their unique aroma. Lemons also grow to a larger size than most limes.

My fave lime is ...

The native Australian finger lime. Its pulp sacs, or vesicles, are like little caviar, bursting pops of lovely citrus. Finger limes have been marketed towards the fine-dining scene due to their intensely colourful and textural properties, but my favourite way to use them is in place of the lime juice in a Vietnamese nước chấm dressing or sauce (see page 74): simply substitute half the vinegar, lemon or lime juice for finger limes to elevate your dish.

When I was wholesaling finger limes more than a decade ago, my friend and grower liaison Mark Johnston gave me some advice about how to squeeze the limes. Mark told me that the volatiles in finger lime skin are intensely bitter, so never let them mix with the juice sacs or you'll taste the bitterness. He was right. Even the oils left on my fingers were almost unbearable to taste.

My fave lemon is ...

The meyer lemon, which is a cross between a mandarin and a lemon. It has the best of both worlds: a sweet taste with strong acidity. It also has the peel qualities and traits of a mandarin, so its perfume is much stronger than the commoditised eureka or lisbon lemon. I love to squeeze meyer lemon over oysters. If you can't find meyer lemons, my tip is to combine mandarin juice with the same amount of lemon juice – mixing citrus is a fun game!

The future

While the focus for lemons has been predominantly on shelf life and supply, growers have made significant investments to produce seedless lemons and limes. This is commonly done by netting the orchard to prevent cross-pollination, so all the lemons of that particular species become seedless.

Growers are also experimenting with new hybrids by crossing lemon and limes with mandarins, tangerines, pomelos and native varieties, such as blood limes or finger limes, with different textures – it's an exciting time in the lemon and lime world!

Choose

1. Mature lemons and limes will give a little when squeezed. They are likely to be juicier and slightly sweeter, with thinner peel, than underripe fruit.

2. Avoid hard-as-rock lemons and limes as they contain less water and tend to be extra sour.

3. Don't worry about uniform colour. While some lemons and limes may be sun kissed, others might not have as much colour. You may see them sold as 'odd-bunch' fruit at the supermarket, but they can still be great.

4. Use your hands to compare two lemons or limes of approximately the same size; the heavier fruit will be juicier than the lighter fruit.

Store

Lemons and limes should be stored in a plastic bag, to prevent moisture loss, in the coldest part of the fridge. Make sure the skin remains dry, as water will encourage mould and bacteria growth.

Prep

Cutting vertically through the core means the segment walls will 'lock up' some of the juice and make it inaccessible. It's better to slice through the 'waist' of the fruit, as the juice in the segments can be squeezed out more easily.

Beware when zesting lemons and limes! Aromatic bitterness is found in the peel, but if you zest too deeply you'll get rind, which has less of the aromatic oils and mainly bitterness.

THANH'S TIPS

I loved lemon chicken when I was a kid. It was the sweet sauce that got me over the line every time, as it was, and still is, the sweetest dish on Chinese menus. Even though my sweet tooth has vanished, I still love ordering it when we're out for a family gathering; we order several dishes that swivel on the lazy Susan! My daughter loves chicken, and so many variations of chicken are cooked in my household. Sometimes I crumb the chicken myself for this dish, but most of the time I am in a rush to feed the kids, so I purchase ready-crumbed chicken or plain-crumbed chicken schnitzels and then I only need to make the sauce, which is very simple to put together. If you purchase pre-crumbed chicken, you can skip straight to the sauce step!

This recipe works best with meyer lemons, but because they're not readily available, I've used my classic combo of lemon and mandarin juice, to try and emulate that meyer lemon flavour. If you happen to have some on hand, simply replace the lemons and mandarins with three meyer lemons.

LEMON CHICKEN

SERVES 4

4 chicken thigh fillets
2 eggs, lightly beaten
90 g (½ cup) rice flour
1 teaspoon sea salt
120 g (2 cups) panko
    breadcrumbs
250 ml (1 cup) vegetable oil
1 spring onion, curled (see Tip)
steamed jasmine rice, to serve

LEMON SAUCE
zest and juice of 1–2 lemons,
    to taste
juice of 2 mandarins
110 g (½ cup) sugar
1 teaspoon rice wine vinegar
500 ml (2 cups) chicken stock
1½ tablespoons potato starch
    mixed with 1 tablespoon
    cold water

Working with one fillet at a time, cover the chicken with plastic wrap on a clean work surface and pound with a meat mallet until evenly flat and 1 cm thick. Repeat with the remaining chicken thighs, then set aside to rest for 15 minutes.

Pour the beaten egg onto a flat plate, combine the rice flour and salt on a separate plate and tip the panko breadcrumbs onto a third plate. One by one, toss the chicken fillets in the rice flour, dusting off the excess, then coat in the beaten egg and dredge in the panko breadcrumbs, ensuring both sides are evenly covered.

Heat the vegetable oil in a saucepan over medium heat. Working in batches, shallow-fry the crumbed chicken for about 3 minutes each side, until golden and cooked through. Drain on paper towel.

Meanwhile, to make the lemon sauce, combine all the ingredients except the potato starch slurry in a small saucepan over low heat. Bring to a simmer and cook for 5 minutes or until the sugar is dissolved. Give the potato starch slurry a stir, then slowly add it to the pan, stirring. Cook for a further 1–3 minutes, until the sauce has thickened.

Slice the crumbed chicken into strips, divide among plates and pour the lemon sauce over the top. Scatter with the curled spring onion and serve with steamed jasmine rice on the side.

TIP To curl spring onions, shred them finely, then place in a bowl of cold water and set aside until curled. Drain well, then use as a garnish.

LYCHEES

Lychees (or litchis) are genuinely loved by most. Their blush-red skin, perfectly bite-sized shape and juicy flesh, with a sweet and sour tang, combine to make lychees the complete fruit package. If you have eaten fresh lychees, you have probably 'peeled and popped' until there are none left, but even from a can, in a jelly or a cocktail, their flavour is unique and unforgettable.

As an Asian kid growing up in predominantly white Australia, there wasn't a fruit that better represented my heritage than lychees! Let's face it, most Caucasians think durians 'stink', and in 2020 a *New York Times* journalist even compared the look of rambutans to Covid-19. Tropical fruits from when I was a kid still get a bad rap, but not lychees.

Lychees are the golden child of what an Asian fruit should be in the Western world. The hero or model immigrant fruit, if you will. Lychees are culturally accepted, genuinely loved and you'll find them on the shelves of most good fruit shops. As an Asian wholesale fruiterer, it's my responsibility to celebrate the produce that I grew up with and is important to my family and my heritage. To me, lychees mean more than you can imagine – they're the fruit that has broken through the invisible bamboo ceiling – and have shown me the future of what other Asian produce can become in Australia and the Western world.

> **Lychees are the golden child of what an Asian fruit should be in the Western world. The hero or model immigrant fruit, if you will.**

Australian-grown lychees owe their beginnings to Wong Wah Day, one of the first Chinese settlers in Far North Queensland, who arrived in 1894. Wong emigrated to Australia from Guangzhou, where lychee trees grow like eucalyptus trees. In 1924, Wong's brother, Wah Hop, brought him two lychee trees from Zhongshan. Wong planted the trees and started the first commercial lychee plantation in Australia. (Incidentally, Guangzhou is a few hundred kilometres away from where my grandparents were born, in Guangdong province, and our family loves lychees, too!) Generations later, the Wah Day family continue to grow lychees in Queensland, and their humble beginnings lead to my own story of lychees in Australia.

In my career in the fruit industry, I have exported lychees to Asia and North America; imported lychees from Thailand, Vietnam and China; visited orchards and packing sheds in many countries; attended the world lychee conference; helped make lychee gin and lychee ice cream; and distributed lychees across fruit shops and supermarkets throughout Australia. You could say that lychee juice runs in my veins! The Wah Day family made my journey into the lychee world possible, and my father's passion to deliver quality fruit to the Asian communities we serve as a business gave me the opportunities to travel and see much of the fruit world.

Lychees: a love story

My favourite lychee moment happened on Hainan Island in China, where my father and I were inspecting our crop of lychees as it was being packed. Our exporter explained to us why the variety of lychees we were purchasing was called fei zi xiao (妃子笑), or in my own translation: 'Concubine Fei smiles at the sight of her hometown lychees'.

In China, fei zi xiao is a specific varietal of lychee famous for its small seed and the story behind its name. Yang Guifei was Tang Emperor Xuanzong's favourite concubine, and he would go to great lengths to impress her. Fei often missed her childhood favourite fruit, lychees, from her hometown, Yongji, which was 200 kilometres from the Imperial Palace in Xi'An. Unsurprisingly, there were no fridges or ice in 8th century China, and lychees do not have a shelf life of more than five days. So the emperor ordered his men to travel non-stop on horses from city to city for four days' straight, so Lady Fei could enjoy fresh lychees. When the lychees arrived at the palace, Lady Fei would smile, and hence the name of this varietal was born: fei zi xiao or 'Fei lychee smiles'. It's no wonder that lychees are a symbol of romance in China.

When our supplier told me this story over dinner, I was in awe of how a name and a story can travel 1500 years into the future. Lady Fei was one of the Four Great Beauties in China, women who held significant influence over the emperors and, subsequently, the Chinese dynasties of their time. Lady Fei's love affair with Emperor Xuanzong even caused a rebellion that ultimately led to the fall of the Tang dynasty! Who knew the names of lychees had such immense meaning?

According to Eastern dietetics, eating too many lychees in one sitting is going to make you 'hot'. This is kind of like saying eating too much chocolate will give you pimples! A balanced diet is important and, although tempting, it might be best to eat only a few lychees at a time, rather than a whole bowl!

Choose

1. Look for deep-coloured tones, such as dark red or bright pink.

2. Avoid lychees with green or white skin, as well as dehydrated browned skin. Lychees can't be picked early because they do not ripen after harvesting. As the fruit approaches maximum maturity, the skin colour changes from green to its ripe hue, indicating it is ready to be picked.

3. Gently squeeze the lychee – it should feel firm yet bouncy. Avoid lychees that are very hard or very soft or have juice oozing from the skin. As the flesh inside a lychee should be very juicy, you should notice some 'give' when you squeeze it. A lychee with a tight and hard skin has likely been stored for a long time, or in inadequate dry conditions. When you squeeze brown-skinned fruit, the lychee will be much firmer. Basically, there may not be any issues with the taste of the fruit but its shelf life will be dramatically shortened.

IMPORTED VS LOCAL

Local lychees have translucent flesh, while overseas lychees have a slightly cloudy and white flesh, having spent several weeks in transit – the longer lychees are kept in storage the more cloudy the flesh gets. Lychees from overseas still have great flavour, but they will be firmer and less juicy than local lychees.

Store

Only buy the amount of lychees you want to eat over the next few days, as they have a short shelf life. Lychees love cool, humid conditions, and, if stored properly, should keep for up to a week. Place a wet paper towel in an airtight container or dunk the lychees in clean water before storing to prevent moisture loss from the skin. Place them in the container or a sealed bag, then store in the fridge.

Prep

Use both thumbs and index fingers to push the suture, or stitch, running around the middle of the fruit – the lychee should pop in half. Squeeze the two halves, then 'peel and pop'.

One of my good friends and cooking mentors, Damien Jones, worked as David Thompson's sous chef at his Thai restaurant, Nahm, and now runs his own fine-dining Thai restaurant, Mr Jones, in Ballarat. He's also one of my customers and often purchases a raft of specific herbs and produce, including lychees, to use in his recipes. Damien taught me how to make Thai red curry paste from scratch, but I've used store-bought paste in this dish to make things a whole lot easier! When in season, Damien sources lychees to make a summer version of his red curry at his hatted restaurant.

Thai red curry paste is spicier than green curry paste because it uses mature red chillies, which contain more capsaicin (the active component that dictates a chilli's heat) than their green counterpart. Thai cooking embraces the concept of balance of the five primary tastes – sweet, sour, salty, spicy and bitter – to create a 'harmonious' meal. Adding lychees to a Thai red curry makes perfect sense, as their intense sweetness balances the deep saltiness of the fish sauce, spiciness of the red chillies, sourness of the lime juice and bitterness of the eggplant and herbs.

My tip is to taste the dish as you're cooking it. If the lychees become too overwhelmingly sweet, add more curry paste, fish sauce or lime juice, to balance things out.

DUCK THAI RED CURRY WITH LYCHEES

SERVES 4

1½ tablespoons vegetable oil

1½ tablespoons Thai red curry paste (or more, depending on the strength of the paste)

2 skinless duck breasts (about 350 g), cut into 2 cm pieces

200 ml coconut milk

150 g fresh lychees (about 8), halved, skin and seeds removed

200 g Thai eggplants (about 7), quartered

1 small green capsicum, sliced or cut into chunks

2 makrut lime leaves, plus 2 leaves extra, very finely sliced, to serve

1½ tablespoons fish sauce, plus extra if needed

1 teaspoon brown sugar, plus extra if needed

1½ tablespoons freshly squeezed lime juice, plus extra if needed

3 Thai basil stems, leaves picked

steamed jasmine rice, to serve

Heat the vegetable oil in a wok over high heat. Add the Thai red curry paste and stir-fry for 1 minute or until fragrant. Add the duck and stir-fry for 3 minutes or until the meat is sealed.

Add the coconut milk, lychees, eggplant, capsicum and whole makrut lime leaves. Reduce the heat to low and simmer for 15 minutes or until the eggplant is cooked through.

Stir through the fish sauce, brown sugar and lime juice, then increase the heat to high and cook for 2 minutes or until you can no longer smell the fish sauce. Taste the curry and check that you have a good balance of sweet, salty, sour and spicy flavours, adding more fish sauce, sugar, lime juice or curry paste, if needed.

Transfer the curry to a serving bowl and scatter the finely sliced makrut lime leaves and Thai basil leaves over the top. Serve with steamed jasmine rice on the side.

MANDARINS

Compared to oranges, mandarins have looser skin and pith making them easier to peel and break into segments. They also have less acid, meaning they're usually sweeter, and have a stronger perfume, especially from the oils in the peel. I only ever remember eating imperial mandarins in Australia when I was young, but now there is a raft of competitor varietals, all with their own unique flair. Some are bigger with thinner segment walls; others are juicier to the point of being watery; and some are more plump and full. The world of mandarins is vast, and most hybrid mandarins marketed today, such as tangerines, murcotts, clementines, afourers, novas and tangelos, carry specific desirable traits. Mandarins are the ultimate convenient citrus fruit, and they were a favourite in my lunchboxes at school.

A quest for juicy mandarins

I once travelled to Gayndah, Australia's mandarin capital, as I was providing translation services for some of our business partners from China who had come to purchase our prized Australian fruit. On this occasion I got to meet up with Brent Chambers, who I'd previously worked with in the avocado industry. Gayndah Packers, or Gaypak, are historically one of the largest mandarin packers in Australia and most of us have probably eaten a mandarin or two packed by Gaypak in our lifetime. You know you've entered mandarin country when you drive past the 'big mandarin'.

"

The idea of citrus being seedless is a relatively modern one in the citrus industry.

Brent knows mandarins; he was the operations manager and general manager in the region for more than a decade and organised everything from farm to supermarket. We discussed honey murcotts, imperial mandarins, seeded versus seedless varieties, flavour and juicy fruit. When discussing fruit with a high water content, or 'juicy' fruit, we also talked about mandarins that eat dry. This unfortunate dry flesh in citrus is called 'granulation', and it's something the industry still struggles to address today. Granulation affects all citrus but is particularly evident in some mandarin varieties. The juice sacs dry up either while the fruit is on the tree or after it has been harvested. I'm sure we've all eaten a dry, lacklustre mandarin before and they're not a great experience.

While discussing the contentious debate of puffy versus tight-skinned imperial mandarins, Brent proclaimed that both eat the same with one big exception: late in the season, large puffy mandarins tend to become very dry. It's this little piece of information that had me completely excited – a hint! A trail to follow and a piece of information about mandarins that no one else had ever told me.

Several weeks later, the mandarin season was reaching its end and I started looking for large puffy imperial mandarins at the fruit shop so I could analyse the fruit and compare it to tight-skinned mandarins. As I firmly grasped and then tossed puffy and tight-skinned mandarins back on the fruit display, I noticed that some were heavier than others. If you're unaware, all mandarins are packed by box, and every box has a 'count' on them. The count represents the number of mandarins in each box, so the greater the number, the smaller the size of the fruit; conversely, the smaller the count, the bigger the fruit.

On this occasion the mandarins were large. The puffy imperial mandarins in the box were relatively light, while the tighter-skinned imperial mandarins felt a touch heavier. I bought a mixture of both to sample and, as Brent informed me, the puffy mandarins were indeed mostly dry. The next day I went to a different fruit shop for work and they were ranging small mandarins. I decided to buy only tight-skinned heavy fruit to test and used my hand to feel the nuance in weight. It's probably worth noting that I touch fruit at least a hundred times a day, so it's easy for me to identify small changes in the weight of the fruit. I picked a light mandarin and to my amazement the fruit had granulation. I then picked a heavy mandarin and it was juicy. This tip has never failed me and it applies to the whole citron family. Armed with this information, you need never pick a dry citrus fruit of any variety again!

I learned from my father that sometimes deep knowledge of a fruit takes a lifetime of work and a desire towards continuous improvement to obtain. I have seen my father discover nuances about fruit and vegetables no one else could possibly know, and it's this that makes him a special fruiterer.

While translating the desires of the buyers in Gayndah, there was a strong emphasis on the premium market honey murcott needing to be seedless. When I was a kid, nearly all the oranges I ate had large seeds and most mandarins had some seeds, which you had to spit out. In the last three decades the most commercially grown varietals of citrus are seedless, and in the future we are probably going to see more citrus varieties without seeds, especially in the mandarin category.

The idea of citrus being seedless is a relatively modern one in the citrus industry, and the privilege of convenience really does elevate the premium on a fruit.

My best mandarin experience

When I exhibited at the Fruit Logistica in Berlin, the world's biggest fruit industry gathering and exhibition, I met Jim Im who is now one of my best fruit mates. He's a second-generation Jeju Island mandarin farmer who travelled to Australia and worked picking oranges tirelessly in the Aussie heat, working his craft. He now exports Korean fruits around the world and is the largest exporter of Jeju Island mandarins, thanks to his family's connection to the island and grower community. In the middle of

a -10°C snow storm in Berlin, Jim handed me a redhyang mandarin grown on Jeju Island. It was a life-changing experience. The segments were big, the segment walls were thin and tasty, the internal pulps were juicy and separable like a pomelo, with an intense sour flavour only outdone by the sweetness, and the aroma in each bite was like scratching the peel over and over again.

When I travelled to Jeju Island I noticed many other mandarin varietals in the Seogwipo pack houses that were sold with green-coloured skin. It's important to note that depending on the varietal and the country, many citrus industries across the world do force citrus, such as oranges, mandarins and lemons, to a have uniform skin colour, and this dispels any myths that the colour of the skin is an indicator of a fruit's ripeness. Don't be deceived by your eyes; use my hand-weighing technique instead. You cannot imagine how heavy the redhyang variety was!

The core of the problem

I've eaten hundreds of mandarins from Egypt, the United States and Australia and I've encountered many varietals that tend to have a thick central core thread and a stringy segment edge. This part of the fruit anatomy annoys me, as when you break apart an individual mandarin segment you're left chewing the pith. I discovered the best way to achieve a great mouthfeel is to remove this thread and any attached thick pith on the segment edge. This can be done with a pair of scissors and is a labour of love, but, if you ask me, it's worth it. You'll have a much better experience that will leave you wanting to eat more mandarins than you originally set out to. Removing the thread means that when you initially bite into the mandarin segment, the gush of juice is linear and hits the side or back of your mouth, giving you a burst of zest and juice. It also removes any stringy fibres and makes the side segment walls much easier to chew and swallow. An elevated mandarin eating experience is one that my two kids love. I can even offer sub-optimal mandarins cut in this fashion and my kids will eat them ... sometimes!

Much more than a fruit

Mandarins originate from China and having Chinese heritage means the fruit has always had a special meaning to my family. During Lunar New Year we would often seek out mandarins to put on the altar. The Chinese word for mandarin – 'júzi' (橘子) – is very similar to the word for gold – 'jīnzi' (金子) – and even the hue of the fruit is akin to gold. This is why mandarins have an auspicious connection to wealth, and placing them on the altar represents our desires for wealth in the coming year.

Mandarins, and specifically the peel – 'chén pí' (陈皮) – have been an important part of Chinese culture and the culinary repertoire for thousands of years. Some mandarins in China are grown specifically just for the peel on the skin, which is dried and either cooked in dishes or used in other fascinating ways. The last time I travelled to Chao Zhou in Guangdong province, where my great grandparents were from, I purchased individual tea gifts. A teaspoon of tea leaves was placed delicately in a brown dried mandarin peel, still in its spherical shape, with the peel releasing a beautiful perfumed aroma from the intense oils in the dried skin.

Choose

1. Do the weight test: select two mandarins of the same size – the heavier mandarin will have more water content and therefore be juicier, while the lighter mandarin may have granulation.

2. To pick seedless segments, hold the peeled segment up to the light to see if there are any seeds.

Store

Store mandarins in a plastic bag or airtight container, to prevent them drying out, in the fridge (ideally 5°C). Because a mandarin's skin is much thinner and more permeable than an orange, it will dehydrate faster and have a much shorter shelf life if not stored correctly.

THANH'S TIPS

When I was a kid, Mum used to dry mandarin peels on the kitchen windowsill and use them whenever we were sick. We lived in such a small house that I don't know how she managed to find space to dry anything, to be honest. Mum would create a citrus skin steam room, where we would inhale aromatic nutrients to relieve us of blocked or sore noses. It was such a simple relief and without modern medicine. All you do is pour boiling water into a large bowl, add the mandarin peels and wait a minute for the temperature to drop slightly. Cover your head with a towel, hold your head over the bowl and breathe gently for a minute or two; you'll feel your nasal congestion slowly disappear.

Dried mandarin peels aren't only used in traditional Chinese medicine, they are also added to dishes, such as congees, soups, stir-fries, desserts and teas. Once you've dried the peels, they will keep for years; in fact, the longer you store them the darker the skins become and the more intense the aroma will be. If you try to purchase aged mandarin (or tangerine) peels in Guangdong, the older ones will cost more, similar to China's famous aged pu'er tea.

Drying mandarin peels is effortless, therapeutic and rewarding. Better yet, it's zero waste! Any varietal of mandarin will do, although each has its unique aroma. Imperial mandarins are very easy to peel, so they are an obvious choice, but choose whatever is available and smells good when you scratch the skin. Today, most commercially grown mandarins are waxed to increase shelf life, so use organic or backyard mandarins if you can find them, as scrubbing the wax off the skin is nearly impossible.

DRIED MANDARIN PEELS

CHÉN PÍ (陈皮)

Wash the mandarins and pat dry with a clean tea towel. Score a 2 cm circle at the top of the mandarin in the skin only. Remove this mandarin skin and peel, then continue to score and peel the skin from top to bottom in six wedges. Set aside the fruit segments to enjoy later.

Using a serrated knife, scrape away the rind and pith from the peel as this is very bitter and tasteless. Place the mandarin peels on a plate and leave them on a windowsill with lots of sunlight to dry out. Turn the mandarin peels over every day for about a week, until the peels are completely dry. Store in an airtight jar in the pantry.

mandarins
the sun

MAKES
1 JAR

In Chao Zhou, China, where my grandparents were born, there are specific cultivars of mandarins that are grown for their peel rather than their flesh. This shows the cultural importance placed on the aroma and taste of mandarin skins after they've been sundried. The last time I went to Chao Zhou, I saw stacks of ten or 20 dried mandarin peels tied in rubber bands, all neatly cut and dried into the same shape, almost like a three-leafed clover. In traditional Chinese medicine, mandarin peels have a 'warming' effect on our bodies. Over thousands of years, many communities in the region have used dried mandarin peels in their dishes for their bitter and aromatic notes. There are many variations of this mandarin peel and beef stir-fry; this is my version, based on the last time I ate it in Chao Zhou. I've been told by my relatives in China that mandarin peel becomes stronger with age, so adjust the amount you use depending on how old your peel is (mandarin peels sold in China are at least three years old).

MANDARIN PEEL & BEEF STIR-FRY

陳皮牛肉

SERVES 2

3 whole dried mandarin peels (see page 161; about 30 g)
250 g porterhouse or sirloin beef, cut into thick strips
3 tablespoons vegetable oil
1 small onion, finely sliced
2.5 cm piece of ginger, peeled and sliced
2 spring onions, white and green parts separated, finely sliced
1 carrot, finely sliced
1 teaspoon Sichuan peppercorns
1 teaspoon soy sauce
1 tablespoon mirin
1 teaspoon rice wine vinegar
1 teaspoon cornflour mixed with 1 tablespoon cold water
1 teaspoon toasted sesame seeds
¼ teaspoon cracked black pepper
steamed jasmine rice, to serve

MARINADE
1 tablespoon soy sauce
1 teaspoon sugar
1 teaspoon cornflour

Place the dried mandarin peels in a bowl, add enough water to just cover and set aside to soak for 30 minutes. Drain, then slice into 5 cm long strips.

Combine the marinade ingredients in a bowl, add the beef and marinate for 2 minutes.

Heat 2 tablespoons of the vegetable oil in a wok over high heat, add the beef and stir-fry for 2–3 minutes, until sealed. Immediately remove the beef from the pan and set aside.

Wipe the wok clean with paper towel, add the remaining 1 tablespoon of vegetable oil and return the wok to medium heat. Add the onion, ginger, white part of spring onion, carrot and Sichuan peppercorns, and stir-fry for 1–2 minutes, until fragrant.

Return the beef to the wok, along with the mandarin peel and the soaking water, and toss to combine. Add the soy sauce, mirin and rice wine vinegar and stir-fry for 2 minutes, then add the cornflour slurry and stir-fry for 1 minute or until the mixture thickens.

Transfer the stir-fry to a serving plate, sprinkle with the toasted sesame seeds, pepper and the green part of the spring onion and serve with steamed jasmine rice.

Everything Natalie Paull bakes is made with precision, care and thought. It's no wonder her bakery, Beatrix Bakes, has a cult following. When I asked Nat if she would contribute a mandarin recipe to my book, she was even more generous than her cakes and agreed. I hope that if you're reading this on a cold wintery day and there are mandarins on your kitchen bench that this delicious recipe inspires you to grease that loaf tin!

NAT PAULL'S SYRUPY MANDARIN LOAF

SERVES 10–12

500 g whole mandarins (about 4; honey murcotts are best if you can get them), washed
cooking oil spray
160 g almond meal
80 g fine polenta
3 g (¾ teaspoon) baking powder
2 g (scant ½ teaspoon) fine sea salt
180 g unsalted butter, squidgy soft
160 g raw caster sugar, plus 60 g extra for the syrup
120 g egg (about 2 jumbo eggs)
juice of 1 lemon
vanilla-spiked whipped cream, to serve

Set up a steamer, add the whole mandarins and steam, covered, for 30–40 minutes, until soft. Remove the mandarins from the steamer and allow to cool to lukewarm.

Preheat the oven to 140°C fan-forced. Spray the base and sides of a 21 cm x 10.5 cm loaf tin with cooking oil spray and line with baking paper.

Place the almond meal, polenta, baking powder and salt in a small bowl and stir to combine.

Using a stand mixer with the whisk attached or with electric beaters, beat the butter and sugar on low speed for 3–4 minutes, until pale and creamy. Add the eggs, one at a time, letting the mixture return to a fluffy, creamy paste after each addition.

When the fruit has cooled, remove the pedicel (a fruit nerd term for where the fruit is attached to a stem) and cut the mandarins in half. Pluck out as many seeds as you can, then weigh out 320 g of mandarin. Transfer to the bowl of a food processor and blitz to a pulpy, porridge consistency.

Scrape the mandarin pulp into the batter and stir well. Add the dry ingredients and fold through thoroughly, then scrape the batter into the prepared tin and smooth the top. Bake for 60–70 minutes, until a wooden skewer inserted into the middle of the cake comes out clean (or the cake has reached an internal temperature of 95°C).

Meanwhile, to make the syrup, finely dice the remaining mandarins and place in a small saucepan with the extra sugar, lemon juice and 200 ml of water. Bring to a simmer over low heat and cook for 5 minutes, until the liquid is a thin, syrupy consistency. Set aside to cool, then spoon most of the syrup over the top of the hot cake. Leave to cool in the tin for 30 minutes.

Carefully invert the cake onto a serving plate. Spoon the remaining syrup over the cake and enjoy warm or at room temperature, with vanilla-spiked whipped cream.

MANGOES

My first memory of mangoes is eating them at home with a bowl of jasmine rice. Mum often served me this when she had no time to cook, and I don't blame her; she raised five kids while working at the fruit shop! When I was young, our family was just getting by, and we usually ate what my parents had available in the store. In the summertime, this often meant mangoes for their flavour and value. As an Asian household, there was always cooked rice in the rice cooker, so it was easy for Mum to slice up some mango and put it on the rice for me. I used to think it was a great meal. I wasn't worldly enough to believe I needed salty, savoury flavours in food; life was simple and delicious.

Mangoes are my dad's favourite fruit – he's obsessed with them. He's wanted to buy a mango farm and is always searching for the best tray of mangoes to bring home to Mum.

Australians often associate and celebrate eating an abundance of mangoes with summer, linked with their extreme value during peak season when they're sold by the tray and for much cheaper than nearly all other fruit. Dad would, on occasion, load the truck full of mangoes, and when he pulled the curtains of the truck to reveal a wall of the fruit, it was like someone spraying mango perfume. Mango season is fruit gluttony at its peak, a sin all Aussies are guilty of, and our stomachs are happy for.

The world of mangoes is diverse and wonderful. Each country tends to celebrate their homegrown varietals and eat mangoes in their own unique way. Arguably the most famous varietal in the world is the alphonso mango from India, where they are often rolled on a table to loosen the pulp before the top is chopped off and the flesh is sucked out. I discovered this fascinating method from a team member with Indian heritage who picked up one of our mangoes and, to my eyes, started bruising the fruit. I was almost disgusted at his treatment of the mango until I found out why!

Unripe mangoes are firm and can be cut into matchsticks and then balanced with salty, sour, savoury and spicy flavours to make a refreshing meal. These 'green mangoes' are often celebrated in Thailand, Vietnam, Laos and Cambodia. My family has been wholesaling ripe and unripe mangoes to the Asian community for decades.

One of my fondest fruit travel memories was visiting Humpty Doo in the Northern Territory to visit our growers at the peak of the mango season. The late grower My Viet Trinh, who grew predominantly green mangoes, walked me through his farm and taught me how to pick ripe mangoes that still have a green appearance on the skin, specifically the Thai varietals nam doc mai and keow savoy. In Australia, the description for mangoes sold as 'unripe' is very loose – they are picked before full maturity and sold for their sour flavour and crunchy texture, with names such as cooking mangoes, salad mangoes, green mangoes, sour mangoes ... the list goes on. To clarify, I will refer to these mangoes as 'cooking mangoes' instead of 'snacking mangoes'. This moment was so educational and mind-blowing for me because most Australians only eat mangoes as sweet snacking fruit. Consumers have been trained to identify a mango as ripe and ready to eat by looking at the colour of the skin: green is unripe; yellow is ripe. But nam doc mai and keow savoy mangoes stay green, so it's important to look at other traits to determine the maturity stage of the fruit. Through this lesson, I taught myself other sensorial cues to help me identify if a mango will be tasty or not, and now it will help you!

It's also a notable fact that the sap in mango trees contains a compound called urushiol, which is found in poison ivy and can cause dermatitis. It often oozes out of the stem, but is also found in low levels under the skin, so for some who are allergic it can be painful to eat mangoes!

Mango season is fruit gluttony at its peak.

A PLUMP BASE IS A SIGN OF RIPENESS.

BLACK LENTICEL SPOTS ARE A SIGN OF MATURITY AND GREAT FLAVOUR.

A ROUNDED SHOULDER SHOWS MATURITY AND RIPENESS.

A FLATTENED BEAK IS A SIGN OF RIPENESS.

Choose (ripe/ snacking mangoes)

IN THIS ORDER ...
AROMA: we all have unique flavour preferences, so enjoying the aroma of a mango will give us a hint as to whether we will enjoy the eating experience too. Also, a strong aroma shows the mango is at the late stage of ripening, where many of the starches have turned to sugars, and this is evident as more gases are released. The fruit will be softer, a tell-tale sign to eat it soon!

LENTICEL SPOTS: these are visual hints that the fruit has matured on the tree and developed complex flavours. Large white spots are good; black dots are even better.

FULL SHOULDER, FLATTENED BEAK AND PLUMP BOTTOM: these areas are the last parts of the mango to expand; when they plump up, it shows the fruit has reached 90–100 per cent maturity on the tree. It's a simple sign that the fruit has developed all its complex flavours and will be very flavourful once it's ripe. Some mangoes only grow one or two of these features.

EVEN COLOUR: mangoes with mostly even colour are more likely to be fully ripe with complex flavour. If a mango is blotchy with green patches, or has uneven colour when it's fully ripe, it could mean the fruit was picked too early and was forced to ripen, or was not stored at the right temperature, resulting in the fruit ripening too slowly. Even colour is irrelevant for mango varietals with green skin that do not turn yellow when ripe.

WHAT TO AVOID ...
RESIN CANALS: black blotches on the skin, which cause black strings under the mango surface. The mango is safe to eat but might not taste as good.

ANTHRACNOSE: this is a fungus that hangs onto the skin of many mangoes. Mango skin naturally has compounds that break down and stop fungi growing, but when the picked fruit sits at room temperature, these anti-fungal compounds start to break down and anthracnose can start to grow. Black dots will appear on the surface of the mango skin, which will turn into blotches that bruise and damage the flesh inside. This may occur if you keep your mango for too long, but if you're at the store and you see some dots on the skin, it's likely the mango has been on the shelf too long and it's best to give it a miss! That's why you should eat a mango as soon as it's ready or freeze the flesh before it goes bad!

Choose (unripe/ cooking mangoes)

1. Look for firm mangoes with a curved beak.

2. Avoid mangoes with lenticel spotting.

Store

Keep mangoes on a fruit plate at room temperature (18–21°C); they'll have more aroma and will ripen correctly stored this way.

Prep

THE MODERN HEDGEHOG
Instead of cutting a mango cheek into a 3 x 3 grid, try a 7 x 7 or even an 8 x 8 grid. If it's still firm, the mango will have much more texture when you bite into it. If there are any strings in the mango, they will be more digestible as they are cut into smaller segments, and you'll have fewer fibres caught between your teeth!

CUT THE SKIN OFF, DON'T PEEL
Most strings lie under the skin of a mango, so if you peel a mango like a banana, it will be really stringy. Cutting a mango using the hedgehog method doesn't remove the strings, so you may still get some stuck in your teeth as you bite close to the skin. The strings in a mango are genetic, so different mango varietals will have more or less string. Stringless mangoes are much more of a desired trait, hence why the nam doc mai is so desired as a cooking mango, because when eaten raw it has little-to-no strings, making it a pleasant textural experience.

The best Vietnamese green mango salad I've ever eaten was at My Viet Trinh's farm. His wife not only served us this classic Vietnamese dish, but she did so farm-style. What I mean by that is she used a combination of mangoes to create different textures: nam doc mai, the classic Thai mango, which is less fibrous and has a smooth flesh and intense sour notes; and xoài tượng (elephant mango), a large and very firm Vietnamese variety, which is super crunchy and has a relatively neutral flavour. I've always been a big advocate of using different varietals of the same fruit in one dish, and this recipe was exemplary of that – it allowed the mangoes to shine without the need for a protein, although if you do want to bulk it out a little you could add a few peeled and deveined boiled prawns. This is my version of the dish using my mum's nước chẩm as a dressing, but remember that you can always leave out the chillies if you don't love spice.

VIETNAMESE GREEN MANGO SALAD

GỎI XOÀI

SERVES 6

3 green mangoes, (a variety if possible), peeled and julienned
100 g finely sliced Asian shallot
1 small Lebanese cucumber, julienned
1 loosely packed cup mint leaves
1 loosely packed cup Vietnamese mint leaves
1 x quantity Nước Chẩm (see page 74)
50 g (⅔ cup) fried shallots
50 g salted peanuts

Combine the mango, shallot, cucumber, mint and Vietnamese mint in a serving bowl.

Pour the nước chẩm over the salad and toss to combine. Allow the salad to stand for at least 5 minutes, for the flavours to meld.

Scatter the fried shallots and salted peanuts over the top of the salad and serve.

MANGOSTEENS

The Queen of Fruits has it all! There isn't a soul I know who has tasted mangosteen and doesn't like it, but this much-loved fruit can be hard to source. Even I, a wholesale fruiterer with connections across the industry and specialising in tropical fruit, can sometimes find it challenging to purchase mangosteen in Australia, thereby elevating its status as a 'rare' fruit. Although I seldom ate mangosteens as a small child, growing up this fruit became one of my favourites, mainly because my dad couldn't stop eating it. Given Dad's access to fresh produce, he is pretty balanced with his fruit intake, but the mangosteen is his Kryptonite. Lucky for me, I got to share this experience during high school when he'd bring a whole box home! The entire box of thick purple-skinned bulbs wouldn't last five minutes, let alone the night – it was crazy!

Most of the world's fresh mangosteens come from tropical fruit-producing powerhouse Thailand, and this is where I've also had most of my fresh mangosteen experiences. On the outside, mangosteens look like pretty purple-skinned balls with a calyx, or leaf, on top. On the inside, they're the bomb. Mangosteens are intensely sour but somehow sweet, too, with juicy flesh and a unique flavour that make it my second-favourite fruit behind the cherry. Its difficulty to grow and transport,

short shelf life and deliciousness make it a highly prized fruit across South-East Asia, where it originates. As the mangosteen is seasonal, it is a fruit that I long for.

The garlic clove–shaped bites of tangy tropical goodness are full of 'sweet umami' – the intense but balanced flavours leading to an unstoppable desire to eat more of the fruit.

A risky business

Our family business has been importing mangosteens for more than two decades, and it's a highly risky venture. You can lose tens of thousands of dollars instantly if you get a bad batch. Remember that the fresh produce trade is often figuring out how to avoid a loss before making a profit. Given that I've seen my fair share of bad mangosteens, from this misfortune comes some good: I know what to look out for. A bad mangosteen will be completely inedible, that's if you can even open the shell to get to the flesh. Given its thick shell, we can't tell with our eyes if the internal flesh is good or not. That's when our other senses need to kick in.

The mangosteen's short shelf life means that it goes from amazing to rubbish within days. There is a mystery behind them, and in our attempts to control and commoditise this fruit, traders have stepped away from the very thing that has brought us this beautiful gift: nature. You see, fruit is alive in the very literal sense. With mangosteens, I plead for you to think of them as such. Even though the skin is inedible (though you can make it into tea), you shouldn't see the skin as an obstacle, but as part of the living fruit. If the skin dies, the flesh dies. It's as simple as that, and you cannot have the deliciously sweet umami flesh if the skin is dead.

If mangosteens are not stored correctly, the skin will ripen, dehydrate or spoil within days, so the industry has stringent packaging rules to control the cold chain. These include keeping the mangosteens away from ethylene-producing fruits and storing them in conditions of 90 per cent humidity and at a temperature of 13–15°C.

> 66
> **The mangosteen's short shelf life means that it goes from amazing to rubbish within days.**

THE DARKER THE SKIN,
THE RIPER THE MANGOSTEEN.

LOOK FOR BRIGHT,
FRESH-LOOKING SKIN.

AND A STRONG,
BRIGHT-GREEN STEM.

Mangosteen roulette

What if the mangosteen skin is soft, but the inside is still bad? Speaking to Thai traders over the years, I have learned there are two technical reasons for mangosteens going bad on the inside. Given there are no English words for these terms, I like to use the literal Thai translations of 'glass meat' and 'tree sap'. Glass meat refers to the flesh being translucent and is a result of excessive rain and water absorption from the tree into the fruit. The translucent flesh lacks flavour and obscures the texture, making the mangosteen firm and unappetising, although still edible. Tree sap is a yellow-looking paint, or mucus, found inside the flesh, usually affecting a small portion or some portions of the fruit. Sometimes you can see tree sap or yellow specks on the skin of mangosteen, but this doesn't always mean that the fruit is affected internally. Tree sap comes from mangosteen trees with a tree sap–type disease, but because mangosteens are harvested en masse, the tree sap–affected fruit gets graded with non-affected fruit, making it problematic to grade out.

Wild mangosteen

My mangosteen journeys have also led me to Central Java, Indonesia, where the Java Fresh team gather wild-harvested mangosteens from the rainforests. There is a distinct difference between wild-harvested and orchard-grown mangosteens, and that difference is sweet umami. The intensity of flavours that a fruit grown on a 30-metre-high tree up a monstrous mountain, with wild galangal and ferns blanketing the floor, are on another level. I travelled to Tasikmalaya and watched locals traipse through the forest and scale these huge trees to harvest the high-hanging fruit. It was insane!

Given the heat in Indonesia, mangosteen trees only grow 800 metres above sea level. It takes eight years for a young tree to yield just 2 kg of fruit and 19 years for the tree to hit maximum maturity and produce 200 kg of fruit. I hope that gives you more of an appreciation for mangosteens!

The Indonesian knowledge of the fruit is also outstanding and growing by the day. While the terminology might be different – 'yellow gum' is used instead of 'tree sap' – their research into the fruit is paying dividends. I spoke to Hilda Sucipto, the head of Research and Development at Java Fresh, who shared some of her knowledge with me. Hilda explained that a healthy mangosteen will have a moist green stem; bright, fresh-looking skin with a dark colour that indicates maturity; and will be soft to touch, suggesting good internal flesh. If the tip on the calyx is visually black, this may be a sign of a defect in the fruit. Possible reasons for this are lack of nutrients or water entering through the top of the fruit, potentially breaking cells and allowing disease or yellow gum inside. Her research also supports my theory that the skin needs to be protected at all costs.

Closer to home

While the mangosteen is native to South-East Asia, a small number of producers also grow mangosteens in Australia. I have found that Australian mangosteens, which I sell, are very small, but there are no seeds so you can eat the entire flesh. The flavour is great, and there is rarely any damage to the fruit. This may be because our soils and drainage systems are good or perhaps because we don't have the excessive monsoonal rains like they do in Asia. Nevertheless, small mangosteens will give you bang for your buck, given the seeds most often haven't developed!

Mangosteens have a neat party trick: the number of stamens or 'wooden stamps' on the base of the fruit reveal precisely how many lobes of flesh are inside. What doesn't the mangosteen have?

Choose

1. Feel the fruit with your hands, especially around the waist – the skin should be soft with some 'give'. If it's hard, don't buy it as the flesh and skin has perished.

2. Look for bright, fresh-looking skin.

3. Pick fruit with strong bright-green stems.

4. Dark-purple skin is best. Green or pink mangosteens are unripe, while red is borderline mature.

Store

Ideally, mangosteens should be eaten on the day of purchase, but they can be kept at room temperature between 18°C and 25°C, away from ethylene-producing fruits, for up to two days.

Prep

DAD'S WAY: push down on the stem to break the calyx, then remove the stem and core if still attached to the stem. Break the shell in half to access the segments.

THANH'S WAY: place the mangosteen between your palms, waist-side up, then press inwards to break the line around the waist and remove the side with the stem. Pull out the segments to eat.

KNIFE: cut the skin around the waist and remove the top half, then break off the segments to eat.

FUN FACT: THE NUMBER OF PETALS OR 'STAMPS' AT THE BOTTOM OF THE FRUIT WILL REVEAL HOW MANY EDIBLE SEGMENTS (ARILS) ARE INSIDE!

MUSHROOMS

ushrooms are a fungi, not a vegetable. This means that from an evolutionary perspective they are more closely related to humans than they are to vegetables! I'm not trying to confuse you, I'm merely trying to point out that even though we consider mushrooms as a vegetable, and indeed we cook them like vegetables, they should be seen, selected, stored and prepared like fungi.

My good friend Jim Fuller, who we'll meet on page 185, recommends boiling then frying mushrooms because they have a completely different structural make-up to vegetables. For this reason I have included two different cooking methods: one for most mushrooms, which you should boil then fry because of their high water content (see page 185); and one for enoki mushrooms, which have a far higher skin-to-flesh ratio, meaning there is less water for them to release during the cooking process (see page 186).

Wild fungi

Foraging for wild mushrooms is a very grounding activity to do. It's like travelling back in time to being a hunter-gatherer. It shows you how alive mushrooms are, knowing that potentially only 24 hours beforehand the fruiting body of the mushroom probably hadn't even shot out of the ground. How does this knowledge help us when it comes to purchasing and storing fungi? It tells us that we should try and replicate the same environment for mushrooms, but at home. If you've ever foraged for pine mushrooms in a pine-tree plantation you'll know how cold yet moist the air is. This is the kind of atmosphere you want to replicate in your fridge and you can achieve this by using a paper bag, which keeps the humidity very high for the mushroom to remain stable in its natural environment, while allowing it to breathe and not sweat. If you ever have the opportunity to forage for mushrooms safely on a tour or with a mycologist, I encourage you to take it – it will change any preconceived ideas you had about how fungi survive and thrive.

I do believe that in a world heavily focused on plant-based meats, mushrooms are one of the closest substitutes we have for replicating meat textures.

Mushrooms are one of the closest substitutes we have for replicating meat textures.

Choose

THANH'S TIPS

1. Look for bright and plump mushrooms.

2. Avoid dehydrating mushrooms, which can appear shrivelled or starting to blacken.

3. Avoid mushrooms with sweat or water on the skin – this is often seen in plastic packaging.

Store

Store mushrooms in a paper bag in the fridge to allow them to breathe in a low-humidity environment. They will still eventually dehydrate, but at a much slower pace than in the open air. Paper bags also prevent mushrooms from sweating, which encourages bacterial growth.

The mushroom industry body suggests mushrooms should be eaten within one week of being cut. For consumers, that means we should eat mushrooms within two to three days of purchasing them.

WHY ARE MUSHROOMS SOLD WRAPPED IN PLASTIC?

Some mushrooms are sold in vacuum-sealed plastic to remove the oxygen inside, preventing the oxidisation of cut mushrooms. However, once the bag is opened the mushrooms are exposed to oxygen, so it's best to store them in a paper bag. What about mushrooms in punnets covered by plastic wrap? The wrap is a special cling film with micro incisions that allow the mushrooms to breathe. Once opened, move the mushrooms to a paper bag.

PAPER BAGS HOLD HIGH HUMIDITY YET ALLOW FUNGI TO BREATHE.

Besides the fruit itself, the next best thing at fruit markets are the people you meet. One of my best produce mates is Jim Fuller, a mycologist, fine-dining chef, chemical engineer and ex-mushroom trader. He was my neighbour at the market – he traded mushrooms, I traded durian – and he's since taken me mushroom foraging, given me his inoculated mushroom bags and empowered me with more mushroom knowledge than I could ever imagine. If I'm the Fruit Nerd, Jim's the Mushroom Nerd. His biggest piece of advice? Boil your mushrooms.

Let me explain: mushrooms are fungi, not plants, and their structure doesn't break down in the same way as plants when boiled. Jim says that as long as there is sufficient water in the pan, you can boil mushrooms for hours and they won't structurally break or fall apart. Because mushrooms are 80–90 per cent water, when cooking them using the traditional French method of high heat and with oil or butter, there is a battle between the water released from the mushrooms and the fat, because the water prevents the fat exceeding 100°C. Browning, also known as the Maillard reaction, can't begin until the fat reaches 145–165°C, but as soon as the water evaporates, the fat is immediately sucked into the mushrooms, getting progressively cooler as it travels away from the pan, leaving you with a violent sizzling battle between the fat and water in the pan.

Jim explains that if you only cook your mushrooms in oil, you would need 150 ml for 250 g of mushrooms, to keep temperatures high enough in the pan to fight the water, but if you add the oil at the end, you only need 15 ml of oil for 250 g of mushrooms. Amazing!

Wok or frying pan? It's easier to boil and then fry the mushrooms in a wok because the base of the wok has a smaller surface area than a frying pan. You only want to add enough water to shallow-boil the mushrooms – the water level should not be higher than the mushrooms. Ultimately, don't be afraid of how much water you add, it just means the mushrooms will need to boil a little longer.

Here is Jim's foolproof method for perfect boiled-then-fried mushrooms.

JIM FULLER'S PERFECT MUSHROOMS

Place the mushroom in a wok and add 100 ml of water to half-cover them. Place the wok over medium heat and bring to the boil, then boil the mushroom for 3–4 minutes, until the mushroom has shrunk by 20–30 per cent and the water has evaporated (add another tablespoon of water, if the mushroom hasn't reduced by this amount).

Add the olive oil, salt, garlic and herbs and stir-fry for 1 minute or until the mushroom has browned. Finish with a splash of water to deglaze the pan, then remove the pan from the heat and add a generous knob of butter. Serve hot.

200 g mushrooms of your choice (but not enoki), roughly chopped
3 teaspoons olive oil
1 teaspoon sea salt
2 garlic cloves, finely chopped
2 herb sprigs, such as rosemary, basil or parsley, leaves picked and finely chopped
knob of butter, to serve

SERVES
4

No sugar, no salt, ultimate umami! When you're hungry and don't have time for food prep, this is the perfect meal that's full of flavour. You can use the mushrooms in various ways – I like to serve them with steamed rice, in a Turkish roll or in a burger. Did I mention they're cooked in under five minutes?

Firstly, mushrooms aren't vegetables, they're fungi, and they absorb lots of flavour, which is why cooking them correctly is paramount. While other mushrooms have an abundance of water, enoki mushrooms do not, and so for this recipe we are not using the wet-fry method (see page 185), but rather a semi-dry oil method.

I've also cooked this recipe using button, flat and Swiss brown mushrooms. For these types of mushrooms, finely slice them and boil in 50–100 ml of water until the water is nearly evaporated. Once the mushrooms are cooked, continue with the recipe below, but shorten the cooking time from 3½ minutes to 1 minute.

5-MINUTE ENOKI MUSHROOM STIR-FRY

SERVES 2–4

2½ tablespoons grapeseed oil
2.5 cm piece of ginger, peeled and julienned
bunch of enoki mushrooms (about 300 g), trimmed
1½ tablespoons soy sauce
1½ tablespoons rice wine vinegar
1 teaspoon mirin
1 teaspoon cornflour mixed with 1 tablespoon cold water

Heat the grapeseed oil in a frying pan over medium–high heat. Add the ginger and leave it to infuse the oil for 30 seconds. Add the enoki mushrooms and use a wooden spoon to separate the strands, then add the soy sauce, rice wine vinegar and mirin and cook, stirring occasionally, for 3½ minutes. Add the cornflour slurry and cook for a further 1 minute or until thickened.

Remove the pan from the heat and enjoy the stir-fried enoki mushrooms with steamed rice, in a roll or in a burger.

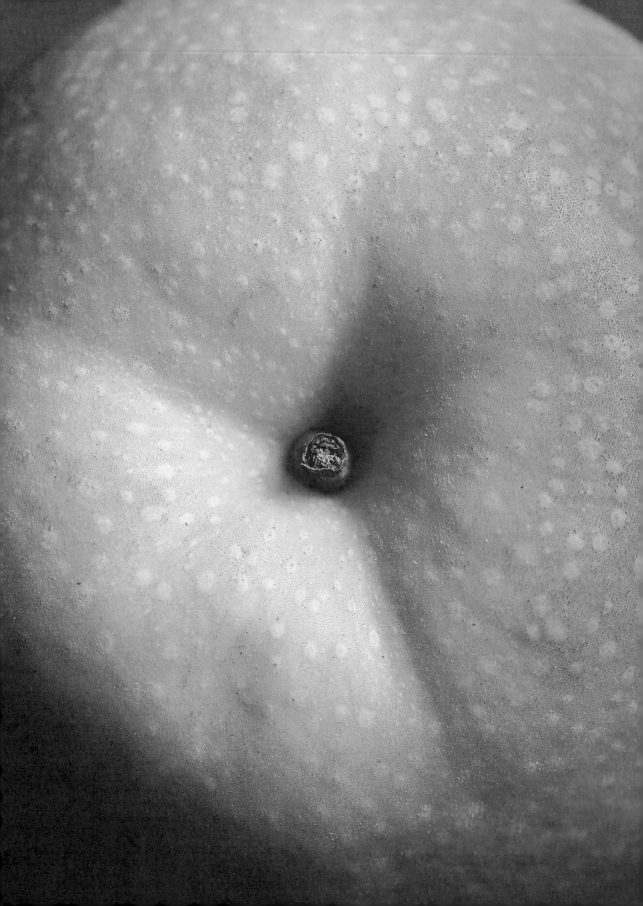

NASHIS

I wouldn't be the Fruit Nerd without nashi pears in my life, or rather in my father's life. Before Dad became a fruit wholesaler he owned a small Asian grocery shop, selling a handful of fruits in the Melbourne suburb of Springvale. He was searching for culturally relevant fruits to sell to the local Vietnamese community when he was introduced to a nashi pear farmer in Shepparton by the name of Jamie Craig. As the market for nashis was very small back in the early 1990s, Dad would drive his truck up to Shepparton and back in the middle of the night to load up just one pallet of fruit for his little shop. As the years went by, the nashi market grew and Dad ended up transporting tonnes of nashi pears back to Melbourne every week, and distributing them to other Vietnamese community fruit shops around the city. Dad went on to sell the small fruit shop and become a fruit wholesaler at the Melbourne Fruit & Vegetable Wholesale Markets, based in Footscray, and Jamie and Dad became best friends. You could say that the nashi isn't just a culturally relevant fruit to the Asian community, but it's also my family's spiritual fruit.

It's worth noting that the word 'nashi' is the Japanese word for the fruit; however, across East Asia it's better known as an 'Asian' pear as opposed to a Western pear. The main difference being that nashis do not ripen after being harvested. We call the fruit nashi in Australia because the first varietals to be planted here were all Japanese. Nashis are mainly grown in Japan, Korea and China. My grandfather would always tell my dad to eat a nashi whenever he had a fever, to lower the 'heat' in his body. Dad didn't know if this was true or not, but good health and a cooling effect have strong associations with nashi pears within the Vietnamese, Chinese, Korean and Japanese communities.

If you haven't had a nashi before, think of the flavour of a pear with the texture of a watermelon. Its flesh is watery and juicy, but it's texturally crunchy and has a floral aroma on its skin. Refreshing is a great word to describe a nashi.

Cultural significance

The Chinese and Korean communities like to steam nashi flesh with herbs to make a lemon–honey tea of sorts (see page 192). In Korea, the tops of nashis are chopped so the spirits of ancestors can access the fruit for Chuseok, Korea's famous autumn harvest festival. The Vietnamese community associate the smooth skin of a nashi to one's hope for a 'smooth New Year' during the Lunar New Year festival, and the fruit is often placed on the 'five fruits plate' offering called 'mam ngu qua'. There is a traditional saying in China called 'Kong Rong lets his pears go', after the scholar Kong Rong, who gave all of his large pears to his brothers. This idiom is used to teach children the importance of sharing and, as such, gifting nashis in the Chinese community is an act of kindness.

My father and I transformed the nashi market in Australia. Firstly, my dad introduced and continues to distribute many varieties of nashi, both Australian and imported, including varietals such as nijisseiki, hosui, hakka, crown, sand, fragrant, snow, shingo, autumn moon, nansui and ya. Secondly, understanding the cultural significance of fruit-gifting led me to change our packaging of nashis into 'gift boxes' for East Asian communities in Australia. While many other distributors copy our designs and our packaging dimensions, their cultural understanding of why we made these changes for our customers is lacking. The first time we changed our packaging, there was a backlash from our customer base and we made a huge loss. It took another two years of trying different designs, during the relevant celebratory events of Chuseok and Lunar New Year, for the Asian Australian community to accept and enjoy our fruit-gift packaging. It's heart-warming to know that I'm able to make a difference to people's lives and the industry in a small but culturally relevant way.

The main difference between nashis grown in Asia versus Australia is that the former are wrapped in a paper bag to prevent pests, increase the juiciness of their flesh and make their skin thinner. Australian nashis have to adapt to the harsh dry winds and strong sun, so they grow a thick skin and usually have cosmetic markings due to leaf rub.

IF YOU HAVEN'T HAD A NASHI BEFORE, THINK OF THE FLAVOUR OF A PEAR WITH THE TEXTURE OF A WATERMELON.

Choose

1. Look for firm fruit.

2. Nashis are delicate, hence why they are often sold in 'socks'. Check the skin for bruising as this could mean the nashi was dropped or damaged.

3. Skin marks and grazes are purely aesthetic and won't affect flavour, although if you are buying nashis as a gift you may want a more presentable fruit.

4. Avoid soft fruit; shrivelled skin suggests incorrect storage.

5. Nashis can deteriorate quickly. If the skin colour starts to become paler it's likely due to incorrect cold storage – the fruit will taste flat and not as vibrant.

6. Skin sun spots are areas where the sun has made the fruit extra sweet. They will show up as a blistering yellow-orange mark on a specific spot on the skin – these are the nashis my dad chooses.

Store

Store nashi pears in a plastic bag, to ensure moisture retention, on the bottom shelf of the fridge.

Baesuk is the Korean version of lemon–honey tea. It's a homely dish, cooked mainly by parents when their children have a cough. Naturally, it has ginger and a few other simple ingredients. Baesuk means 'cooked pear' and I first ate it in South Korea while visiting shingo pear orchards in Jinju. It was hot, and the growers invited me to a lunch where the soup was served chilled at the end of the meal as a light dessert. It was much needed after all the pan makgeolli (chestnut rice wine) that I had drunk! I loved it, but can't remember its taste so well, given my inebriated state.

I asked my good friend John Choi, whose father is a farmer in South Korea and has helped me with my grower connections there, to give me an insight into his baesuk recipe, which he cooks for his kids. He told me that the amount of honey you add is personal, and that his son Joshua likes one tablespoon of honey, while his other son Daniel likes it much sweeter with two tablespoons! Each to their own ... John also adds a small piece of cinnamon stick to give the soup a gentle herbal flavour, but you can also use a little ground cinnamon powder.

After the pear is steamed, some juice may leak out, which is why it's important to capture it in a bowl. The whole pear, including the skin, is edible, and the juice is also rejuvenating. While, traditionally, roasted gingko nuts are used in Korea, they're not so accessible for me, so I've added pine nuts instead, but you can also use walnuts. Steaming the nuts will release their oils and make the soup gently richer. If you prefer a clean drink, omit the nuts. Don't overdo it with the dried jujubes, as they are really rich and overpowering in flavour; if you prefer a lighter drink, use one jujube.

NASHI HERBAL SOUP

BAESUK

SERVES
1

1 large brown nashi pear
   (500–700 g), washed well
2.5 cm piece of ginger, peeled
   and finely sliced
2 dried jujubes, pitted and
   finely sliced
30 g pine nuts
1 tablespoon honey
½ teaspoon whole black
   peppercorns
½ cinnamon stick

Bring a steamer to the boil.

Meanwhile, slice the top 1 cm off the pear and reserve. Using a teaspoon, dig out the seeds and discard them, then remove enough pear flesh to make a large cavity, leaving a 1 cm border. Reserve the pear flesh.

Fill the inside of the pear with the ginger, jujube, pine nuts, honey, peppercorns, cinnamon stick and reserved pear flesh and pop the pear lid back on top.

Place the pear in a tight-fitting heatproof bowl, to catch any pear juice that leaks out during steaming. Add the bowl to the steamer and cook over low heat for 1 hour or until the pear is tender and fragrant, but still firm enough to hold its shape.

You can serve the baesuk hot or cold. If serving cold, place in the fridge, covered with plastic wrap, for 2–3 hours, until chilled.

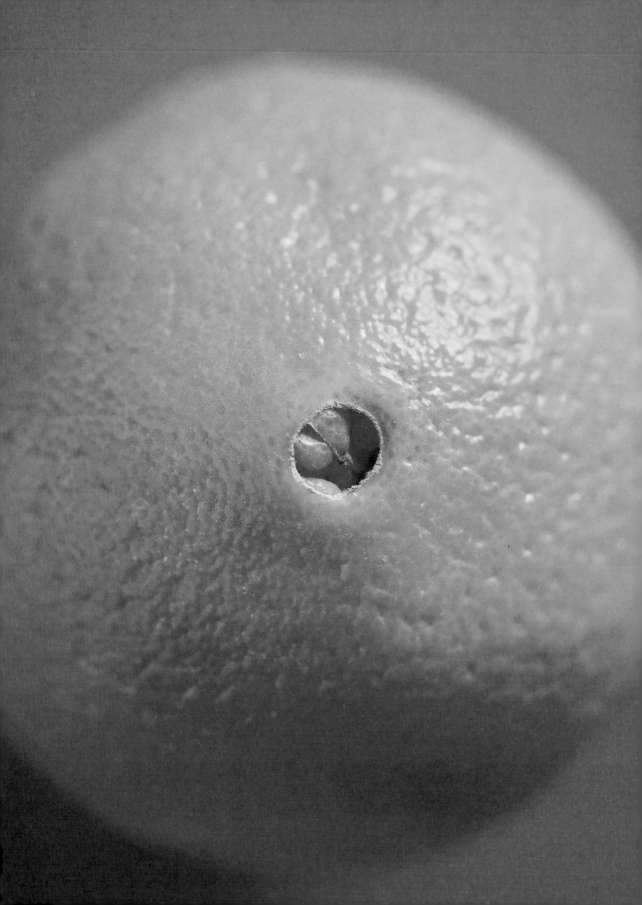

ORANGES

On a cold winter Saturday morning at the local football oval, the whistle blows, indicating halftime; the team gathers, with all the kids muddy and puffing with exhaustion and squeezing water bottles like they've just been rescued from a desert. Out come the plastic containers filled with cut fruit: it's oranges. This is a fond childhood memory for many of us, because oranges were the juicy and flavourful hydration we needed to keep going.

I'm not a sports scientist, but NBA great LeBron James eats about five oranges when he's resting on the bench, so they must be good for us. Besides a bit of potassium, which helps with cramping, oranges really reign supreme as a hydration fruit, perhaps only topped by coconuts and watermelons, which are less convenient to eat, especially while playing sports. Knowing that we love oranges for their hydration ability tells us that what we seek in an orange is a fruit full of juice and a high water content. It also tells us what a bad orange would taste or feel like: dry and not juicy.

There's nothing worse than a dry orange. All citrus can be affected by drying, otherwise known as 'granulation'. It is a physiological disorder that causes the juice vesicles, or juice sacs, to wither and dry up. It occurs both on the tree and post-harvesting. Much research has been conducted, but still no one knows exactly what causes granulation, so it's something the industry and farmers have to work around until we can address the issue.

Why doesn't the industry grade out granulated fruit? After growers do their first and second picking on the farm, strip picking occurs where all the fruit, both good and bad oranges, are harvested in the same basket. This is because it's more efficient and cost-effective to pick everything off the tree at once, than to feel all the fruit and only harvest a few. As long as this process continues, both dry and juicy oranges will be sold alongside each other.

The best orange I have ever eaten was from a batch of organic navels from a smaller grower in Mildura. It had the most intense yet balanced sweet and sour flavours and was brimming with juice. I've never experienced that heightened state of orange since, but I've had plenty of excellent oranges. Most orange varietals grown today are hybrids of navels, and many are grown for their thick skin, which increases shelf life, and low acid, for a naturally sweeter taste. There's a big difference between a bland orange and one with intense sour and sweet notes. My favourites are the late-season navel varieties, which hang on the tree longer, develop more sugars and tend to have lingering sour notes, which I love.

Valencia vs navel

If you're an orange fan, you might've wondered about the difference between valencias and navels, the two most common orange varietals commercially grown in the world. Navels are picked in winter and valencias are picked in summer. Generally, navels are sweeter and have more pronounced and textural pulp to bite into, making them better as a snacking fruit, while valencias tend to have thinner pulps, making them better for juicing. Navel orange juice tends to go bitter and lose flavour within 24 hours, while valencia juice can be stored for several days and still hold good flavour without turning bitter. Regardless, these two varieties mean that you can have locally grown oranges for most of the year!

NBA great LeBron James eats about five oranges when he's resting on the bench, so they must be good for us.

COLOUR IS
NOT AN INDICATOR
OF RIPENESS; BE GUIDED
BY TOUCH AND WEIGHT.

Why commercially sold oranges are completely orange in colour

Anyone with an orange tree in their backyard, will have noticed that, generally, the fruit never becomes uniformly orange in colour. It always tends to have spots of green, which is natural. In fact, the valencia orange generally turns greener the closer it gets to summer, developing its own form of sunscreen to protect itself from sunburn. The industry intentionally colours oranges by placing them in a room with controlled ethylene to induce full colouring on the skin. This is to make them look more aesthetically pleasing. We may argue that this is unnecessary, but our over-biased use of our eyes reveals that we tend to select uniformly coloured oranges, instead of those with green parts.

Touch picking

Given my knowledge of the industry and knowing that the majority of the best oranges are exported overseas to Asia, I spoke with Karen Leary, an Authorised Export Officer 'AO' based in Mildura, who inspects thousands of containers of oranges every season before they are shipped across the world. I asked Karen to explain how growers select the best oranges or know when the fruit is ready to pick. Karen explained that growers select fruit using the 'touch picking' method. This involves gently squeezing the orange; if the orange is firm and hard, then the fruit is not ready to be harvested. If the fruit has a slight 'give', then it's reached its final stages of maturity. The fruit plumps up and builds some final juices and expands, making the skin slightly thinner and, therefore, squeezable. If you have a citrus tree in your backyard, you'll notice that the fruit is rock hard in its early stages, and only softens once it's nearing maturity.

When it comes to oranges, colour is not an indicator of ripeness; instead be guided by touch and weight to pick a good fruit.

Choose

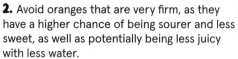

1. Use your hands to compare two oranges of approximately the same size; the heavier orange will be juicier than the lighter orange. Very light oranges will most definitely suffer from granulation.

2. Avoid oranges that are very firm, as they have a higher chance of being sourer and less sweet, as well as potentially being less juicy with less water.

The aesthetic grading of oranges is so perfect that it's nearly impossible to spot granulation or dryness by eye, so using your hands to feel the fruit is critical. I have found that your dominant hand gives the sensation that the fruit is lighter, so I suggest using your non-preferred hand, as this arm appears to be more sensitive to slight changes in weight. The difference between a 200 g and 240 g orange is 20 per cent, which is easily noticeable, but most often you will find differences of 10 per cent; think about it like this – you're picking a 10 per cent juicier orange every time!

Store

Store oranges in a plastic bag or airtight container in the coldest part of the fridge.

Prep

I remember cutting oranges and really not enjoying biting and chewing the bitter core thread. I used to bite around it. It was annoying, it was stringy, and it always got caught in between my teeth. When I moved out of home I began cutting oranges in different ways, until I found a method that satisfied the mouthfeel (kou gan) I was looking for. I love biting into an orange, ripping the vesicles, segmenting off the skin and enjoying the juicy pop when taking a bite. As I started cutting oranges for my kids, I figured out more efficient ways to maximise an orange's mouthfeel experience.

THE ANATOMY OF THE NAVEL

Understanding the anatomy of an orange will allow you to dissect the fruit and make logical decisions for the best eating experience. Cut an orange in half horizontally and work from the outside in. First there's the skin where the oils are, and beyond that there's the rind and the pith. Next are the segments, which contain the pulp and vesicles where all the juice is, and in the middle you'll find the central core, which is quite fibrous and bitter. At the base of a navel orange you'll notice a hard protrusion, which are the remnants of an underdeveloped second fruit. To achieve maximum juice and flavour, here are a few cutting methods I live by:

FOOTY HALFTIME METHOD

1. Cut the orange in half horizontally through the middle.

2. Slice either side of the central core – you'll have two perfect wedges and a third wedge that predominantly has just the core.

3. Now cut either side of the core to give two small perfect wedges. Suck or enjoy the juice around the core, then discard.

ULTIMATE METHOD

1. Cut through the whole orange on either side of the core, from the stem to the base. You will have three sections of orange.

2. Take the section with the core and slice either side of the core, to give you two smile-shaped wedges.

3. Now slice the two remaining sections in half. You will have six perfect wedges without any core.

LABOUR OF LOVE METHOD

1. Remove the top and base of the orange, then score the skin in wedges, from the base to the top.

2. Peel away the skin, then use a slightly blunt knife to scrape away the rind from top to bottom. You'll be left with just a little pith along the segments.

3. Break the orange in half and tear away the remnants of the underdeveloped fruit at the base, which has very little juice.

4. You now have perfect segments with only the segment walls and thin membrane covering the segments. This membrane adds to the overall flavour, because oranges are naturally sour.

FOOTY HALFTIME VS ULTIMATE METHOD

PEAS

GARDEN PEAS, SUGAR SNAP PEAS, SNOW PEAS & SNOW PEA TENDRILS

I'm sure you have eaten frozen green peas in fried rice, a pea soup or on the side of a pub meal before, but have you ever cracked opened a fresh garden pea pod and eaten the peas raw? Do you know the differences between garden peas, sugar snap peas and snow peas? The differences are very subtle, and one can think of them as peas at different stages. Garden peas have tough inedible pods, but contain big peas which we love, and these are the ones we eat frozen. Snow peas are a cultivar that grows relatively flat, with a thin membrane in the skin. They are often picked young when the pods are tender and crunchy so the whole vegetable can be eaten. Sugar snap peas are somewhere in between garden peas and snow peas; their skin is thicker than snow peas but still edible, and their peas grow relatively large. I only realised all of this when I started selling the latter two at the wholesale market where I work.

The combination of pasteurising and freezing garden peas has made them accessible to most of us year-round. Garden peas that are frozen are often sweeter than their fresh garden-pea counterparts, because they are nearly always picked at full maturity when the peas are sweetest. Fresh garden peas, on the other hand, are usually picked a few days before they reach their maximum sweetness. I think fondly of frozen green peas, that is until I unleash the deliciousness of snow peas, sugar snap peas and snow pea tendrils!

> I think fondly of frozen green peas, until I unleash the deliciousness of snow peas, sugar snaps and snow pea tendrils!

No strings attached

Tossing snow peas or sugar snap peas in a stir-fry is one of my favourite ways to eat these vegetables; what haunts me was having to peel the stringy strands off the spines of each pod when I was kid. Ironically, I find this process therapeutic now. I only do so because of a work trip to Guangzhou, China, where I visited a snow pea and sugar snap pea packing facility. Our family imports all kinds of vegetables for the hospitality industry in Australia, with many Chinese restaurants desiring juicy sugar snap varieties that aren't grown in Australia.

The snow pea supplier Mr Zhang picked a bunch of freshly harvested snow peas and drove us to a nearby restaurant for a late dinner after our visit. At the restaurant he ordered a few dishes and then started chatting to my dad while peeling the stringy strands off the snow peas himself. He did so with care but also patient enthusiasm, knowing they were going to be the hero of the meal. After around ten minutes of careful peeling, he handed a bowl full of snow peas to the owner and asked for them to be stir-fried with cured meat. I almost didn't believe it … this was a BYO vegetable situation! While I have been to many restaurants that have BYO wine, the idea of BYO vegetables in Australia wouldn't be acceptable – most chefs wouldn't cook anything not on their menu, let alone produce from a customer. I always think about this when I'm at a pancake parlour or dessert bar and wish I could bring my own cut fruit to add, simply because I can source much better-tasting fruit to go with the pancake, waffle or crepe that I want to order. After seeing Mr Zhang skilfully peel the snow peas, I gained a greater appreciation for their preparation. I've replicated a similar dish to what Mr Zhang ordered, with Chinese sausage, on page 206.

What's most important is simple ingredients that shine, and preparing the vegetables well.

The joy of tendrils

While snow peas and sugar snap peas are cooked and enjoyed by many cultures around the world, the Chinese community love to stir-fry the actual tendrils themselves. While far less celebrated, I argue that they are one of the most underrated vegetables, which will have their moment. These new buds are nutty, crunchy and almost like a denser and more delicious version of baby spinach.

I love snow pea tendrils and my cousin Raymond Chau, who owns a fruit shop in Preston Market, is the master at selecting the finest. Raymond's family used to own a Chinese restaurant many years ago and the head chef taught him how to select the most tender snow pea tendrils. 'They're picked like tea leaves', says Raymond, and only the top buds and one leaf below the top bud is picked.

Raymond told me about his snap test to check if the tendrils are fresh: if you can push your thumb through your index and middle finger while the stem is being held in that position, then its fresh. If the stem bends and doesn't snap then the snow peas are old and will be chewy. There is a fine line between a clean snap and flexible resistance and stringiness. It's the difference between chewing the vegetable and biting the vegetable. Use this tip when purchasing snow pea tendrils: it won't fail you.

To cook snow pea tendrils you can't go past a simple stir-fry with garlic, salt, sugar and a bit of sesame oil (see page 204). Simple is best.

FLAT POD AND SMALL INTERNAL PEAS INDICATES TENDERNESS.

Choose

THANH'S TIPS

SNOW PEAS AND SUGAR SNAP PEAS

1. Look for crisp and firm pods that snap easily.

2. Avoid floppy or shrivelled pods.

3. Choose vibrant green pods, not pale ones.

4. For snow peas, curling inwards is a sign of over maturity and stringiness, as are peas that are longer than 10 cm.

5. Very large peas are a sign of sweetness but also over-ripeness and stringiness. Compare like with like.

6. Avoid peas with grey dimples, which may be the beginning of blight – the pea skin will turn black after one to two days.

SNOW PEA TENDRILS

1. Look for small delicate leaves; larger leaves may be tough and the tendrils less tender.

2. Each tendril should only be two shoots in length from the top; any longer and the stem tends to be fibrous and stringy.

3. Stems and leaves should be light green. Yellow leaves indicate the vines are too mature or have been stored for too long, leading to dehydration and stringiness.

4. Do the snap test: push your thumb through your index and middle finger while the stem is being held in that position – if the stem snaps cleanly, it will be tender and crispy.

Store

Keep snow peas, sugar snap peas and snow pea tendrils in a plastic bag with the air pushed out in the fridge. Eat within two days.

CURLING INDICATES STRINGINESS.

While most people love Chinese broccoli with oyster sauce at yum cha, I love wok-tossed snow pea shoots. I'd even argue that it's my favourite dish at yum cha; the leaves are rich, the stems are crispy and nutty, and the sauce is both sweet and salty. It's got all the elements of a moreish dish, and I could honestly eat it with nothing more than rice and be satisfied! Nothing beats simple ingredients cooked well.

Recreating this restaurant dish at home without a wok burner isn't easy, but this recipe comes pretty close. The trick is to cook the vegetables in small batches, in addition to using a heavy-based pan that can retain a high heat. As with nearly all fried vegetable dishes, you want to avoid overcrowding the pan as this boils your veggies to death; instead, you want to sear the vegetables by ensuring the pan never drops below 150°C. Don't be tempted to multiply the ingredients and add them all to the pan at once – it won't turn out the same. The cooking time below is less than 2 minutes, so ensure you have everything ready and within reach when you fire up the stovetop. I cook with wooden chopsticks because I find it easier to toss the vegetables and they don't harm the pan; otherwise, I use non-metal tongs.

STIR-FRIED SNOW PEA SHOOTS

清炒豆苗

SERVES 2

2 tablespoons vegetable oil
2 garlic cloves, grated
1 teaspoon grated ginger
300 g snow pea shoots, washed well, dehydrated stems trimmed
1 teaspoon sugar
½ teaspoon chicken stock powder
½ teaspoon sea salt
1 teaspoon sesame oil

Heat the vegetable oil in a large heavy-based frying pan over high heat until smoking. Add the garlic and ginger and stir for 10 seconds, then immediately add the snow pea shoots and toss for 20 seconds, moving the shoots around the pan to ensure the garlic doesn't burn.

Add the sugar, chicken stock powder and salt and stir-fry for 1 minute or until the snow pea shoots just wilt. Drizzle with the sesame oil, toss to combine and serve immediately.

Anytime Mum wants to add a quick salty protein to either congee or rice, she heads to the pantry to find lap cheong (Chinese sausage), which in Vietnamese is called 'lạp xưởng'. If she's making congee, she steams it in a pan, but otherwise she usually cuts it up and stir-fries it with whatever Asian greens she's bought from the market. Mum only buys snow peas when they're tender and young, instead of old and stringy, but this dish is also great with other crunchy Asian greens like garlic shoots, sugar snap peas and chive flowers. While my parents were born in Vietnam, my grandparents were born in China, and this recipe definitely leans more towards a Chinese-style dish. Removing both ends of the snow peas is a must in Chinese tradition, to ensure no stringy parts are left for a better mouthfeel experience. My dad used to work as a chef in a Chinese restaurant decades ago, when he first moved to Australia, and he always says that adding vegetable oil to the boiling water keeps the vegetables a vibrant green, but I've never worked out the science to this! The trick to this dish is to cook the snow peas quickly, so they remain crisp and firm, and all the sweetness of the peas remains inside.

FRIED SNOW PEAS WITH LAP CHEONG

SERVES 4

300 g snow peas
2 tablespoons vegetable oil
sea salt
150 g lap cheong (Chinese sausage), cut into 5 mm thick slices
2 teaspoons rice wine vinegar
steamed jasmine rice, to serve

Snap and remove the ends of the snow peas, peeling away the string along the spine.

Bring a saucepan of water to the boil, add 1 tablespoon of the vegetable oil and 1 tablespoon of salt and stir. Add the snow peas and blanch for 40–60 seconds, until they just change colour, then drain and immediately plunge into a bowl of cold water for 2 minutes. Drain and set aside.

Heat the remaining vegetable oil in a saucepan or wok over low heat, add the lap cheong and sauté for 1–2 minutes, until the sausage fat turns translucent. Add the rice wine vinegar and cook for 15 seconds, then add the snow peas and ¼ teaspoon of salt. Toss well for about 1 minute, for the snow peas to soak up some of the oil, then divide among plates and serve with steamed jasmine rice.

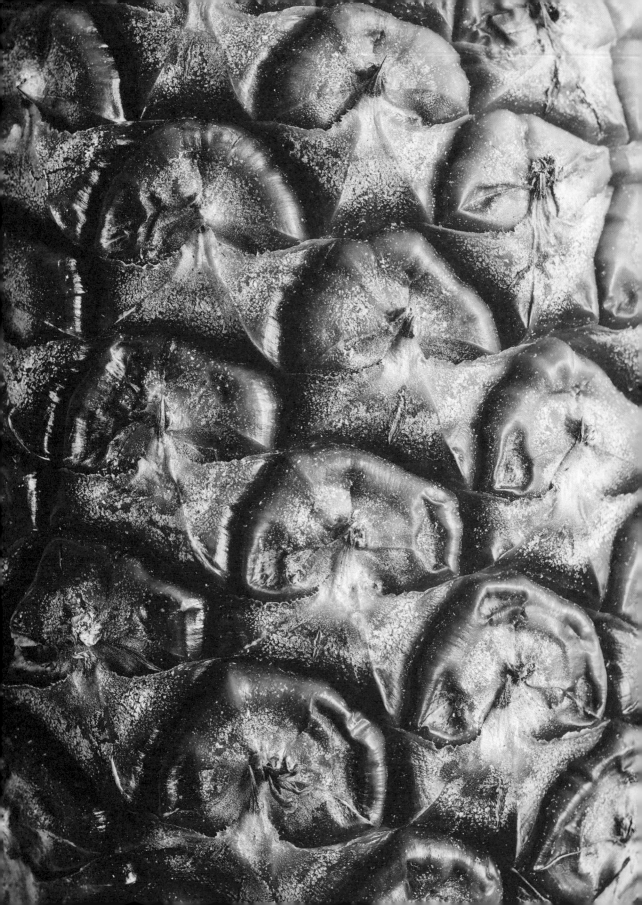

PINEAPPLE

Nothing says 'tropical' like pineapples! Their unique appearance, with criss-crossed rough skin and scaly leaves, has made them the unofficial icon of sunshine, beaches and holidays. The best ice cream I've ever eaten was at the Dole Plantation in Hawaii, where fresh pineapples are crushed and churned daily to make a soft-serve unmatched in the world! Like all things brilliant, the ice cream had an intense level of aroma, while combining an acidic sour tang with a super-sweet juice to create a 'sweet umami' pineapple flavour unlike any I have experienced in a dessert before.

It's all about balance

While pineapple in desserts is commonplace, pineapple in savoury dishes is not. Pineapple on pizza is seen as blasphemy by the Italians and polarises the rest of the world, and I can understand how the pineapple's intense flavour can put off those who may be accepting of the fruit's sourness but not its sweetness in savoury dishes. My mum uses pineapple in a sweet and sour soup called canh chua (see page 214), to add to the complex sourness of the tamarind paste in the dish. Given a pineapple plant takes between two and three years to produce just one fruit, I think it's so important to take the care to ensure every pineapple is at its best.

"

Store pineapples at room temperature, as fridge temperatures may bruise the flesh if very cold.

Balance is so important in fruit flavours, but this is even more critical in pineapple, especially when eaten as a snack. Often I find that pineapple in a fruit salad, or served as aeroplane food, is too sour and imbalanced. I detest these experiences because I know that pineapple can be so much better.

Smooth vs hybrids

There are two types of pineapples in Australia: smooth pineapples, and hybrids. Smooth pineapples are the more traditional fruit, sometimes with the tops or crowns still attached to the main body, and they tend to taste more sour than sweet. Hybrids, on the other hand, usually never have their tops attached as they are chopped off to produce the next-generation plant. As hybrids have a high sugar content and low acid profile, they tend to go off very quickly and you often see them with minor mould on the skin. Until recently, the majority of pineapples grown in Australia were the smooth variety, but the tide is shifting and both smooth and hybrid pineapples are now grown in large volumes, with hybrids potentially taking over the smooths in years to come. Hybrids are cultivars that have been curated with the best traits of other pineapples.

My trusted friend and Sydney wholesale fruiterer Adrian Buchanan sells bins of pineapples every day. He says there is almost no need to selectively choose a hybrid pineapple as they're all consistently super sweet. Smooth pineapples, on the other hand, have a few signs that show if the fruit was picked mature off the plant. A grower can tell if the smooth pineapple will be sweet or not by looking at its eyes, better known as the individual flowers along the skin. Although dark yellow-orange colours suggest that the fruit is sweet, it's commonly harvested when it's white or green and arrives at the fruit shop unripe. Adrian says that as a smooth pineapple grows to full maturity, the skin will expand and stretch, flattening the eyes from sharp peaks to smooth plateaus. Looking at the consistency and shape of the eyes and running your hand along the rough skin can show how mature and sweet the fruit is and will become. If you see a very bumpy-skinned pineapple it might taste sour even after it's been allowed to ripen for several days. This visual tip adds to my aromatic sensory tip that if the pineapple is not exuding a nice sweet perfume, it's not ready to eat.

The art of cutting a pineapple

There seems to be no better place to eat pineapples than in the tropics; whether in Vietnam, Hawaii or Brazil, they always seems to ripen and sweeten up better in warmer temperatures. Pineapple plants grew around Mum's home in Kien Giang, Vietnam, and they would often be cut and sold at the floating boat markets on the Mekong Delta. During my last trip to Can Tho in Vietnam, I bought a pineapple from an old aunty on a boat that was cut to perfection. There is a real art in removing the eyes and cutting chunks that can be held by the leaves – it's a symphony and the sweet flavour of the pineapple was delectable.

While I love the pineapples in Vietnam, the core thread is still a bit much to eat. In Australia, I do remove the core after cutting the pineapple, as I find it makes the whole textural mouthfeel much more pleasant without chewing on something where the fibres will be stuck in your teeth, requiring a flossing session afterwards!

Cutting and processing a pineapple is a labour of love. While many of us have been taught the pineapple boat method, this method still keeps part of the eyes intact, which I find very sour and detracting from the overall mouthfeel experience. In Vietnamese culture, it's known as 'scratching your tongue', as there is often a single hair left behind by the flower, which causes irritation when eaten. Maybe you haven't noticed it, but I bet once you eat a pineapple cut using my mum's method – the Vietnamese street-food way; see page 212 – you won't go back!

Choose

1. Flat, smooth eyes suggest the pineapple is mature and will be sweet. If the eyes have rough, sharp peaks, it shows the fruit isn't as mature as it could be.

2. Another variety, rough-skin pineapples, have jagged leaves, while smooth skins have straight leaves.

3. Generally, yellow-orange pineapples will eat sweeter, but check for firmness – if the fruit is firm and fully coloured, you know it's been ripened off the plant. Softer pineapples have taken time to ripen post-harvesting.

4. Most new cultivars are hybrid varieties that have a high sugar content and taste super sweet. This also means they go mouldy more quickly, but if the fruit is still firm and the mould is only minor, the pineapple is still good to eat; in fact, it's likely to be super sweet.

Store

Store pineapples at room temperature, as fridge temperatures may bruise the flesh if very cold.

THANH'S TIPS

My favourite Vietnamese street snack is a delicately cut pineapple dusted in salt and chilli. This method of cutting pineapple is synonymous with Vietnam – we try to minimise waste, maximise the area of edible pineapple flesh and retain the flesh closest to the skin as this is the sweetest part. I was always mesmerised watching my mum cut pineapples when I was young. She would say that the eyes will cut your tongue if you don't remove them! Taking the care to remove each eye is very therapeutic, and the end result is well worth it. With practice, it actually doesn't take very long at all.

'Muối ớt' literally means 'salt chilli'. Bird's eye or bullet chillies are traditionally used for their sweet-smelling skin, which is released when the chillies are bashed using a mortar and pestle. Avoid using table salt or iodised salt, as they are too salty and bitter. I prefer to use sea salt flakes or Korean solar salt, which I find very clean when eaten raw. I add caster sugar to my mix, but you may not need it if your pineapple is very sweet. Eat immediately after seasoning, as the salt will start to draw out moisture from the fruit once it's marinated. Alternatively, place the muối ớt in a dipping bowl, dip the pineapple sticks in and eat. This way you can control the amount of seasoning.

SALTED CHILLI PINEAPPLE

MUỐI ỚT TRÁI THƠM/KHÓM

SERVES 8

1 pineapple
75 g Korean solar salt or
    sea salt flakes
3 bird's eye chillies, deseeded
    and finely diced
2 teaspoons caster sugar

Cut the top off the pineapple and place the pineapple on its side. Using a large sharp knife, remove the skin, keeping the eyes intact. Make diagonal incisions either side of the eyes and remove, then continue working your way around the pineapple until all the eyes are removed. Trim any remaining green skin.

Stand the pineapple upright and slice into eight wedges. Remove the central core if it feels very hard. Insert a bamboo skewer lengthways into each pineapple wedge.

Using a mortar and pestle, bash and grind the salt and chilli until combined, then tip the mixture onto a small plate, add the sugar and stir to combine. Dip the skewered pineapple wedges in the seasoning and enjoy immediately.

Canh chua was a weekly soup in my mum's repertoire. It's traditionally made with fish and there's a real kick from the tamarind and pineapple, giving the soup its famous tang. My dad was a fisherman back in Vietnam, so he has always been in charge of purchasing fish for Mum. The Vietnamese are very particular about what fish they use, especially for this soup. Depending on where you live in Vietnam, either cá lóc (snakehead fish) or cá bông lau (pangasius fish) are the preferred fish for canh chua. In Australia, Dad thinks Murray perch or Murray cod are the best fish to use. If these aren't available, then select the freshest fish available at your fishmonger. The traditional garnish for canh chua is bac ha, better known as giant elephant ear or giant taro (see Tip). It's not easy to find in Australia, but sliced celery is a good substitute as it has a similar textural crunch. This soup does not require an overly sweet pineapple, so a slightly sour pineapple will add to the complex tang – it is sour soup, after all! The trick is balancing the intense sourness with the sweet and salty flavours.

VIETNAMESE SOUR SOUP

CANH CHUA

SERVES 4

1 x 750 g whole firm white fish, such as Murray perch or cod, gutted and cleaned
1 lemongrass stalk, top third removed, stalk bashed
1 tablespoon tamarind powder
1 small pineapple, peeled, cored and cut into 2 cm pieces
2 teaspoons sea salt
3 tablespoons sugar
½ teaspoon MSG (see Note on page 82)
1 tablespoon fish sauce
2 large tomatoes, each cut into 8 wedges
50 g okra, trimmed

DIPPING SAUCE
3 tablespoons fish sauce
4 Thai red chillies, thickly sliced

TO SERVE
100 g bean shoots
bunch of ngò ôm (rice paddy herb), roughly chopped
1 celery stalk, cut diagonally into 5 mm thick slices
steamed jasmine rice

Wash the fish and chop the head and body into 2.5 cm pieces. Bring a large saucepan of water to the boil, add the fish and blanch for 1 minute to remove any impurities. Drain the fish and set aside.

Wipe out the saucepan, add 1.5 litres of water and bring to the boil. Reduce the heat to medium, add the fish, lemongrass, tamarind powder, pineapple, salt, sugar, MSG and fish sauce and stir to combine. Cook for 2 minutes, then add the tomato and okra and simmer for another 2 minutes. Turn off the heat.

To make the dipping sauce, combine the fish sauce and chilli in a dipping bowl.

Divide the bean shoots, rice paddy herb and celery among four bowls and ladle the soup over the top, making sure each bowl has an equal quantity of fish and pineapple. Serve with steamed jasmine rice and the dipping sauce on the side, for dipping pieces of fish.

TIP If you manage to find giant elephant ear, use kitchen gloves when preparing it, as the latex from the vegetable can irritate your skin. Peel the outer skin using a knife, then cut diagonally into 5 mm thick slices, soak and wash twice thoroughly. Use as per the celery opposite.

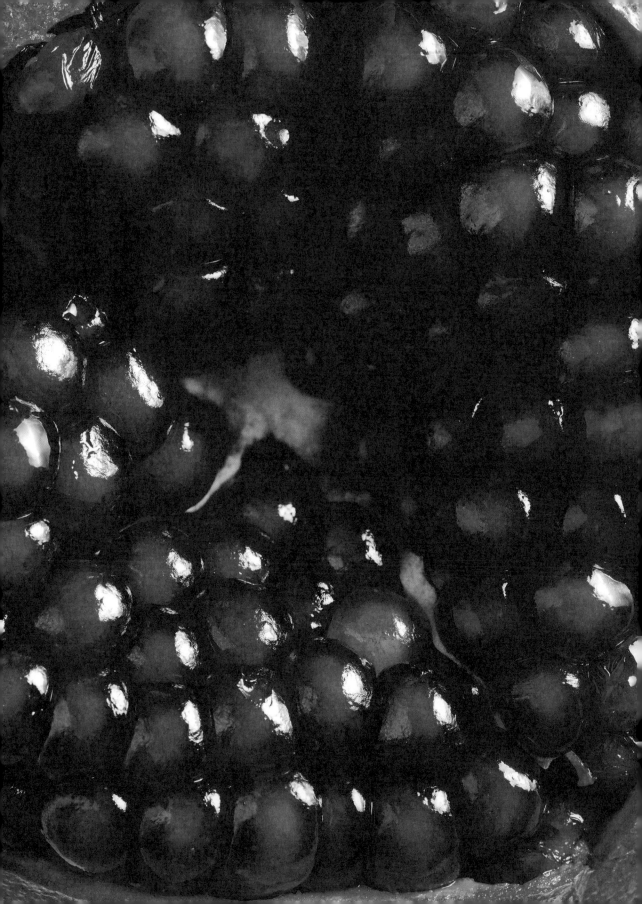

POMEGRANATES

Before working in the produce trade, I rarely ever encountered pomegranate. Once or twice in a salad, and once as a drink, but never fresh. It's one of those fruits that if you haven't come it across before, can be somewhat daunting to approach, mostly because it's anatomically so different to all other fruits. Understanding how pomegranates grow on the tree will help you select a juicy, sweet fruit every time and, importantly, help you conceptualise how to process it with ease. I've only ever sold pomegranates on the wholesale floor for one season, and my Middle-Eastern customers purchased more than 90 per cent of the stock I had. I asked my customers a whole raft of questions and discovered that pomegranates have been part of Middle-Eastern and Mediterranean cuisines and cultures for centuries; in fact, their use can be traced back more than 5000 years in the Middle East.

The growth cycle of pomegranates

Good friend and Sydney agent wholesaler David Hatem is a big pomegranate distributor in Australia, who has taught me a thing or two about how pomegranates develop on the tree. David, who has Lebanese heritage and loves pomegranates, explains that the fruit starts off small and green but as it matures it not only changes colour, the growing fruit stretches the skin and changes from a spherical shape to an angular pentagonal or hexagonal shape. If the fruit looks like it's about to burst its seams that's because it literally will if it's not harvested from the tree.

This knowledge helped me deduce two things: firstly, that mature and sweet pomegranates will look angular rather than spherical and look like they're about to burst; and secondly, that juicy and full pomegranates are heavy for their size and not dehydrated. A light pomegranate is often perceived to be an immature fruit, but it can also be a ripe fruit that isn't full of juice. These two tips will help you find a top pomegranate.

Although you shouldn't disregard skin colour, as dark tones represent maturity, there are many varietals of pomegranates, varying from pink to dark red, so don't let your eyes deceive you.

Once you've picked a juicy and sweet pomegranate, processing it isn't difficult as long as you understand that the angles are the weak points of the fruit, and that the internal white segment membranes need to be removed as they can taste very astringent and bitter. Thankfully, removing the arils isn't hard if you make the correct incisions and follow the instructions on the opposite page. Processing pomegranates can get messy, so a big bowl to capture all the arils is required.

Once you've removed the arils, the refreshing and sweet red jewels bring any dish to life. That's if you don't eat them all first!

> **Once you've removed the pomegranate arils, the refreshing and sweet red jewels bring any dish to life. That's if you don't eat them all first!**

Choose

1. Look for plump and angular fruit – pomegranates start off spherical and become pentagonal or hexagonal as they mature. Look for sharp, angled edges.

2. Heavy pomegranates indicate a fruit full of juice; light fruit suggests dehydration.

3. Don't rely too much on skin colour, as pomegranate varietals range from pink to dark red.

Prep

1. Score around the top of the pomegranate and then along the ridge lines from top to bottom.

2. Use your hands to remove the top/flower end of the fruit along the score marks, then break the segments apart, keeping the base stem area intact.

3. Remove any white segment walls before turning the pomegranate upside down and holding it in your non-dominant hand with the cut top facing downwards over a large bowl. Use a large spoon to whack the pomegranate and let the arils fall through your fingers into the bowl (this will help prevent too much juice splashing).

When I sold pomegranates at the Melbourne Market, I discovered that the Lebanese community are the biggest consumers of this jewelled fruit. They love them, culinarily and culturally. I asked one of my Lebanese customers, chef turned rare-produce provedore Boudi Haddad, which Lebanese dish best celebrates pomegranates and he responded 'sawda djej' – chicken livers with pomegranate molasses and fresh pomegranate arils. Boudi says he grew up eating this traditional dish, served with Lebanese bread and toum (garlic dip).

Chicken giblets and the liver are such underrated parts of the bird that rarely get the love they deserve. Liver is my Kryptonite, especially in pate. The sweet and sour punch of the pomegranate seeds, along with the lemon juice, which adds acidity, balance the strong flavour of the liver. I also go overboard with the fresh pomegranate arils, just because I can!

FRIED CHICKEN LIVERS WITH POMEGRANATE MOLASSES

كبدة الدجاج بدبس الرمان

SERVES 2–3

300 g chicken livers
1 tablespoon butter
2 tablespoons extra-virgin olive oil
2 tablespoons olive oil
3 garlic cloves, crushed
juice of 1 lemon
3 tablespoons pomegranate molasses
sea salt and cracked black pepper, to taste
chilli powder, to taste (optional)

TO SERVE
1 pomegranate, arils removed (see page 219)
1 tablespoon chopped coriander leaves
Lebanese bread
toum (garlic dip)

Rinse the chicken livers, remove the central membrane and cut into bite-sized pieces.

Heat the butter and extra-virgin olive oil in a frying pan over medium heat, add the chicken livers and sauté for 5–6 minutes, until golden and just cooked through. Remove from the pan and set aside to rest.

In another frying pan, heat the olive oil over medium heat, add the garlic and cook for 1–2 minutes, until golden. Add the chicken livers, lemon juice and pomegranate molasses and stir for 30 seconds, until well combined.

Turn off the heat and season to taste with salt and pepper and a little chilli powder, if desired.

Serve the chicken livers in the pan on a wooden board, topped with the pomegranate arils and coriander, and with Lebanese bread and toum on the side.

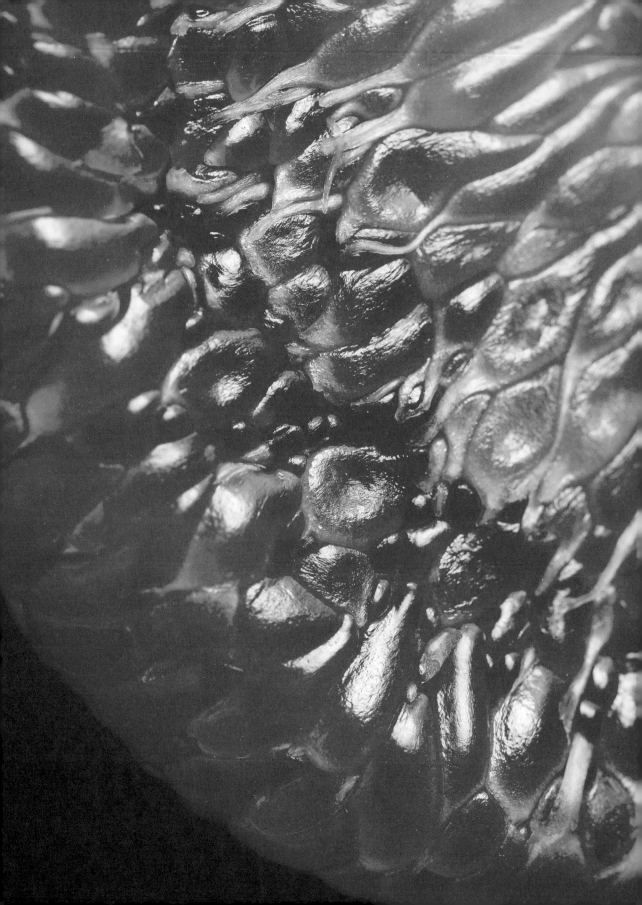

POMELOS

When you've been given the botanical name Citrus maxima, you've got a lot to live up to. Luckily, the pomelo has many positive traits that do this. For those unfamiliar with the pomelo, its size alone can be intimidating, and even more potentially challenging is how to best extract its goodness!

Along with the citron and mandarin, pomelos are one of the original citrus species, and it is the ancestor of many of the citrus fruits we love today, including oranges, tangelos and grapefruits. Pomelos are large citrus fruit that can grow bigger than a human head! The rind is usually much thicker than other citrus fruit and is soft and spongy; while the segment walls are also thick and mostly inedible.

The vesicles, better known as pulp sacs, make the pomelo's texture unique among the citrus family. The sacs tend to be individual and can be separated – each one firm on the outside but juicy on the inside. There are many pomelo varieties with unique flavour profiles, and the pulp can taste sour, bitter and sweet – a combo made in culinary heaven when it comes to savoury dishes. The honey pomelo, which has a predominantly sweet flavour and mild aroma, is preferred in Malaysia and China, while in Vietnam prized varietals have a balance and intensity of sour, bitter and sweet notes. Thailand, meanwhile, enjoys pomelos that are sweet and sour.

The pomelo world is colourful, with varietals in various hues and pulp that can be yellow, green, red and pink.

Receiving peeled pomelo segments is one of the ultimate expressions of love.

Pomelo vs grapefruit

While grapefruits are loved and enjoyed by those in Europe and other parts of the world, pomelos are primarily enjoyed in South-East Asia, from where the fruit originates. One could say that pomelos are the grapefruit of Asia! Pomelos and grapefruits are distinctly different in taste. The membrane of the grapefruit's segment walls has strong bitter notes, and because the juicy pulp sacs cannot be easily removed from the segment walls due to the fruit's anatomy, grapefruit is often eaten in wedges (like an orange). This eating experience usually leaves me with an astringent mouthfeel and texture, due to biting into the skin wall membrane. Grapefruit pulp can also be too tart and lacking in balance with sweetness, although I can understand those who love grapefruit enjoy the intense sour flavours and bitter notes.

As a juice or a combination fruit juice, grapefruit has many great qualities, but as a snacking fruit, it falls behind the greatness and versatility of the pomelo.

Why peeling pomelos is a must

The membrane of a pomelo's segment walls is thick and bland, bordering on bitter. It is considered inedible and needs to be discarded, so an efficient technique to remove the segments from the fruit is required.

Given that, second only to China, Vietnam produces the most pomelos and is arguably the greatest consumer of pomelos per capita, it's logical that the Vietnamese have this technique down to a fine art. While I was travelling through Vietnam, my regular go-to fruit snack was pre-peeled pomelo segments. Street traders would artistically work the peel, rind, pith and segment membranes to curate a perfect tray of bright pomelo segments. It was such a luxury to purchase fruit peeled with such skill and attention to detail.

After being blessed with peeled, not cut, fruit, with no broken pulp sacs and no pith threads attached, I had to live up to my ancestors, and master how to process the pomelo by hand. My cousin and second-generation fruiterer Raymond Chau taught me the technique that the Vietnamese aunties who work in his fruit shop taught him. Fruiterers who peel fruit daily and display them are always on another level! Like all things, the more you do it, the quicker you become, and the experience of eating pure pomelo pulp sacs is worth it.

You may have seen the culinary technique of removing orange segments by slicing or cutting the skin and rind completely and then cutting between the segment walls to remove the segments of orange. I disdain this technique for both the orange but even more so for the pomelo! A significant amount of juice is left on the chopping board, and the textural bite and bursting of juice are lost, especially with cut pomelo vesicles. This technique disrespects the pomelo; as one of the original citrus fruits, it has taken centuries of figuring out, and we owe it to the generations before us to process pomelos the way they best discovered and continuously improved on. I promise you'll have a much better textural experience peeling pomelos, instead of cutting into them.

Why peeled pomelo, to me, means love

In Eastern cultures, it's often considered a motherly show of love to cut, peel and process fruit for children. My parents were refugees who moved to Australia for a better life; this meant English was their fourth language, while for me, it was my first. My parents were always serious and busy, and communication between us in Vietnamese to 'get by' was only okay. When I wanted to express my feelings and emotions in English, or they wanted to express theirs in Vietnamese, our communication broke down.

Whenever I was upset with them, or they wanted to show their support for me, cut fruit would always turn up in my room, and occasionally it was peeled pomelo. This would often happen when they found me studying or when they finally had a chance to breathe late at night after a tiring day at work. I'm sure this will sound familiar to many migrant families – where language is a barrier, a show of love can be expressed through carefully cut-up fruit.

Like my parents before me, I carefully cut and peel pomelo like it's my last meal and offer it to my son Oliver and daughter Rayla. Seeing them and my wife Sonya enjoy the fruit I lovingly prepared for them is one of my great joys in life.

I think that everyone must attempt to prepare a pomelo for a loved one at least once in their life. For me, receiving peeled pomelo segments is one of the ultimate expressions of love.

Do pomelos get sweeter after harvesting?

Many aunties have told me that if I leave my pomelos at the door for a few weeks they'll become sweeter. This is common practice throughout Vietnam, and even though I have done this before and it seemingly works, I have always questioned this method. Knowing, scientifically, that citrus fruits do not develop more sugars after harvesting, how can pomelos possibly get sweeter? It's likely due to the ascorbic acid, better known as vitamin C, in the pomelo degrading over time in high-temperature environments. This loss of acid gives the impression that the fruit is sweeter.

I have shelf-tested pomelos at room temperature and they last up to a month in an ambient environment, as the fruit has a thick skin and rind, and the pulps sacs themselves are whole and individual.

Choose

1. Select pomelos that are heavy for their size, as this suggests good orchard management where the fruit has been picked ripe and is full of juice.

2. Avoid light pomelos, as they may have been harvested light and dry from the orchard.

3. Try different varietals until you find your favourite balance of flavours, then stick with it!

If you want your pomelo to be a little extra sweet, then leave it out for a week or two. If you prefer a balance of sweet, sour and bitter flavours, then eat it as soon as possible!

THANH'S TIPS

Store

Given that you're likely to only buy one pomelo at a time, I don't think storage suggestions are required. A pomelo will keep in the fridge or on the table for at least two weeks. If you do remove all the segments and don't finish them, wrap the leftovers in plastic wrap and store in the fridge for up to two days.

Prep

1. Cut the base off the pomelo. Use a sharp knife to score from the stem to the base eight to ten times around the pomelo. Take care not to break the segment walls and cut the flesh.

2. Starting at the base, peel the skin and rind, leaving behind the pith and segments.

3. Stick your two thumbs into the base cavity of the pomelo and break it into two halves.

4. Using a knife that's longer than the entire segment, and working with one segment at a time, slice through the core thread to detach the segment wall, including the two ends, then use your hand to peel back and remove the segment wall.

5. Run the knife the entire length of the segment to detach the pulp sacs, or vesicles, from the next segment wall, then use the palm of your hand and thumb to separate the segment pulp from the skin wall.

6. Still holding the segment firmly, use your other hand to hold the pith and roll the segment away from the pith entirely.

7. Discard the leftover skin and pith and repeat with the remaining segments.

TIP: If too much rind is still attached to the pomelo, the base pith will be very difficult to remove. Use a paring knife to gently scrape away some of the rind.

Whenever I'm in Thailand, I always order pomelo salad. Yam sam o has all the classic Thai flavours of sweet, sour, savoury and spicy, and I think it's the most complex version of this salad in South-East Asia. Balancing these flavours is the hardest part of this dish, as the ratio of sour and sweet will depend on the pomelo varietal you use, so you'll need to adjust the amounts of lime juice, fish sauce and palm sugar based on taste. I love biting into the chunks of pomelo, its textural pops of juice gush sweetness, bitterness and sourness all at once. This is definitely not a quiet salad; on your first bite you'll be hit by all the bright flavours of the dressing!

THAI POMELO SALAD

YAM SAM O

SERVES
4–6

2 pomelos
2 tablespoons shredded
    coconut
40 g (⅓ cup) unsalted peanuts
1 Thai red shallot, finely sliced
2 makrut lime leaves, finely
    shredded
4 sprigs of mint, leaves picked
bunch of coriander, stems and
    leaves finely chopped

DRESSING
40 g (⅓ cup) dried shrimp
1 garlic clove, roughly chopped
1 Thai red shallot, roughly
    chopped
1 red bullet chilli, roughly
    chopped
2 tablespoons fish sauce, plus
    extra if needed
1 teaspoon lime juice, plus extra
    if needed
1 tablespoon palm sugar, plus
    extra if needed

Follow the instructions on page 227 to peel the pomelo. Save the rind for the pomelo rind pudding on page 230, if you like! Use your hands to tear the pomelo segments into 2.5 cm pieces, then place in a large serving bowl.

To make the dressing, using a mortar and pestle, pound the dried shrimp to a fine powder. Remove half the shrimp powder and set aside, then add the garlic, shallot and chilli to the mortar and pound the mixture to a paste.

Place a small saucepan over medium heat, add the shrimp paste, fish sauce, lime juice and palm sugar and heat, stirring occasionally, for 1–2 minutes, until you have a thick and fragrant dressing. Taste and adjust the fish sauce, lime juice and palm sugar, if needed. Remove from the heat and set aside to cool.

Heat a dry frying pan over low heat, add the shredded coconut and toast, tossing constantly, until golden. Transfer the toasted coconut to a plate, then return the pan to the heat, add the peanuts and toast, tossing occasionally, until evenly browned. Tip the hot peanuts onto a chopping board and roughly chop.

Add the coconut, peanuts, shallot, lime leaves, mint and coriander to the pomelo, pour over most of the dressing and gently toss to combine. Serve immediately, with the remaining dressing and shrimp powder on the side.

TIP Pick the pomelo that is the heaviest for its size, as this indicates that the fruit is juicy and not dry inside!

Chè bưởi is a light and tasty Vietnamese dessert, where the hero of the dish is not the pomelo flesh but the pomelo rind! You can't actually buy this dish at restaurants in Australia, although I have purchased it from Vietnamese aunties who make it at home and sell it to the community. It's laboursome to create, but well worth it once you do.

VIETNAMESE POMELO RIND PUDDING

CHÈ BƯỞI

SERVES 4–6

1 pomelo (see Tip), peeled following the instructions on page 227, rinds reserved (save the fruit for snacking or make the Thai salad on page 228)
220 g table salt
2 tablespoons sugar
100 g tapioca flour
crushed salted peanuts or toasted sesame seeds, to serve

CHÈ – SWEET SOUP
2 pandan leaves, each tied in a knot and bashed with the back of a knife
200 g rock sugar
150 g split mung beans, rinsed
3 teaspoons tapioca flour

NƯỚC CỐT – THICKENED COCONUT MILK SAUCE
400 ml can coconut milk
1 teaspoon sea salt
1 tablespoon tapioca flour
2 tablespoons sugar
2 pandan leaves, each tied in a knot and bashed with the back of a knife

Dice the pomelo rind into 1 cm cubes. Place in a large bowl, cover with water and stir through 2 tablespoons of salt. Leave to soak for 1 hour, then gently squeeze about half the water from the rind cubes, ensuring they retain their shape. Rinse with fresh water. Repeat this process, using fresh water and 2 tablespoons of salt each time, five times.

Place the rind cubes in a dry bowl, then toss through the sugar and chill in the fridge for 1 hour to marinate and firm.

Sprinkle the tapioca flour over the rind cubes and toss to evenly coat. Prepare a bowl of iced water.

Bring a saucepan of water to the boil, add the rind cubes and simmer for 4–5 minutes, until they are translucent and float to the surface. Drain and immediately plunge the rind into the iced water to cool. Drain on paper towel.

Meanwhile, to make the chè, place the bashed pandan leaves in a saucepan, cover with 1 litre of water and bring to the boil. Add the rock sugar and stir to dissolve, then add the mung beans and cook at a medium boil, skimming off any surface foam, for 40 minutes or until tender.

Combine the tapioca flour and 2½ tablespoons of cold water in a small bowl to make a slurry, then add it to the pan and stir for 3–4 minutes, until the chè has thickened. Add the pomelo rind cubes and cook over medium heat until the mixture comes to the boil. Remove and discard the pandan leaves, then set aside to cool.

To make the nước cốt, place the coconut milk and salt in a small saucepan. Warm over medium heat until hot.

Combine the tapioca flour and 100 ml of cold water in a small bowl to make another slurry. Stir the slurry through the coconut milk for 2 minutes or until the mixture has thickened. Add the sugar and stir to dissolve, then add the bashed pandan leaves to the pan. Cook, stirring, for

2 minutes, until it's the consistency of thickened cream. If it's not thick enough, continue to cook, stirring, for another minute or until you reach the desired consistency. Remove the pandan leaves, then transfer the sauce to a heatproof bowl and set aside in the fridge until cold.

Divide the chè and pomelo rind cubes among bowls. Drizzle with the thickened coconut milk sauce, sprinkle with a few crushed salted peanuts or toasted sesame seeds and serve.

TIP You need to use a pomelo variety with a thick rind for this dessert; otherwise, you won't have many textured pomelo rind cubes! Your best bet is to ask for a recommendation at a Vietnamese fruit shop.

POTATOES

Much of my inspiration to become the Fruit Nerd comes from the humble spud. The art of being a great fruiterer is knowing your produce inside out. At the beginning of my career in fruit and veg, a younger me once walked through the sheds of the iconic Queen Victoria Market looking for produce to cook for dinner. I stopped at a stall where a potato I had never seen before was on display and I asked the fruiterer what it was. They asked what I was cooking, which was a simple oven roast, and the fruiterer went on to suggest a variety of waxy potatoes, explaining that they held up in the oven after boiling. I ended up buying that unique potato just to see how it tasted alongside the others. I noticed the difference in texture but not so much the flavour – my palate wasn't refined. This experience both inspired and caused me to question my own feelings and thoughts about produce in general. Why aren't all fruit and vegetables given as much attention when being purchased and sold? Why aren't different varietals of fruit and vegetables sold with every produce line? Why can't all fruiterers offer this level of expertise and knowledge when quizzed? What does waxy even mean? It was both a traumatic and revelatory life event, and led me to want to become the fruiterer who could offer this level of advice to anyone purchasing any fruit or vegetable ... in essence, the Fruit Nerd.

A brief history lesson

Being a nerd is cool, but when I was a kid in primary school, nerds were bullied by the big sporty kids like the Hollywood stereotypes of old. Today, if being a techy is cool, then so is being a fruiterer. That's what I hope the Fruit Nerd can represent – engagement and knowledge through flavour. I studied food systems and gastronomy just to articulate how cool fruit and vegetables are. In one of my food history lessons, we traversed time to discover what effect the potato had on humanity. It's dramatic. Many argue that the potato changed the modern world. Before the 'discovery' of potatoes, most communities relied on grains, but potatoes are nutritionally far superior and entire civilisations came to depend upon them. The reliance on grains could lead to famines during poor weather years, but the potato offered a great diversified solution to food security and population growth. High in energy, simple to prepare and easy to pluck out of the ground when needed, the potato was one of the main sources of energy that helped fuel the industrial revolution. Given the growth and dominance of Western society, particularly in the culinary world, you can see why there are so many varietals of potatoes still offered today.

Starchy vs waxy

In Australia, a lot has changed for the humble spud; it's not quite as popular as it once was, yet it still holds a special place in the world of fruit and vegetables. Generally, potatoes are put into the 'waxy' or 'starchy' buckets. I never understood what waxy meant, but the opposite description of 'starchy' is much clearer to me. Personally, I describe potatoes as being starchy – spuds with lots of tiny granules that break apart easily when cooked – and non-starchy – waxy potatoes that hold their shape, density and texture after being cooked.

While these two descriptions refer to a potato's textural traits, they don't explain the flavour. Wait, do potatoes even have different flavours? Of course they do! Try comparing a Dutch cream potato with a simple white washed potato – the washed potato will likely be linear in flavour, with a neutral and bland taste and aroma compared to the velvety Dutch cream. Simply oven-bake both potatoes without oil and only add salt at the end after breaking them open. You may be thinking that potato with just salt sounds terribly bland. Well that's because the only varietals that most of us eat are grown for intensive yield without consideration of flavour. There are plenty of other potato varietals that are brimming with interesting flavours and can be eaten with just a little seasoning.

It's important to note that in the final phase of commoditisation of potatoes, which has already begun, only one cultivar will reign supreme and that's a completely neutral potato, which is neither starchy nor waxy. It's simply marketed as being able to do everything; in other words: the 'all-rounder'. Other trending varieties include 'low-carbohydrate' or 'lite' potatoes that have less starch in them, or a very waxy potato, but note that a low-starch potato, such as a desiree, contains a very similar amount of carbohydrates as a 'low-carb' potato.

By substituting the word 'starch' for 'carbohydrate', companies have created a great marketing slogan for these potatoes.

The right potato for the job

The question I had that changed my fruit nerd life might be same question that you have, and that's 'what potato should I purchase for the dish I am cooking?'. The answer is that it simply depends on the type of dish you are making. Potatoes have permeated nearly every cuisine on the planet and there are so many different ways to cook them that the possibilities are endless. Take into account not only what texture you're looking for, but also what flavour the potato can offer you. All potatoes have different nuanced flavours, some being more minerally than others. In addition, the availability of a variety of potatoes depends on where you live and what markets you have access to. I hope you're able to ask someone for advice. If not, then buy two different potato varieties for the one dish and see if one tastes better than the other. I've supplied my favourite potato dish called potato threads, or tu dou si, on page 236. It's a unique textural and moreish experience that might be described as the 'French fries of China'.

Choose

1. Look for firm, heavy potatoes. If they've been cleaned, a bright skin is a great sign the potato will eat well.

2. Avoid potatoes with shooting roots or that are slightly soft to touch.

3. While not inedible, it's best to avoid buying green potatoes, as it means sunlight has caused the formation of chlorophyll, allowing some of the solanine toxic compound to develop. If this happens in your pantry, you can remove the green flesh and still cook the potato.

Store

An important storage fact about potatoes is that they should be kept away from both direct and indirect sunlight. You'll find new packaging completely blacks out potatoes, with only a few holes to allow airflow. So make sure you store your potatoes in a very dark area of your home, with a cool and stable temperature. If your potatoes do become green for any unknown reason, you can still eat them as long as you remove a lot of the green-coloured flesh under the skin. Of course this isn't advisable if you're pregnant or have underlying medical conditions, but if you're healthy you'd probably need to eat several kilos of green potatoes to get sick.

Basically, store potatoes in a cool, dry and, most importantly, dark place. Even indirect sunlight will cause the formation of chlorophyll. Storing potatoes near ethylene-producing fruits, such as bananas, will cause potatoes to shoot roots, so store them away from other produce. I keep my potatoes in a fruit box on the floor in my pantry, as I can close them off from any light and there are usually some holes in the box. Or keep them in a paper bag if you have only a few spuds.

In the Western world, we are used to eating potatoes that are baked, fried, boiled or mashed, but in Chinese cuisine they are often enjoyed stir-fried. This dish is called tu dou si (土豆丝), which translates to 'potato threads'. The threads are tossed with moreish numbing Sichuan peppercorn and chilli oil and are usually eaten chilled. It is such a flavourful dish that it's often eaten as a condiment to steamed rice – carb on carb! – although I prefer to enjoy it with beer. Tu dou si is one of my wife Sonya's favourite dishes, and she's always excited when I cook it!

There are only a few ingredients in this recipe, so the most important element is the selection and preparation of the potatoes. Longer threads are more desirable, so choose the longest potatoes you can find, which will be easier to julienne. I like crunchy potatoes, so select a low-starch and all-round variety for better textural results. This dish comes together very quickly – basically the threads need to be 'just cooked'; overcooking the potato will soften the threads and ruin the dish.

POTATO THREADS

TU DOU SI (土豆丝)

SERVES 2

- 2 long low-starch potatoes (about 500 g), such as nicola, julienned into long 2 mm wide strips
- ½ green capsicum, julienned into long 2 mm wide strips
- ½ teaspoon white vinegar or rice wine vinegar
- 1 teaspoon sea salt
- ½ teaspoon MSG (see Note on page 82)
- 2 tablespoons vegetable oil
- ½ teaspoon whole Sichuan peppercorns
- 2 whole dried red chillies

Agitate the julienned potato in a large bowl of cold water to rinse off the starch. Drain and repeat until the water runs clear. Prepare a bowl of iced water.

Bring a large saucepan of water to the boil, add the potato and allow the water to return to the boil. Blanch the potato at a roiling boil for about 30 seconds (the total time the potato is in the water should be no more than 2 minutes), until just cooked but still with a bite to it. Drain and plunge the potato into the iced water – this helps the potato say firm and crispy.

Once cool, drain the potato and dry in a salad spinner or with a clean tea towel to remove excess water, then transfer to a large heatproof bowl. Add the capsicum, vinegar, salt and MSG and gently toss together with chopsticks.

Heat the vegetable oil in a small frying pan over low heat, add the Sichuan peppercorns and dried chillies and cook for 2 minutes, until fragrant. Remove the peppercorns and chillies using a slotted spoon and transfer to a paper towel to drain. Increase the heat to high and allow the oil to almost reach smoking point – the oil should be shimmering, with wisps of smoke rising from it. Very carefully pour the hot oil over the julienned potato mixture and toss with chopsticks. The heat of the oil will be enough to cook and slightly char the potato threads, though they will still have a firm bite.

Serve the potato threads immediately, or, to serve chilled, allow to cool to room temperature, then cover with plastic wrap and chill in the fridge until cold.

While travelling through Basque Country in Spain, Sonya and I would eat tapas every night and tortilla de patatas every morning. Interestingly, I first made this recipe with an ostrich egg, which tasted outstanding, but it took us a few days to finish such a big omelette! I recommend using duck eggs as their yolk is rich and flavourful. I use Dutch cream potatoes as they have a lovely creamy flavour and hold their shape well, which provides a gentle contrast to the texture of the bouncy eggs. Nicola potatoes are also a great option. The Spanish strongly believe in using the best local produce available, from earthy olive oils to yolky eggs. Seek out good-quality ingredients, make this on the weekend and you'll never think of making poached eggs again! This recipe is big – you only need to eat a slice to feel satiated, so I suggest packing some for lunch the following day!

SPANISH POTATO OMELETTE

TORTILLA DE PATATAS

SERVES
6–8

1 kg non-starchy potatoes, such as Dutch creams, peeled and cut into 5 mm thick slices (use a mandoline if you have one)
200 ml extra-virgin olive oil
1 onion, finely sliced
8 duck eggs (or 10 regular eggs)
3 teaspoons Korean solar salt or sea salt flakes

Place the potato in a colander and rinse under cold running water to remove the starch. Dry the potato in a salad spinner or with a clean tea towel.

Heat the olive oil in a frying pan over medium-low heat and add the potato, making sure the slices are submerged in the oil. Gently cook for 15 minutes or until the potato is cooked through, then remove using a slotted spoon and strain in a fine-mesh sieve. Reserve the leftover oil.

Heat 1 tablespoon of the reserved oil in a frying pan over low heat, add the onion and cook for 10 minutes, until caramelised. Remove the onion from the pan and set aside.

Crack the eggs into a bowl, add 1 teaspoon of the salt and whisk to combine. Add the caramelised onion and mix well.

Heat 1 tablespoon of the reserved oil in a deep 28–30 cm cast-iron frying pan over low heat and add enough of the egg mixture to coat the base of the pan. Add a layer of potato, with the slices overlapping, a layer of egg and onion mixture and a sprinkle of salt. Cook for 2–3 minutes, until the top egg layer is just cooked through, then repeat with more layers until the ingredients are used up. Once you've added the last layer of egg and onion mixture, turn off the flame, cover with a lid and let the residual heat continue to cook the omelette for 3 minutes.

Remove the lid, place a large plate on top of the pan and flip the tortilla onto the plate. Season with salt and pepper, slice the tortilla into pizza-like portions and enjoy.

TIP If the top layers of the tortilla haven't set but the base is overly browned, pop the pan in a preheated 180°C (fan-forced) oven for 5–10 minutes, to firm up the tortilla.

RED PAPAYA

A good papaya can be great; and a bad papaya can be terrible. I can never liken the fruit to anything else; it is genre defying. Please do not describe it as a 'tropical burst similar to a mango', because that simply devalues how great and unique the flavour of a red papaya can be. Its texture can be a softer, more watery rendition of a soft musk melon, which some find challenging. Unlike other fruits, where an average fruit can still be passable, an old papaya can taste 'soapy'. Dad used to bring home fruit that Mum likes, except now it's me looking for the fruit given that Dad knows how much of a fruit geek I am. If I'm ever at the market looking for papaya, Dad always tells me to pick one up for Mum. They are nostalgic for her, as she use to have papaya trees at her home in Vietnam.

What's in a name?

I always find naming conventions fascinating, and one that almost stumped me completely was the difference between paw paw and red papaya. As a seasoned fruiterer, if I'm confused then I'm pretty sure others will be too. It took Candy McLaughlin from Skybury Farms, which produces more than one-third of Australia's papayas, to clarify this for me. While papaya is the more commonly used term, in different parts of the world paw paw is used interchangeably with the botanical plant and fruit Carica papaya. To clarify, Carica papaya is not related to the American paw paw, or Asimini triloba, which is a small tree that produces fruit more closely related to the custard apple. To save confusion, the industry body Papayas Australia decided to define paw paw as 'yellow paw paw', which is the more oval fruit with yellow flesh and a soapy flavour, generally found in backyards around Australia. Papaya was defined as 'red papaya' having pink or red flesh, being very sweet and more often the commercially grown varietals closely related to the Thai and Brazilian cultivars. You could say the industry sacrificed the paw paw name to uplift the papaya. In any case, what you most regularly see in Australia today is red papaya on sale and not paw paw.

A totally modern fruit

'Don't use your eyes, use your hands when picking a modern papaya,' says Candy. 'Just like an avocado, gently squeeze the fruit anywhere and if it "gives" it's ready to eat. Unlike the avocado, however, a gently pressed papaya won't bruise.' I am electrified by this idea of the 'modern papaya'. Candy explains that in days' past papayas were left to ripen on the tree, where they would develop full colour, turning from green to yellow. This process simply doesn't happen to modern papaya, given our need to transport the fruit across the country. Today, modern papayas are picked at about 30 per cent mature to allow the fruit to ripen during transit, on sale and on our fruit plate (not bowl; see page 10!). Red papayas humble me because as scientific and nerdy as I want to get in understanding a produce item, sometimes I need to trust my instincts and understand that mother nature is uncontrollable.

Papayas are the rebels of the fruit world – sometimes they don't fully colour up on the skin but still fully ripen inside, making our selection process almost purely reliant on our sense of touch.

One of my team members, who I secretly dub my 'fruit padawan', is Long Ngoc To. I trained with him for more than five years to become a fruiterer and I'm happy to say that he's taught me things about fruit that I didn't know myself. He is a keen fruiterer who opens more boxes, checks more fruit and looks more keenly with his young eyes than me. Many years ago we were selling red papayas on the market floor and he asked me to source smaller fruit, because they were sweeter. I didn't know why and he explained that these papayas were the fruit from the male flowers, and hence much smaller and sweeter. There is no scientific reason that I've found as to why the smaller male-flowered fruit tastes sweeter, but I have tasted papayas from the same batch of fruit and eaten both female-flowered and male-flowered fruit and they are, in my opinion, up to 20 per cent sweeter.

While different cultivars have different shapes, male tree flowers tend to produce skinnier papayas. I asked Candy about the technical reasons for this and she explained that the modern papaya can be more complex than skinny fruit, given that many commercial plantations grow hermaphrodite trees that are self-pollinating male flower fruits. While looking for skinny fruit is very technical it is something to keep in mind.

While Long Ngoc To swears by male-flowered fruit, Dad uses his instincts and looks for sugar spots that look like sugar crystals coming out of the skin. These are a dead giveaway that the papaya is going to be bursting with sweetness. Candy calls these spots 'sun-kissed freckles'. I rather like this name and think that if you see these freckles on a papaya, it should be the first fruit in your shopping basket. Why? Mother nature is showing you it's red papaya time.

Choose

1. Gently press the fruit; it should have a slight 'give' like an avocado.

2. The skin should have a sweet aroma.

3. Although the shade of yellow or orange on the fruit does suggest ripeness, pale-coloured fruit can be sweet, too. A papaya's skin colour is dependent on many variables, such as cultivar, mother nature, season and post-harvest treatment. Of course, if the fruit is predominantly green this is a sign that the fruit might be immature and not sweet.

4. For an added sweet bonus, look for papayas with sun-kissed freckles.

5. Generally speaking, male-producing flower trees produce skinnier and smaller papayas that taste sweeter. However, this isn't a hard and fast rule as mother nature and the weather have the final say in what the shape and size of the fruit will be.

Store

Store red papayas at room temperature and eat within three days.

THANH'S TIPS

YELLOW TURNING ORANGE CAN INDICATE RIPENESS, BUT NOT ALWAYS.

SUN-KISSED FRECKLES ARE A GREAT SIGN OF SWEETNESS.

WHITE SUGAR CRYSTALS? EVEN BETTER!

After Sonya struggled with her breast-milk supply with our firstborn, I was determined to feed her everything I could to help boost her supply for our second child. In traditional Chinese medicine, green papaya is seen as a nutritious and milk-boosting food for mums in their confinement period, which is the first month post birth. Given that both my grandfathers were traditional Chinese herbalists, I grew up surrounded by many of these practices but never fully understood them. So when our second child arrived, I made Sonya a selection of confinement recipes, including this green papaya soup with a fish broth (black chicken is also used). Post birth, hydration and plenty of nutrients are super important, so soups offer an excellent solution to both. Green papayas are full of vitamins and minerals that are believed to help boost milk supply. It's hard to translate the correct terminology of the benefits in this soup, as it's so different to Western scientific thought, but it's been tried and tested for thousands of years. I have to say, the herbs are ridiculously rich, so taste the soup as you go and amend it to your liking: add salt and sugar for more flavour, or less or more of each herb, but don't remove any ingredients entirely. Unripe green papayas are very firm, so I recommend looking for fruit that is half ripe, as it will still have the benefits of unripe papaya but be softer and more pleasant to eat, especially if you have a sensitive digestive system. If you see food as medicine, then food can not only nourish the soul but also boost and replenish your bodily fluids. That's my herbalist heritage coming into play!

CONFINEMENT SOUP

SERVES 4

1 x 750 g whole firm white fish (such as barramundi), gutted and cleaned
sea salt
1 tablespoon sesame oil
5 cm piece of ginger, peeled and sliced
½ semi-ripe green papaya (see Tip), peeled, seeds removed, cut into 2.5 cm cubes
2 whole dried jujubes
1 tablespoon whole dried goji berries
1 tablespoon whole dried longan
fish sauce, to taste

Wash the fish and chop the head and body into 2.5 cm pieces. Pat dry with paper towels and rub with 2–3 teaspoons of salt, depending on the size of the fish. Set aside for 1 hour at room temperature.

Heat the sesame oil in a frying pan over medium heat, add the ginger and fry for 1–2 minutes, until fragrant. Add the fish and cook for 2–3 minutes, to seal. Using a slotted spoon, remove the fish from the pan and set aside.

Bring 1 litre of water to the boil, add the fish, papaya, jujubes, goji berries and longan, then reduce the heat to low and simmer for 30 minutes. Season the soup with salt or fish sauce, to taste, and serve.

TIP You can identify a semi-ripe papaya by its skin – it will be half green and only just starting to colour up. It will still be relatively firm to touch.

SOFT-LEAF HERBS

Growing up in a Vietnamese household, we ate soft-leaf herbs every night at dinner. Vietnamese cuisine uses soft-leaf herbs almost like a pseudo vegetable, rather than a garnish. They instantly make two-minute noodles luxe and a curry vibrant and alive; they add fragrance to salads and complex flavours to sauces; and their clean freshness lifts meals and adds another layer of texture. Soft-leaf herbs must be the greatest x-factor in any dish.

Soft-leaf herbs refer to the group of herbs with soft, delicate leaves and thin stems. Basil, mint, spring onion, parsley and coriander are all herbs in this category. The higher moisture content in soft-leaf herbs, such as basil and mint, helps release their volatile oils into the air, which gives them a strong perfume when fresh, but also means they are quicker to dehydrate and will lose more of these oil compounds and aromas when they are dehydrated to become dried herbs. The opposite is true of thick-leaf herbs, such as rosemary, bay leaves, oregano and thyme, which are categorised by their woody stems and sturdy leaves that retain more moisture and oil content. When dehydrated, the oil in these herbs is concentrated, making them more suitable for drying. Refrain from drying soft-leaf herbs without proper dehydrating equipment as their aroma will be lost.

Always select soft-leaf herbs that have a fresh aroma to add more flavour to your dishes.

Making soft-leaf herbs go the extra mile

The downside of soft-leaf herbs is their perishability. Picking the freshest herbs available and storing them in optimum conditions is key to minimising waste and ensuring maximum aroma. My father was one of the pioneers to offer Thai basil to the Melbourne community in winter, when local basil doesn't grow. He asked growers in the Northern Territory to grow the basil, and then air and road freight the herbs the 3,700 km to Melbourne. This meant creating optimal transport conditions, but three decades ago packaging technologies for transporting herbs over long distances weren't fully developed. It was a wild west of trying to establish the best approach; experimenting with different bags, the humidity, package size and temperatures. When the thought of losing money is involved every week, you want to ensure that the product lasts the journey. My father was relentless in his approach to preserving Thai basil, and his discoveries were driven by ensuring no box was wasted. Given the competition and advancements in transport over the years, he moved from preserving the produce to maximising the quality and fragrance of the herb, given its long travels. Today, we service a large percentage of the Vietnamese pho restaurants in Melbourne, where there can be no compromise on the quality of Thai basil.

To test the freshness of Thai basil, every day we shake the bunches of herbs upside down; if any leaves fall off, it's a sign that the leaves are becoming dry and weak, meaning the shelf life is very short.

Against the backdrop of my father's vision to offer restaurants Thai basil year-round, local Victorian growers started to develop greenhouses that could grow Italian basil in winter. Rick Butler from Butler Market Gardens is one of these pioneers. At the beginning, once picked, greenhouse-grown soft-leaf herbs would only survive a short time and have minimal aroma. However, as a trained horticulturalist, Rick has continually improved the nutrition and aroma of soft-leaf herbs by 5–10 per cent year on year for the last decade. I used to lament that these herbs didn't have enough punch or perfume, but now I'd argue that they're 80 per cent as aromatic as field-grown herbs. Rick also busts the myth that placing herbs in water keeps them fresher for longer. This is only partially true: the stems have such small xylems (water channels) that they often get blocked at the base and start to grow mould rather than keeping the herb hydrated.

One of the reasons most herbs are sold in plastic sleeves or packaging is because they're grown in a protected environment and generally don't fare well when they're sold loose on the shelf in the open air. The noticeable difference between field-grown herbs and protected cropping is the thickness of the leaves: field-grown leaves are thicker to protect themselves from the elements, while protected cropping herbs are thinner due to constant humid conditions. Unsurprisingly, field-grown herbs survive longer once harvested and can handle a wider range of temperatures in storage.

The future of herbs is very much in the tech space. Whether it's in greenhouses, tunnels or vertical containers, the methods for growing herbs have changed significantly. No doubt improvements in nutrition, aroma, shelf life and packaging will continue as growers become more sophisticated and improve their growing technologies.

The coriander snap test

One of my great joys in life is to ask fruit and vegetable shoppers how they pick produce and why. Many are led by cultural preferences and perhaps decades of experience in buying fruit and veg. One day, I was visiting a fruit shop in the very multicultural suburb of Lalor, Victoria, and I saw a Middle-Eastern woman picking coriander and being very selective about it. There were small and longer bunches for sale; I went to pick the longer bunches, because, to me, they represented better value for money. Contrary to my selection, she picked all the smaller bunches, so I asked her why. She explained that longer-stemmed coriander is often more stringy and, therefore, old and past its best. To test, snap one stem – if the broken stem looks stringy, or if the stem doesn't snap at all but simply bends, this shows the coriander has aged significantly. Shorter bunches, on the other hand, are more likely to be young and tender. Given coriander's prominence in Middle-Eastern dishes, I have used the snap test often, and it has worked brilliantly. Occasionally long stems do snap cleanly, but more often than not, my coriander lady is correct.

Growers like Rick Butler have also taught me how to pick the best spring onions. As a major grower, he explains that a spring onion's diameter determines its spiciness and aroma. Wide stems denote less aroma but more spiciness, while thin stems have few spicy notes but a lot of aroma. The sweet spot to balance spice and aroma is a stem thickness of 8 mm.

Always select soft-leaf herbs that have a fresh aroma to add more flavour to your dishes. It is equally important to store them in optimum conditions to retain the aromas in the leaves for several days.

THANH'S TIPS

Choose

ITALIAN AND THAI BASIL; MINT:
Shake the bunch upside down – no leaves should fall off. Inspect the bunch for any curled leaves; crush a leaf 30 cm away from your face – you should be able to smell the herb's sweet or strong perfume.

CORIANDER: Do the snap test; you are looking for tender stems that snap cleanly. Avoid stringy stems. Generally, shorter stems are younger and more crisp and herbaceous.

SPRING ONIONS: Look for stems that are about 8 mm thick for the best balance of spice and aroma. Spring onions should stand tall; avoid floppy stems or any that indicate wetness or decay in the shoots.

Store

With the exception of spring onions, store soft-leaf herbs in their plastic sleeve (if applicable), covered in wet paper towel, inside a container or plastic bag in the fridge. Depending on the herb, the optimal fridge temperature will vary. Hardier herbs, such as coriander and mint, can withstand colder temperatures of 5°C. The cooler temperature and humidity will also prevent dehydration and prolong ageing. Warm-climate herbs, such as Italian and Thai basil, should not be stored below 12°C. Any colder and the leaves will burn and turn black. Store basil in the warmest part of your fridge, which is usually in the door at the top in the protected dairy section. If you're in a hot climate, store basil in a cool part of the pantry.

For longer storage, place chopped herbs in ice cube trays, cover with water and freeze. Place spring onion stems in a glass of water in the fridge or on the kitchen bench. As they have roots, they will continue to absorb water and grow.

Prep

To pick most soft herbs, hold the top of the stem in one hand, and use your other hand to strip the leaves in a downwards motion. Alternatively, pull the stems through the large hole of a box grater.

> "
> **For longer storage, place chopped herbs in ice cube trays, cover with water and freeze.**

TO TEST, SNAP ONE STEM — IF THE BROKEN STEM LOOKS STRINGY, OR IF THE STEM DOESN'T SNAP AT ALL BUT SIMPLY BENDS, THIS SHOWS THE CORIANDER HAS AGED SIGNIFICANTLY.

I know coriander can be polarising, but I love it. Did you know that in the West coriander root is the herb's most wasted and underrated part, even though it has more aromatic notes than the stem itself? In Eastern cooking, however, it's added to all sorts of dishes, from Thai green curry pastes to chicken stocks. Think of this dish as a pesto pasta, except with coriander. Obviously, given we are using the coriander root, you need to source bunches with large roots attached, so you can create a more flavourful spaghetti. The dish is relatively light, given there is no meat, and it's easy to make.

CORIANDER ROOT PASTA

**SERVES
2–3**

120 ml olive oil
3 garlic cloves, grated
45 g coriander leaves and
    stems, roughly chopped,
    plus extra leaves to serve
1½ teaspoons coriander seeds,
    ground using a mortar and
    pestle (or use ground
    coriander)
juice of ½ lemon
sea salt
45 g (⅓ cup) salted shelled
    pistachios, crushed
cracked white pepper (see Tip)

CORIANDER SPAGHETTI
100 g coriander root (from
    about 2 bunches), scraped
    clean and finely sliced
100 g (⅔ cup) 00 flour
100 g semolina flour, plus extra
    for dusting

To make the spaghetti, place the coriander root in a bowl and use a stick blender to blend it to a smooth paste.

Combine the flours and coriander root paste in a large bowl, add 2½ tablespoons of water and use your hands to bring the mixture together to form a rough dough. Transfer to a work surface and knead, adding a touch more water if the dough is very dry, for 8 minutes or until you have a smooth and cohesive dough. Form the dough into a ball, wrap in plastic wrap and set aside to rest for 30 minutes at room temperature.

Lightly dust a work surface and roll out the dough until it is just thin enough to fit through the widest setting of a pasta machine. Pass the dough through the pasta machine, then fold the dough into thirds (as if folding a letter) and repeat this process until the dough is smooth. Continue to pass the dough through the machine, increasing the number each time, until the pasta is 1–2 mm thick. Cut the pasta into three segments and pass through the spaghetti attachment. Gently toss in semolina flour and cover loosely with plastic wrap.

Bring a large saucepan of salted water to the boil.

Heat the olive oil in a frying pan over medium heat, add the garlic, coriander and ground coriander seeds and cook for 2–3 minutes, until fragrant.

Add the spaghetti to the boiling water and cook for 1 minute, then, using tongs, drag the spaghetti into the coriander sauce, along with 1 tablespoon of the pasta cooking water. Stir to coat the spaghetti in the sauce, until the sauce thickens slightly, then season to taste with lemon juice and salt.

Divide the coriander spaghetti among plates, top with the pistachios, extra coriander and a little white pepper, and serve.

TIP White peppercorns can be purchased from Asian grocers or specialty delis.

Jelly noodles, chilli oil, fried garlic and fresh coriander – wham! Not just a summer favourite, but a moreish bowl of umami that exemplifies simple ingredients done well. The coriander not only flavours the dish, it's also eaten like a vegetable given how many stems are thrown in! Sonya's mum cooks this dish very well, and I learned this recipe from her. Make sure you purchase tender bunches of coriander as you want the stems to 'snap', and trim 2.5 cm off the base of the stems as they tend to be stringy (freeze them and add to your next stock).

MUNG BEAN JELLY NOODLES

LIÁNGFĚN 凉粉

SERVES
6

120 ml vegetable oil
400 ml cold water
100 g fine mung bean flour
(see Tip)
1 teaspoon Korean solar salt
or sea salt flakes
2 garlic cloves, roughly
chopped
125–165 ml crispy chilli oil
bunch of coriander, roughly
chopped

Bring 5 litres of water to the boil in a large stockpot, then reduce the heat to low so the water is barely simmering.

Meanwhile, divide 2 tablespoons of the vegetable oil between two large stainless-steel bowls and smear the oil around the bowls to make them non-stick.

Combine the cold water, mung bean flour and salt in a separate large bowl and stir well to dissolve the flour. Pour the mixture slowly into the stockpot and stir constantly with a wooden spoon or rubber spatula for 2–4 minutes, until the mixture resembles thickened cream. Ensure you stir around the side and base of the pot to stop the mixture sticking. Evenly divide the mixture between the two greased stainless-steel bowls. Set aside at room temperature for at least 3 hours or until set.

Heat the remaining oil in a frying pan over low heat, add the garlic and cook for 1–2 minutes, until just starting to colour. Immediately pour the garlic and the oil into a heatproof bowl and set aside.

When the mung bean jelly has set, invert one of the bowls onto a large chopping board and let the jelly fall out. Using a large knife, preferably a cleaver, cut the jelly into long 1.5 cm wide noodles, about 5 mm–7 mm thick. Ultimately, the thickness of the noodles is up to you – I recommend starting with 1 cm thick noodles if this is your first time making this dish. Repeat with the remaining bowl of jelly.

In a mixing bowl, combine 150 g of the jelly noodles, 1 tablespoon of the chilli oil, 2 teaspoons of garlic oil and 1 tablespoon of the chopped coriander. Toss well, then transfer to a serving bowl, scatter with another tablespoon of coriander and serve. Repeat as needed to make six to eight serves.

TIP Use a good-quality fine mung bean flour for this recipe, as it will ensure the flour-to-water ratio works well. If the flour is grainier than fine icing sugar, you will need less water.

You know how when something is scarce, it makes you want it more? Well, that's the case for me and holy basil. Sometimes referred to as 'hot basil', it's a species of Thai basil with a very thin leaf. It only has a few days of shelf life once picked, which means it's almost impossible to find in the colder states of Australia, where it can't grow. It's also the basis of one of Thailand's most famous dishes: pad krapow. Holy basil has a strong, but delightful, aniseed aroma, a light peppery kick in flavour and a chewy texture. Seemingly, with each bite of the herb, more aromas are released. Unfortunately, substituting regular Thai basil doesn't really reflect the flavours of this dish.

While pad krapow is usually made with minced chicken, if you can find frozen crab claw meat, I suggest you go for it. If you do use minced chicken, however, add it after frying off the aromats, but before the sauces, as it takes longer to cook than crab. When I cook this for my kids, I usually cut up Thai, long or Lebanese eggplants and fry them in the oil for several minutes before adding the aromats, so feel free to do this if you would like to add some vegetables. Pad krapow is one of the most aromatic, if not the most aromatic, stir-fries I know, so definitely try it at a Thai restaurant, and then venture out and try to source this rare basil at the market!

CRAB PAD KRAPOW

ผัดกะเพราปู

SERVES 2

1 red cassette chilli
5 garlic cloves
1 coriander root, scraped clean
1 teaspoon soy sauce
2 teaspoons fish sauce
1 teaspoon oyster sauce
1 teaspoon brown sugar
3 tablespoons coconut oil
200 g crabmeat
4 holy basil stems, leaves picked (about 1 cup leaves)
steamed jasmine rice, to serve

Using a mortar and pestle, pound the chilli, garlic and coriander root to a rough paste, but not too fine.

Combine the soy sauce, fish sauce, oyster sauce and brown sugar in a small bowl.

Melt the coconut oil in a saucepan over medium heat, add the pounded aromats and fry for 1 minute or until fragrant. Add the soy sauce mixture and cook briefly until it just starts to simmer, then add the crabmeat and toss to combine. Cook the crabmeat for 1 minute, then add the holy basil leaves and stir until just wilted and the crabmeat is cooked through.

Divide the pad krapow between plates and serve with steamed jasmine rice.

STONE
FRUIT

When I was a kid, I used to climb the 10-metre-tall trees in our backyard on summer afternoons and pick juicy red plums and peaches. I'd bite into them, but more often than not, they were very sour. Mum and Dad used to harvest the fruit by using a milk carton with a square cut out and attached to a long broomstick in order to reach the high-hanging fruit. We lived in that house until I was 10 years old, and then moved. Dad planted three stone-fruit trees at our new home: one apricot and two nectarine. The apricots were always eaten by birds and the nectarines were plentiful but never sweet.

We often hear stories of amazing backyard fruit grown by grandparents and aunties and uncles, but I had quite the contrary experience. Dad grew up with durian and papaya in Vietnam, so it was novel for him to grow stone fruit. Although he loved having fruit trees at home, he never had the time to care for them because he worked so much, so the trees never really yielded great fruit. Like him, I think many people love to grow fruit and veg, but for whatever reason they don't achieve a great bounty.

As I've learned throughout my career, growing food isn't just science, it's also an art.

> ## When you can't physically stop yourself from eating more, that's the marker of an amazing fruit.

Sweet nostalgia

The first experience we have of a food often determines our future idea of its taste and whether or not we are going to like it. As such, I never expected stone fruits to taste good, and I still don't. Growing up, I mainly ate firm clingstone peaches and can't recall any wonderful nostalgic experiences until my 20s. Sour plums, tart apricots and bland nectarines are my baseline. This is why I'm so delightfully surprised whenever I do eat a good stone fruit, and why it is unforgettable. I think many people probably have similar mediocre experiences and it is my challenge to change this!

My first nostalgic stone fruit experience came when I was living in Fukushima, Japan. My host mother brought home some white peaches (momo), removed the skin and then cut the flesh into perfect bite-sized segments for me to eat with a toothpick. They were to die for. I can still taste the candy-like juice with its mild tartness holding the sweetness in balance. I had never experienced what I call 'sweet umami' in stone fruit before, or what I define as intensely sweet and sour notes balanced in harmony to give you a 'moreish' feeling. When you can't physically stop yourself from eating more, that's the marker of an amazing fruit.

My second nostalgic experience was while travelling through Campania, Tasmania. I visited a packing shed for exporting stone fruit, and they were kind enough to open their doors and sell a box of stone fruit to me, even though I was a stranger. They had so many rare varietals such as greengage plums, which were apple-like crunchy, vinegar-like sour and sweetcorn-like sweet. My senses almost couldn't compute what I was experiencing. Greengage plums are an heirloom variety from Europe and not widely grown in Australia, certainly not on any commercial scale. This was one of those 'wow' moments that change your idea about something forever. My wife and I also visited some U-pick orchards in Campania and the amount of apricot stones we left on the ground was rather embarrassing. I'd never eaten so many apricots in one sitting.

USE YOUR NOSE! APRICOTS MUST SMELL SWEET BEFORE THEY'LL EAT SWEET.

These amazing experiences, which pushed my boundaries of what good stone fruit should taste like, left me questioning why stone fruit, generally, is so average the majority of the time we buy it. One of the main issues is that most of the fruit is harvested too early and the complex flavours and sugars are yet to fully develop. The industry focuses so much on aesthetics, shelf life and yield that flavour is one of the last things considered.

After speaking to growers and technical scientists in the industry, and distilling their vast experience and knowledge, I realised that achieving an amazing stone-fruit experience requires not only knowledge of varietals, but also the technical differences in flavour. So, I've put together some general tips to help you level up your stone-fruit game and give you agency to pick the best among the pack!

INFORMATIVE AND MIND-BLOWING FACT

Nectarines, peaches, plums, apricots and cherries contain little-to-no starch when harvested ripe, meaning there is nothing left to convert to sugars. So why does stone fruit get softer and sweeter when left on the table? The sugar level actually remains relatively constant, but the fruit begins to dehydrate, causing the existing sugars to concentrate. The acid in the fruit can also drop up to 20 per cent as the fruit ages off the tree, so we perceive it to be sweeter, even though it's not developing any more sugars. This is why it's so important that growers pick the fruit at the right maturity.

Choose

THANH'S TIPS

PEACHES

Use your nose! The skin of a peach is very permeable, so you can smell if the fruit is going to be sweet or not, regardless of how firm or soft it is. Peaches that are not aromatic have been picked too early and are unlikely to reach full flavour.

When is the optimal moment to eat a peach? I enjoy peaches that are just starting to 'give', meaning they are still crunchy on the skin and firm but soft when biting into the flesh. The fruit hasn't over-ripened and still has a firm texture, while exuding sweet over sour notes. If the fruit becomes too soft, it is generally sweet but without its acid and flavour. If it's eaten too early, it's likely to be overly tart. Whether you like to eat peaches firm or soft, you should still be able to smell its aroma. It's worth noting that in Asian cultures, peaches are often preferred firm and hard with a crunchy bite, while many in the Western world prefer a sweet experience, with juices dripping down the chin.

When squeezing a peach to check maturity levels, gentle press the 'seam' of the fruit, where the line runs from the stem to the base. This line is called the 'suture', or the 'stitch', and is the weakest point of the fruit that shows the first signs of 'give'.

NECTARINES

Use your eyes! Nectarines that develop freckles or small dots (known as 'sugar spots') on the skin will usually be sweeter than ones without them. These sugar spots generally occur when the fruit has been exposed to more sunlight, from growing on the outer or top branches of the tree. Specifically look for sugar spots on the top half of the fruit closest to the stem, as this indicates that the fruit is extra sweet from top to bottom, instead of just the bottom, which tends to ripen faster on the tree.

Sugar spots are the damaged pores of the fruit skin from sunlight, which cause greater transpiration and water loss, and a concentration of sugars in these areas. Unlike other fruits, stone fruit can handle a lot of UV!

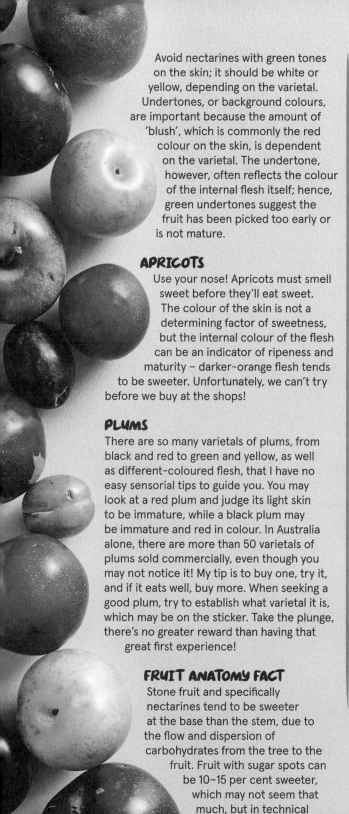

Avoid nectarines with green tones on the skin; it should be white or yellow, depending on the varietal. Undertones, or background colours, are important because the amount of 'blush', which is commonly the red colour on the skin, is dependent on the varietal. The undertone, however, often reflects the colour of the internal flesh itself; hence, green undertones suggest the fruit has been picked too early or is not mature.

APRICOTS

Use your nose! Apricots must smell sweet before they'll eat sweet. The colour of the skin is not a determining factor of sweetness, but the internal colour of the flesh can be an indicator of ripeness and maturity – darker-orange flesh tends to be sweeter. Unfortunately, we can't try before we buy at the shops!

PLUMS

There are so many varietals of plums, from black and red to green and yellow, as well as different-coloured flesh, that I have no easy sensorial tips to guide you. You may look at a red plum and judge its light skin to be immature, while a black plum may be immature and red in colour. In Australia alone, there are more than 50 varietals of plums sold commercially, even though you may not notice it! My tip is to buy one, try it, and if it eats well, buy more. When seeking a good plum, try to establish what varietal it is, which may be on the sticker. Take the plunge, there's no greater reward than having that great first experience!

FRUIT ANATOMY FACT

Stone fruit and specifically nectarines tend to be sweeter at the base than the stem, due to the flow and dispersion of carbohydrates from the tree to the fruit. Fruit with sugar spots can be 10–15 per cent sweeter, which may not seem that much, but in technical terms (1–2 brix*), this is often the difference

between sour to acceptable, acceptable to sweet, and sweet to super sweet! Size also matters: fruit that is small (smaller than a yoyo) tends not to develop the best flavour. So pick mid-sized fruit and upwards!

*Brix is the term for the amount of sugar generally found in a fruit. The rating spans from one to 25 and is calculated using a refractometer, which measures how much light goes through the juice of a fruit. The less light the fruit receives, the more sugar will be present.

Store

Don't store stone fruit in the fridge! Contrary to popular belief, storing stone fruit in the fridge may cause the fruit to lose flavour and be rubbery in texture. Buy stone fruit that you'll eat over the next two to three days and store it at room temperature.

Why? Total geek moment here. Between 3°C and 10°C the expression of genes in a fruit, which tell it to produce enzymes to make proteins and ripen, shuts down. This means that when you transfer fruit from the fridge to the table, it won't ripen properly, it won't become juicy and it may taste bland. John Lopresti, a stone-fruit researcher, calls the temperature of the fridge, the 'killing zone'. Please don't kill your stone fruit! Of course, if you own a commercial fridge and can store your stone fruit at 2°C then you don't need to worry, as the genes don't change in the extreme cold.

Prep

Always make sure your stone fruit is at room temperature before eating. Room-temperature fruit will exude more aromas and have better flavour than cold fruit.

My wife Sonya has Russian heritage, and her love for plum jam comes from her grandma. As a kid, every weekend, she would visit her grandma's house with her cousins; they would play and then head inside for snacks. There would always be an abundance of Russian treats, and the one that she loved most was piroshki (hand pies), with either apricot or plum jam. The last time I was at her grandma's place, I couldn't stop eating them! The pastry is dense and bread-like on the edges, but airy and cake-like in the middle. They go so well with this loose jam!

This jam recipe is very low in sugar, as Sonya's grandma's jams were never overly sweet, and I find this makes it less sickly and very moreish – you get much more of the plums' lovely delicate sour tang notes. In addition to not being particularly sweet, this jam isn't thick like store-bought ones, as it doesn't have added pectin. The jam is probably the least viscous jam I have eaten. I guess that's how Sonya's grandma, and her great-grandmother before her, made it back in the Soviet era, when ingredients were scarce, and you had to make do with very simple produce.

When I last made this recipe with Sonya, I used queen garnet plums, which are famous for their high sugar content. I recommend taste-testing the jam as you cook it to check the viscosity and levels of sweetness. Add more sugar if you want, and if you want it to be thicker in texture, cook it for longer.

NATURAL PECTIN

Pectin is a natural thickening agent found in the stone, flesh and skin of all stone fruits, but some contain more than others. Adding lemon juice to the jam mixture increases the acidity, which helps activate this natural pectin. If you prefer a thicker jam, or if you're using apricots instead of plums, add a couple of teaspoons of pectin powder when the jam reaches 110°C and stir well.

SONYA SUN'S PLUM JAM

MAKES
2 kg

2 kg plums, halved and stones removed
1½ tablespoons freshly squeezed lemon juice
250 g granulated sugar

Combine the plums, lemon juice and 100 ml of water in a large saucepan over low heat. Bring to a simmer and cook, stirring occasionally, for 40 minutes.

Using a potato masher, mash the plums to your desired consistency, then add the sugar and bring to the boil. Reduce the heat to a simmer and continue to cook the jam, stirring frequently, until it thickens and reaches 110°C on a kitchen thermometer.

Remove the pan from the heat and allow the jam to cool for 5 minutes. Carefully divide the jam among sterilised jars (see Tip; page 275) and set aside to cool completely.

Unopened plum jam will keep in the pantry for up to 1 year. Once opened, store in the fridge for up 3 months.

LOOK FOR SUGAR SPOTS NEAR THE STEM FOR EXTRA SWEETNESS.

A DEEP YELLOW UNDERTONE IS A GREAT SIGN OF RIPENESS.

THE AMOUNT OF BLUSH IS DEPENDENT ON THE VARIETAL AND ISN'T INDICATIVE OF MATURITY.

AVOID SKINS WITH A GREEN UNDERTONE. THEY'VE BEEN PICKED TOO EARLY.

I've made this salad a few times to bring to parties. The grilled peaches really elevate the dish, and you'll find that everyone tries to sneak a few extra onto their plate because they taste so bloody good – I suggest grilling more than you need! I like to prep the ingredients at home, then simply toss everything together when I arrive or just before serving. Alternatively, this salad makes the perfect light lunch, dinner or side dish at home.

I love this salad, as the ingredients work so well in harmony: the sweetness of the peaches pairs well with the tanginess of the balsamic vinegar, the creaminess of the avocado, the bitterness of the salad leaves and the textural crunch of the pine nuts. I prefer to use rocket for its bitter, peppery leaves, but any salad mix works well. You can also substitute nectarines for the peaches.

My fruit nerd tip is to use a mixture of white and yellow peaches – it adds a dynamism to the dish that will have people saying, 'Have you tried the salad?!'.

SUMMERY GRILLED PEACH SALAD

SERVES 8

8 firm peaches (preferably 4 white and 4 yellow), halved and stones removed
olive oil, for drizzling
sea salt and cracked black pepper, to taste
100 ml balsamic vinegar
2½ tablespoons honey
450 g salad leaves (preferably rocket)
1 avocado, sliced
100 g pine nuts or raw cashew nuts

Preheat a barbecue grill to high or heat a chargrill pan over high heat.

Place the peach halves in a large bowl, drizzle over the olive oil and massage it into the fruit. Season with salt and pepper.

Grill the peach halves, cut-side down, for 2–3 minutes, until grill marks char the flesh and the peach has a smoky aroma. Remove from the grill and set aside to cool, then cut the peach halves into thin wedges.

Meanwhile, in a small bowl, whisk together the balsamic vinegar and honey to make a dressing.

In a large salad bowl, toss together the salad leaves and dressing, add the avocado, pine nuts or cashews and peach, and gently toss to combine. Serve immediately.

STRAWBERRIES
& BLUEBERRIES

The sight of perfectly blush-red strawberries are a category-defining image. The fruit is almost universally loved – I actually don't know anyone who doesn't enjoy strawberries. Maybe it's because we enjoy their flavour in so many desserts, such as ice cream and cakes, and the unique aroma has a nostalgic string that pulls all of our hearts. While fresh strawberries in punnets almost always look spotless, without an insect bite or leaf disease in sight, the reality of growing a strawberry is far from the romantic view we see in the store. Given its notoriety I wonder how many people have even seen a strawberry growing from a plant before?

If you've ever grown a strawberry plant at home, you'll realise how hard it is to yield just a handful of strawberries, let alone harvest them before worms or birds get to your unripe fruit.

My first trip to a strawberry farm was an eye-opening experience that gave me a huge appreciation for how much goes into producing and selecting a punnet of strawberries.

In my first year working for Coles, I had the opportunity to travel to a strawberry farm in Silvan and pick strawberries destined for the stores. As if picking strawberries in the summer heat wasn't taxing enough, the amount of insects in the field were almost like a mini swarm because the farm had introduced a number of 'predator insects' to prevent over reliance on pesticides and insecticides. It was like being in a warzone of ladybugs eating aphids and all kinds of insects that I'd never seen before buzzing around the plants. The summer heat was extreme too, and not just from the sun but the hundreds of rows of strawberry plants covered with black plastic. The plastic not only absorbed the heat but kind of reflected it back at your face and made you even more hot! The use of plastic materials to help support efficient agriculture practices is called 'plasticulture' – what a name, right? Underneath were the strawberries themselves, many of which were not the right shape, size or uniformly red.

My first trip to a strawberry farm was an eye-opening experience that gave me a huge appreciation for how much goes into producing and selecting a punnet of strawberries.

While I lament the fact that, more often than not, strawberries are not sweet enough for my own liking, I do appreciate that strawberries are available year-round across most of the country because of the industry's efforts to make the fruit accessible to everyone all the time. Not only do commercial producers cultivate strawberries to be big, red and heart-shaped, they also grow them to have no insect damage and harvest them with a shelf life that can last days and travel thousands of kilometres. These are things that a consumer may not ever realise when they select a punnet of strawberries, but knowing these intricate details allows me to give you some worthwhile tips to ensure you eat sweeter strawberries, more often.

The first tip is to understand strawberry colour. Pickers pack strawberries with the pointy end of the fruit facing the lid of the plastic punnet. This allows the consumer to see more of the red blush and it looks more visually stunning. What you may not know is that the area around the strawberry leaf, known as the calyx, is the last part of the strawberry to ripen. Therefore if you see a full red-coloured fruit it is likely to be sweet. Turn the punnet over and look at the colour of the fruit – if you see lots of white around the calyx of the strawberries, they might not be sweet.

The second tip is to use your nose to smell if the strawberries have a strong aroma or not. Strawberry punnets have small air gaps in the plastic to allow the fruit to breathe, but it also means you can smell the fruit. The stronger the aroma, the more likely the strawberries will be delightfully sweet.

My third tip is to know that strawberries respond well to prolonged warm weather, which is why there is usually a flush of strawberries in summer. When the fruit ripens all at once, the regions usually struggle to pick all the strawberries early, so more of the fruit is picked at a mature stage. You'll know this has happened when you look at the underside of the plastic punnet and most of the strawberries are fully red. They don't say summer strawberries for no reason! While looking for great-eating fruit is always at the front of my mind, there can also be a lot of bruising, bleeding and breakdown of the fruit, which you should be on the lookout for when selecting a punnet of strawberries. Generally, if you spot a strawberry that is leaking juice or is bruised heavily, it's likely there will be other fruit in the punnet that aren't quite right, so use your instincts.

THE AREA AROUND THE STRAWBERRY LEAF IS THE LAST PART TO RIPEN, SO IF YOU SEE A FULL RED-COLOURED FRUIT IT IS LIKELY TO BE SWEET.

The blueberry is like the cool kid at school that isn't as popular as the strawberry, but everyone still loves.

While the overall berry category is huge – in fact, the fastest growing fruit category by volume in the last decade – I want to talk about blueberries. When grown well, blueberries are tangy and sweet and full of antioxidants (the sight of blue gives off super-food vibes), as well as being convenient to eat. During my time as a national fruit buyer for Coles, I sat next to the blueberry buyer for the best part of a year. One afternoon, one of the suppliers brought in 50 varieties of blueberries to try. I didn't even know there were more than one or two varieties. What I did discover was that some were bland, some were sweet, some were tangy and others were soapy. Nearly the entire berry category, not just blueberries, has been commoditised so that brands hold a stronger place in consumer minds than varietals. When testing these blueberries, it occurred to me how much we've lost by removing the varietel name; just because they all look the same does not mean they all taste the same. Think about if red delicious apples and granny smith apples were both sold as just 'apples'; it's almost unfathomable.

One summer, I went blueberry picking at a U-pick orchard in Scottsdale, Tasmania, and I got another opportunity to taste-test this fruit. There were at least 20 rows of blueberry bushes, and each row was a different varietal. Just like other fruits, each varietal has their own ripening period; some earlier, some later. I noticed plenty of green-to-white fruit, which was unripe and tasted sour, as well as overripe berries that were shrivelled and had lost much of their tang.

Based on these experiences, my tips for selecting blueberries are similar to inspecting a carton of eggs: open the blueberry punnet and inspect the fruit – if any are green or white in colour, they will be unripe. Also be on the lookout for any shrivelled fruit, as this may be a sign that the blueberries are dehydrated and no longer fresh, or the fruit was picked overripe.

The berry market is dominated by some big distributors, and although our choice of blueberries may be becoming more commoditised, it's still worth using your instincts and visually inspecting the fruit before buying a punnet.

> **The blueberry is like the cool kid that isn't as popular as the strawberry, but everyone still loves.**

Choose

STRAWBERRIES

1. Full-coloured fruit (especially around the calyx or leaf) shows maturity and sweetness.

2. Flip the punnet upside down and check for any white flesh around the stem. This suggests the fruit has been picked early to increase shelf life and won't be as sweet.

3. While checking the bottom of the punnet, check for any fruit that is bruised or bleeding.

BLUEBERRIES

1. Like strawberries, look for full-coloured fruit. Green or white blueberries suggest immaturity and the berries will taste sour.

2. Avoid punnets with shrivelled or mouldy blueberries – even if there are only one or two. It's an indicator that the punnet is old and the other berries will turn quickly.

BLACKBERRIES AND RASPBERRIES

1. Look for vibrant and plump fruit.

2. Open the punnet and look at the berries – don't be shy, it's like opening a carton of eggs to check none of them are cracked.

3. Avoid blackberries and raspberries with any bruising, leaking or mould.

Store

Store berries at the back of the middle or top shelf of the fridge for one to two days. Only store for longer if you know they're really fresh, and even then by only another one to two days.

FLIP THE PUNNET UPSIDE DOWN TO CHECK FOR WHITE FLESH OR BLEEDING.

Inspired by my friend Mandy Hall, a fermentation enthusiast based in Adelaide, these raw honey–fermented strawberries are a little fizzy and full of microbes and depth of flavour! Once fermented, the strawberries can be eaten like jam, but they are healthier and not as sickly sweet. Strawberries already contain natural yeast and lactic acid bacteria, so as soon as you pop them in a jar with the raw honey, the fermentation process begins as long you close the lid and keep the air out. Keeping the temperature warm also helps the microbes eat the sugars faster. It's a simple recipe that packs a punch, and is especially great in summer when strawberries are abundant; you'll have an extra couple of weeks of strawberry goodness! Pair the fermented strawberries with salad dressings, pancakes, cakes, ice cream, yoghurt and granola, or add them to tonic water!

MANDY HALL'S RAW HONEY—FERMENTED STRAWBERRIES

MAKES
500 ml

250 g punnet of strawberries
250 ml raw honey
1 rosemary sprig

Sterilise a 500 ml Mason jar or any jar without a metal lid (see Tip).

Wash the strawberries well, then remove the calyx or leaves (halve or slice any large strawberries) and place in the prepared jar. Pour the honey into the jar, making sure the strawberries are completely submerged and there is a 2.5 cm gap at the top of the jar for the ferment to bubble. Add the rosemary sprig to the jar.

Loosely screw on the lid and place the jar on a plate (in case the ferment bubbles over). Leave to ferment at room temperature, stirring every day, for 3 days. If the weather is really hot, the fermentation will be quicker, so taste after 2 days – if it's delicious and to your liking, then place the jar in the fridge. Consume within 2 weeks.

TIP To sterilise your jars, simply wash them in hot, soapy water, then rinse and dry them in a warm oven. If the lids cannot go in the oven, boil them in a saucepan of water for 5 minutes, then allow to air-dry.

SWEET POTATOES

Whether you bake, boil, fry or mash sweet potatoes, there's so much to love about them. When I was a kid, Mum mostly steamed sweet potatoes, but I found out later in life that roasted sweet potatoes are mind-blowing once you discover how to caramelise the sugars (see page 281). Whenever I travel through South-East Asia for work, I always find myself purchasing steamed sweet potatoes from the street hawkers and it definitely gives me nostalgic feels for when Mum cooked them. That's the interesting thing I find about sweet potatoes; every fruiterer has a different view about them. While many swear by roasted sweet potatoes, others love them in fresh salads. I've also seen many recipes where sweet potatoes are mashed and spread over a shepherd's pie instead regular potatoes ... genius, I reckon.

The ultimate tuber

The reason why I think sweet potatoes are the ultimate tuber and snacking vegetable is because they're so convenient. We don't roast potatoes or yams and walk around eating them, but we do with sweet potatoes. Regular potatoes need to be salted or slathered in oil or butter to be commonly enjoyed, but that's not the case with sweet potatoes. Like potatoes, not only do sweet potatoes come in various colours – purple skin and yellow flesh, red skin and white flesh, white skin and purple flesh, orange skin and orange flesh – but textures and flavours also vary wildly. Some are really dense, while others are juicy and almost to the point of being mushy. Flavours vary also, with some being light and others earthy and candy-like.

A great roasted sweet potato comes in its own packaging and is completely compostable.

Sustained energy

Arguably as a fruiterer, the sweet potato's greatest marketing point is its low GI factor, which stands for Glycaemic Index. Ask any fruiterer what low GI means when it comes to sweet potatoes and they'll most likely say 'it's healthier than potatoes'. That's what I used to say as well ... until I became a complete fruit nerd and questioned everything I was told until I actually understood it. I am no nutritionist, but I am fascinated how produce is marketed from a health perspective. A sweet potato's low GI basically means that your body slowly digests the sugars and that there is a slow release of energy, instead of, say, eating a chocolate bar and getting a spike of sugars and energy followed by a low. It's been given the 'healthier' tick of approval because it gives you sustained energy, makes your tummy work for that energy and keeps your tummy full for longer so you don't need to eat more and have peaks and troughs of energy. However, as I explain in the roasting potato technique on page 281, depending on the cooking method, the 'low GI' of a sweet potato can change.

Keep it sweet and juicy

I was fortunate enough to speak to Sweet Potatoes Australia general manager and grower Claire Maslen at a fruit conference. Claire gave me the lowdown on how to best store sweet potatoes so we get the best eating experience. She says that sweet potatoes should not be stored under 10°C, otherwise the skin wrinkles and dehydrates. Instead, 12–20°C is best.

Given it is impossible to know how a fruit shop has rotated its stock, look for bright, firm sweet potatoes that are heavy for their size when making your selection. In addition, generally, sweet potatoes will be great for around 2 weeks after harvesting, which means the consumer has about a week to eat them. Longer than that and your sweet potatoes may be heading towards their best-before date and lots of moisture may have escaped. What we really want is to retain that moisture, so we're not left with a dry eating experience.

If you've ever eaten a sweet potato and been left with a dry mouth searching for a glass of water, this is likely due to incorrect storage or cooking the potato incorrectly.

After cooking sweet potatoes with either the skin on or off, the steam evaporates out of the flesh very quickly, so, just like resting a steak to retain its juices, letting the sweet potato rest, covered, is key. I like to turn the oven off and let the sweet potatoes cool gradually in the oven, instead of removing them and seeing all the juice evaporate! A good eating experience is key to coming back for more and this is why I believe sweet potatoes never really hit their peak potential. With our time-poor lives, there are too many steps to get through for a consumer to see the sweet potato as 'convenient produce'. While most of us enjoy eating sweet potatoes, perhaps not many of us have the knowledge or the time to prepare them correctly.

I believe sweet potatoes are the ultimate tuber. They can be as flavourful as a taro, as filling as a potato, as textural as a yam and as convenient as a cassava.

One of my more memorable work trips was visiting the Asian fruit shops of Sydney with two of my most trusted Sydney fruiterers, Adrian Buchanan and Peter Le. I discovered that the sweet potatoes were displayed very differently from anywhere else that I'd travelled. Specifically, I was in Bankstown walking along Bankstown City Plaza where there are seven fruit shops within eye distance of each other, all vying for customers. Each store had chopped the ends off their sweet potatoes with the ends facing outwards for customers to see. The colour was mesmerising, especially the dark-purple-flesh potatoes. The display was to show customers that their sweet potatoes were the sweetest. Peter explained to me that the sweet potatoes were about the length of my hand because the Asian community enjoy smaller portion sizes that can be eaten by one person, but also because smaller sweet potatoes cook quicker. Where competition thrives, innovation and customer service flourishes and this rings true for fruit and veg. If you're able to find a fruiterer who chops off the ends of a sweet potato for their display, you know they know what they're doing!

Choose

1. Select firm, heavy sweet potatoes. Light sweet potatoes suggest dehydration.

2. Small-to-mid-sized sweet potatoes are the most convenient as they cook more quickly and are a better snacking size than large sweet potatoes.

3. If possible, ask to cut the end to see the colour – the darker the flesh the sweeter it will be, as simple as that. It needs to be freshly cut, so this is difficult as most fruit shops do not offer this service.

4. If roasting, choose sweet potatoes of the same diameter so they cook evenly.

Store

Store sweet potatoes in a dry, dark and cool place with a stable temperature between 12°C and 20°C. Do not store below 10°C, as this can lead to dehydration and wrinkling. Eat within a week of purchase. You can store them for longer but they will start to lose flavour and dehydrate.

THANH'S TIPS

A GREAT ROASTED SWEET POTATO COMES IN ITS OWN PACKAGING AND IS COMPLETELY COMPOSTABLE.

My study semester in Shanghai was in the middle of winter and the weather was miserably cold. Underneath the elevated rail lines, street-food vendors, who had moved from the countryside to make a living in the city, sold charred sweet potatoes from coal-fired barrel-sized iron ovens. Kǎo dì guā (烤地瓜) is a favourite snack for Shanghainese during winter and the vendors roast them to absolute perfection. The flavour is incredible and nothing like any sweet potato I had eaten before. How did they do it? I assumed it was the char from the coal oven or the variety of potato they grew. In honesty, I didn't know until a decade later.

One day, my good friend Otis Hsu was talking about sweet potatoes and he explained in Mandarin that I needed 'to push the sugars out' of the potatoes by cooking them for a long time. I went home and air-fried some sweet potatoes at 220°C for an hour and noticed that the sweet potato skin looked visually burnt and the flesh just below the skin was a touch dry. Still, the flavour and sweetness were the best I had eaten since Shanghai. The next time I air-fried sweet potatoes I reduced the temperature, but forgot to pierce the skin. When I opened the air-fryer lid, the sweet potato was sizzling from the inside, and when I pierced it with my fork black caramel started oozing out. I tasted it, and it was bitter. I realised I had pushed the sugars out of the potatoes and turned them into a dark bitter caramel.

I needed to find a way to cook the sweet potatoes for long enough for their sugars to caramelise. White sugar caramelises between 155°C and 182°C, and the internal core of a sweet potato needs to 180°C before it will caramelise. I continued to refine the cooking time to obtain a golden, but not dark, caramel, but increasing the roasting time dried out the potato skin and the outer sugars would turn dark brown, while the inside was cooked.

Only through trial and error was I able to establish a cooking time and method where the 'sugars are pushed out', meaning you've caramelised the sugars in the sweet potato, but more importantly you've cooked it through evenly. I did this by starting with a lower heat below the caramelisation point of 170°C; when the sweet potato core reached this point I finished the cooking at 200°C to gently caramelise the sweet potato instead of unevenly darkening the caramel near the skin. I also realised that if I removed the sweet potato from the oven straight away, the potato would lose moisture, so I left the sweet potato in the oven to lower its temperature gradually. The result was that the moisture remained inside the sweet potato and when I cut it open, it was still piping hot, but far juicier.

The worst thing is eating a dry sweet potato, and even worse is when you don't eat it after 5 minutes and the moisture has escaped, leaving you with a dry, bland mouthfeel. By trying to replicate the coals in the barrels in Shanghai, but without having coals and a barrel, the method opposite was the best I could come up with. It will change your life and how your palate understands sweet potatoes!

To release some of the bubbling caramel and prevent the sweet potato from bursting, especially during the second half of the cooking time, I fork the sweet potatoes mid-way through roasting. Some people fork their potatoes before placing them in the oven, but I find they cook better without being forked initially, as they lose a touch of moisture and they're not hot enough in the first half of cooking to require air holes anyway. I also recommend placing baking paper underneath, as the caramel that drips from the sweet potato is a pain to clean afterwards!

A note on the glycaemic index: by roasting sweet potatoes at high heat you destroy the resistant starches, meaning roasted sweet potatoes are a high GI food, not a low GI food. So if you want a slow release of energy from your sweet potato, instead of quick energy, it's best to boil them. However if you want flavour, roasting them is the only way to go!

TIP Sweet potato cooking times can vary between 5 and 10 minutes, depending on the density and fibre content of the varietal.

REPLICATING A COAL OVEN FOR ROASTED SWEET POTATOES

KǍO DÌ GUĀ (烤地瓜)

Preheat the oven or an air-fryer to 170°C. If using the oven, line a baking tray with baking paper.

Place the sweet potatoes in the oven or air-fryer and roast according to the below cooking times:

· Small (2 cm wide): 45 minutes

· Medium (3 cm wide): 1 hour

· Medium–large (4 cm wide): 1 hour + 10 minutes at 200°C

· Large (more than 4 cm wide): 1 hour + 20 minutes at 200°C

Halfway through the cooking time, pierce the sweet potatoes with a fork.

At the end of the cooking time, turn off the heat and leave the sweet potatoes in the oven or air-fryer for 30 minutes, to finish cooking in the middle.

sweet potatoes of your choice

SERVES 4

TOMATOES

When I was young, our Italian neighbours grew tomatoes in their backyard. One time our lovely aunty next door taught my mum how to cook a simple tomato and egg dish, which Mum still cooks today. Italians are synonymous with tomatoes; in fact, I was once taught how to pick truss tomatoes by an elderly Italian woman who saw me looking puzzled one day at the fruit shop. She told me to use my finger to swipe the 'gold dust' across the shoulder of the tomato – if the smell on my finger was sweet, then the tomato would be sweet. I didn't know the science behind this but it intrigued me.

There is something mysterious about the sour-sweet taste of a tomato that makes us love them so much. Cooked into a sauce, sliced in sandwiches, spread on pizza, chopped into salads or eaten like an apple, the tomato's culinary versatility is incredible.

A story of classification

Of all the fruit and vegetables in the world, tomatoes have the most storied journey of them all. Their classification has seen them travel from a fruit to a vegetable and, in the last decade, back to a fruit. The traditional botanical description of fruits with a seed have tomatoes firmly placed in this category, but they were classified as a vegetable for the better part of the 20th century as they were predominantly used in cooking. The beginning of the 2010s saw the rise of snacking tomatoes in punnets, with their mind-boggling sweetness that leans towards being a fruit snack eaten on their own. While snacking tomatoes grow in popularity, traditional field, truss and roma tomatoes are still purchased predominantly for cooking, placing tomatoes firmly in the versatile bucket of being both a fruit and a vegetable. As a fruit, they are the most-grown produce in the world, with 180 million tonnes grown as of 2021, compared to bananas at 115 million tonnes.

When I reflect on the tomatoes I ate as a kid and the tomatoes of today, they are vastly different in flavour, varieties and availability.

Changing with the times

'They don't grow them like they used to', or 'they don't taste the same', are the common phrases I hear about tomatoes. Before you read on, I challenge you to think about your own preconceived ideas about tomatoes. Are you happy with the tomatoes of today? Are they better or worse than in times' past? I say this because the world of tomatoes is likely to be far more sophisticated than you might think, for the world's most-grown fruit has also had the most investment placed in it.

I spoke with my friend and neighbour in the wholesale market Grant Nichol, who heads up part of Flavorite, one of Australia's largest protected cropping tomato producers, to find out how the snacking tomato has changed in my lifetime. Answering my first question about flavour, Grant says that so much of a tomato's flavour comes down to the variety grown. He also says that the modern tomato is far more technically and scientifically produced than most other vegetables or crops.

Just like strawberries, tomatoes 50 years ago used to be a seasonal fruit only available two months of the year. Passata sauce bottles and canned tomatoes preserved excess summertime produce and ensured consumers had access to year-round fruit. Efficient transportation, investment in greenhouses, development of new varietals and different growing methods changed the game. Table tomatoes for cooking and snacking tomatoes for eating are now available every day of the year; tomatoes that contain less water were specifically invented for sandwiches, as were tomatoes that could literally be dropped from a roof and not splat or bruise. You could nickname these 'machine tomatoes' because they're all harvested by machine and can withstand the rigours of steel, rubber, conveyer belts and the weight of many tomatoes stacked on top of them. You might be thinking who eats these machine tomatoes? Every tomato sauce we squeeze on a pie, every pizza we eat with tomato paste, and many of the tomatoes we buy in cans are these varietals.

Glasshouse tomatoes

A huge percentage of Australia's tomatoes are grown in some form of protected cropping scene, often in glasshouses. Glasshouse tomato plants are often planted in grow bags with spun wool or hay. These materials allow the tomato root to sit neatly and draw on nutrients fed into the root holding material. Whatever the plant requires, it's fed via a hydroponic system controlled and managed by humans, and the water used is often recycled. Grant says that 1 kg of hydroponic tomatoes may require 18 litres of water to grow, but the same amount of field-grown tomatoes might require 120 litres because irrigation can run into the soil, while in protected cropping, water can be recycled using filters. It's amazing sustainable water science in practice!

Given that every plant is grown using the same root base, it means that every plant should yield the same consistent type of tomato. If the tomato plants were grown in soil, there could be different soil types from one side of a property to the other, thereby making the tomato fruit vary drastically, regardless of whether the soil was in a glasshouse or not. That's why planting in soil is not often used in greenhouse systems. In glasshouses, the farmer will control the leaf matter, snipping off any unnecessary growth to give the fruits more energy. Grant says this is a balancing act as the leaves are also required to perform photosynthesis. Given the capital investment in glasshouses, every tomato plant in a glasshouse needs to generate more sales than one grown in the field. Often the main expense is heating the glasshouse during winter, but this practice can allow a single plant to produce tomatoes for ten months of the year, as opposed to a field-grown tomato plant, which only produces fruit for two months of the year. Grant also informs me that the first crop from a plant is usually the best, and then the following crops tend to yield less and not be as strong.

Glasshouses allow growers to control each plant and every component of the growing process, from temperature and nutrients to leaf density, height and water control.

Comparing 'tomatoes with tomatoes'

Circling back to 'they don't grow them like they used to', I think this one-liner has negative connotations as it suggests the previous method was better than the current. I argue there is a place for field-grown and glasshouse-grown tomatoes, even though glasshouse tomatoes make up the majority of tomatoes in Australia, especially in winter. The statement 'tomatoes don't taste the same' is correct given that older varietals are different to the ones we eat today, even though they might share a name such as 'truss tomato'. I asked Grant, hypothetically, to compare a like-for-like field-grown versus glasshouse-grown tomato. Hypothetical being the key word because the modern tomato varietal that is grown in a glasshouse is not the same as one grown in the field. Grant says that plants in the field are often stressed from the sun, wind and rain. Stressed plants tend to produce fewer and smaller fruits, with hardier, blemished skin and more intense flavours. However, if the plant is too stressed it could start to draw back nutrients from the tomato fruits themselves to survive, causing all sorts of issues with the fruit. But overall the flavour can be very intense, depending on mother nature.

Perhaps our nostalgia for tomatoes of old are for these intense field-grown tomatoes. I do think it's unfair to compare a summer crop to an all-year crop. In the past, tomatoes grown in the field weren't available in winter and the fact that a consumer demands tomatoes in winter shows that the industry has come a long way to make this happen for us. I think we are blessed to have year-round availability of tomatoes, and although the idea of 'seasonal tomatoes' is somewhat gone, I'd prefer consistently good tomato experiences, rather than none at all. In fact, a large percentage of tomatoes are still grown in the field, but as the move towards protected cropping tomatoes continues, we should understand the industry's position to secure availability and work on improving quality of flavour. Those of us looking for flavours of old can still seek them in late summer when the glut of field-grown tomatoes are available.

I do, from time to time, have a poor tomato experience, but it's almost never in the summer and when I do eat one, it's more likely to do with the variety of tomato I've bought. Snacking tomatoes sold in punnets are generally picked ripe and ready to eat, though they have a short shelf life. Selecting cooking tomatoes can be trickier, as we are not privy to the type of tomato being purchased. In the case of a cooking tomato, the industry often picks these green and lets them ripen during transport. Use your instincts: when the fruit is firm, has good colour and smells good, it's likely to be a good fruit. It's always best to buy a few good tomatoes rather than many average ones, as one tomato goes a long way to making your next dish have that extra bit of umami.

So how do you spot a field-grown tomato? They'll likely have marks of all kinds on the skin, compared to protected cropping tomatoes which are blemish free and perfect-looking to the point of seeming fake! Given tomatoes are now grown to be 'fit for purpose', try purchasing a specific tomato variety for every occasion!

Finally, going back to the 'gold dust' the Italian nonna told me to look for on tomatoes, I asked tomato-growing expert Chris Millis, the Chief Operating Officer from Flavorite, to provide his insights. He explained to me that they are plant hairs called 'trichomes'. They are like glands that secrete oils to help protect the plant, and they show that the plant is healthy.

It's amazing when ordinary people who have the care and insight to figure out these small details share their secrets. It's even more amazing when these tips aren't just 'old wives' tales' but are backed up by the horticulturists and growers. This is a solid A+ tip, given a healthy plant always produces healthier and, more often, tastier fruit.

Choose

THANH'S TIPS

1. For cooking tomatoes, such as field, truss and heirloom varieties, look at the vine and shoulder of the tomato for 'gold dust' – this is the good stuff. Swipe the top of tomato near the stem; the sweet fluro dust should make your finger smell very aromatic and sweet.

2. Check the colour and health of the vine if it's still attached. A green vine has been freshly picked, but a brown or dehydrated vine suggests the tomatoes were picked up to a week ago.

3. Avoid soft, dull-coloured tomatoes.

4. Different varietals have their own colours but, generally speaking, the darker the tone, the more ripe the tomato will be.

5. Snacking tomatoes should look bright and plump. Avoid any tomatoes that are wrinkled or starting to shrivel.

Store

Store tomatoes at room temperature, ideally between 15°C and 25°C. Don't store tomatoes in the fridge unless you have no choice, and by that I mean if you live somewhere really hot and the ambient room temperature is above 28°C. If this is the case, store tomatoes in the warmest part of your fridge, which is the top drawer for dairy products.

SWIPE THE GOLD DUST ACROSS
THE SHOULDER OF A TOMATO.
IF YOUR FINGER SMELLS SWEET,
THE TOMATO WILL TASTE SWEET TOO.

A staple vegetable in many Asian cuisines, I call water spinach the broccoli of Asia. It goes by various names: kang kung in Malaysia and Indonesia; rau muong in Vietnam; and ong choi (Cantonese) and tong xin cai (Mandarin) in China. The name morning glory also pops up. Water spinach is yet to be embraced in Western food culture, so it's only sold in Asian markets and grocery stores in Australia, where it's invariably sold as one of the above names, depending on where you buy it.

Texturally, water spinach is a delight because it has the best of both worlds: crunchy stems and rich leaves. It is most commonly stir-fried with belacan (fermented shrimp paste) in Malaysia and Indonesia, fermented bean curd in China and fish sauce in Vietnam, where it's also shredded and added to soups. While it's considered 'peasant food' in Vietnam and is grown in the rice paddy fields, its deliciousness means it's loved by all. Growing up, it was one of my favourite vegetable stir-fry dishes to eat with rice. I needed nothing else!

Every year during winter, when locally grown summer water spinach is unavailable, my family business becomes one of Melbourne's largest water spinach distributors. We source it from Queensland and every Monday and Thursday, when the load arrives, my father is the first to open the cartons and check the vegetables' condition, age and stem size. While you may only see decent-looking produce at the store, we see the good, the bad and the ugly. Insects, disease, transport and cold-chain issues and packaging are all common problems, especially as our produce travels 2,500 km from the farm to our distribution facility.

The biggest difference between local and far-travelled water spinach is the stem size. Local water spinach is more likely to be cut and harvested when young, as the vegetable is more tender and suitable for stir-frying. It has a short shelf life, but this is more economical for farmers as they can harvest their crops quicker. Far-travelled water spinach is usually harvested with thicker stems for a longer shelf life that enables the vegetable to travel long distances. Thicker-stemmed shoots are easier to split or shred as a soup vegetable, but the bottom root section tends to be stringy.

Choose

1. Look for firm stems that snap cleanly and easily.

2. Avoid leaves that are yellow, slimy, dehydrated, wilted or curled up.

Store

Place water spinach in a plastic bag or wrap in paper towel to prevent moisture loss, and store in the fridge for up to three days.

Prep

1. Trim any dry roots, then cut the water spinach into 4 cm lengths.

2. Separate the larger stems from any thinner stems with leaves.

3. Cook the larger stems first for about 1 minute, then add the thinner stems and leaves towards the end of cooking. If you throw everything in together, the leaves tend to be overcooked.

4. If eating raw, shred the water spinach and place in a bowl of iced water with a few citrus wedges to give it zest and vibrancy. The colder the water, the more crispy the water spinach will be.

THANH'S TIPS

REGARDLESS OF WHETHER WATER SPINACH STEMS ARE THICK OR THIN, THEY SHOULD ALWAYS SNAP CLEANLY WHEN YOU BREAK THEM.

LARGER STEMS ARE EASIER TO SHRED TO USE AS A GARNISH.

SMALLER STEMS ARE MORE TENDER, PERFECT FOR A STIR-FRY.

This dish is as common in Vietnamese households as a Greek salad is in Greek homes. Mum would cook this dish, along with a meat and soup dish, and serve it with steamed jasmine rice. The trick to cooking this is to make it well balanced and moreish enough to eat on its own, while also being salty and flavourful enough to pair well with the rice. Fermented bean curd can be very salty, depending on the brand, so make sure you season the dish cautiously. The water spinach cooks very quickly, so have all the ingredients ready, including the cornflour slurry. I always set a timer, so I know how long the ingredients have been in the pan or wok, as once the water spinach leaves wilt in the heat, the dish is almost ready.

Once you master this dish, I promise you'll go back for more. Also, if water spinach isn't available in your area, regular baby spinach is fantastic; simply shorten the cooking time as there are no stems. It's worth noting that my parents were born in Vietnam but have Chinese heritage, as my grandparents migrated to Vietnam from China. The fermented bean curd is a Chinese condiment, so there's a mix of cuisines in this dish. In Vietnam, it's common to see fish sauce replace the fermented bean curd; both are delicious, but I think the creaminess of the bean curd adds another layer. Enjoy a piece of my family in your home!

STIR-FRIED WATER SPINACH WITH FERMENTED BEAN CURD

RAU MUỐNG XÀO

SERVES 2

2½ tablespoons vegetable oil
2 garlic cloves, finely chopped
bunch of water spinach (about 250 g), stems and leaves separated, stems cut into 8 cm lengths
2 cubes of fermented bean curd with chilli
1 teaspoon sea salt
1 teaspoon sugar
2 red bullet chillies, diced
1 teaspoon cornflour mixed with 1 tablespoon cold water
steamed jasmine rice, to serve (optional)

Heat the vegetable oil in a wok over high heat, add the garlic and stir-fry for 10 seconds. Add the water spinach stems and cook for 30 seconds, then add the leaves and cook for 1 minute. Add the fermented bean curd, salt, sugar and chilli, and stir vigorously to break up the bean curd. Add the cornflour slurry to the pan and toss vigorously until the sauce is thickened.

Serve immediately with steamed jasmine rice or as part of a Vietnamese meal.

WATERMELON

How good is seeded watermelon? Said no one ever. The last seeded watermelon I cut and ate annoyed me no end, largely because I didn't want my kids to accidentally eat the seeds. That moment re-affirmed to me why seedless watermelons fit our lives so well. In Australia, seeded watermelons only still exist because they are required to pollinate seedless varieties of watermelon.

A well-grown modern watermelon is an absolute crowd-pleaser. It's hydrating, sugary, juicy and moreish. Texturally, it's easy to eat and the absence of seeds allows you to eat more of it than you otherwise might. The only area where watermelon falls down is its inconvenience to process. If it was more convenient to carry and cut, we would probably eat watermelon as often as we do apples and bananas. Have you ever seen pre-cut watermelon in a plastic cup in the ready-to-eat fridge of a convenience store and thought that's a great snack, ignoring the packaging and the fact that it's likely multiple times the price of a whole watermelon? Not many people want to go to the lengths of buying, transporting and cutting a whole watermelon anymore, which is why in Australia the majority of watermelons are sold cut and cling-wrapped, whereas elsewhere in the world, they're still mostly sold whole.

All wrapped up

I spent many of my early days working in the fresh produce team at Coles in Bentleigh, cutting and wrapping watermelon. The hand-wrapping station bench was my weapon of choice to perfectly stretch the plastic wrap to achieve seamless film tension before stamping the watermelon on the hot plate to seal the film. A clear, glossy red pane of watermelon flesh and tightly fused plastic wrap on the bottom skin was the goal. I learned from cheese connoisseurs the Studd siblings that the term for wrapping cheese tightly in plastic wrap to achieve a pristine view of the cheese is called 'glassing', and this is no different to wrapping watermelon.

Every morning I'd rotate the cut watermelon on the shelf, and even though yesterday's watermelon would be fine to eat that day, its shelf life was significantly shortened given it was cut and left at room temperature for 24 hours. While some stores may have less-seasoned team members who don't tightly seal their plastic wrap, you can always tell a watermelon or pumpkin has been wrapped that day by looking at the plastic wrap itself. It will have strong tension and a glass-pane reflective shine, even if it's not properly sealed. Day-old plastic-wrapped fruit is likely to have a little condensation due to the fruit being moved from the fridge back to the shelf. The edges of the watermelon may also start to shrink and come loose.

With seedless watermelon, the empty seed cavities still produce the sugar crystals that develop when the watermelon is mature and ripe. Look for these crystals in cut and plastic-wrapped watermelon!

Did you know that in Australia, seeded watermelons only still exist because they are required to pollinate seedless varieties of watermelon?

SUGAR GRANULES IN THE FALSE SEED ARE A SIGN OF SWEETNESS.

LOOK FOR STRONG PLASTIC WRAP TENSION AND A REFLECTIVE SHINE!

LOOSE PLASTIC WRAP OR CONDENSATION IS A SIGN THE CUT WATERMELON IS A DAY OLD.

Tap, tap, tap

How often have we seen others tap a watermelon at a supermarket and wonder what in the world they are doing? Does it help their selection and, if so, how? Before I became a fruiterer, I thought this was an old myth, largely because not a single person could explain to me why it was helping them select a good watermelon. That is, until I met Matt Russo and Vince Brancatisano at Prestige Produce. Matt has been in the produce industry for decades and has a family who still owns produce farms today. Matt explained to me that the 'tap' produces a sound which can indicate a defect, but it won't necessarily tell you if the watermelon will be sweet. If the fruit is bruised due to being dropped or poor handling, then the bruise will absorb the sound when you tap the watermelon, giving off a flat sound. Cracks inside a watermelon are purely cosmetic, but a crack will also absorb the sound of a tap, so the noise will also be more flat. If the internal flesh of a watermelon is without these two issues, then the sound will be like bouncing a basketball – the thud of your hand will bounce back towards you. A simple, insightful and clear explanation of the myth. Matt, thank you!

Vince explained that the tapping test also determines the density of a watermelon. Vince has sold millions of watermelons in his lifetime, as has his father before him. He used to help his family during school holidays in the 1980s and remembers watermelons being transported on loose trucks filled with hay to prevent bruising in transit. Every watermelon was then moved from the trucks into bins by hand.

Colour and skin

Four decades later, Vince has travelled the world visiting watermelon farms and continuing the family fruit wholesale trade. I asked him to bust a few more myths and he was keen to get the good word out. He first explained to me that there are more varietals of watermelons than people can imagine, in all their own shades of red and yellow. He also shared that watermelons continue to ripen after they are harvested, although they lose their crisp texture in lieu of sugary sweetness, much like mangoes. This means that the colour of the flesh continues to darken. Keeping in mind that all watermelons have different shades of red, I think it's best not to overly rely on the colour, although do avoid excessively light white-pink tones in the flesh. Generally speaking, most of us know that the white area near the rind isn't very sweet.

Shiny or dull-skinned whole watermelons are likely a trait of varietal, rather than an indicator of the fruit's sweetness, and excess webbing and scarring on the skin is simply a marker of growing conditions due to fruit rubbing onto the plant or leaves. White or yellow blotches on the skin can either indicate the spot the watermelon sat on the ground or it can be genuine sunburn. While sunburn spots can be a factor for a slightly sweeter fruit, Vince explains that this spot also rots faster so the shelf life is shorter. Other exciting nerdy insights that only a grower or a wholesaler would know include how the thickness of the rind can determine sweetness and maturity, and how the look of the stem can reflect the maturity of the watermelon at harvest time.

Choose

WHOLE WATERMELON

1. Do the tap test: a dull sound will reveal if the fruit is bruised or has a crack in the flesh; a bouncy sound (like bouncing a basketball) indicates the watermelon is full. It will not reveal if it is sweet.

2. If the stem area is green, then the fruit may have been picked too early. If it is brown, it potentially shows the melon reached late maturity on the vine and was attempting to drop the fruit.

CUT WATERMELON

1. Check the plastic wrap: if it's tight, then the fruit was wrapped that morning; if it's loose, it could be yesterday's cut fruit.

2. Look for sugar granules in the seed and false seed area. This is the easiest way to tell if the watermelon will be sweet or not.

3. All watermelon varieties have different-coloured flesh, so this is not a good indicator of ripeness.

Store

Store whole watermelon in a cool, dry area such as the pantry. A stable temperature will extend the fruit's shelf life. For cut fruit, keep plastic-wrapped pieces in the fridge and only for one to two days.

Thanks

To my 'Ba', Ai Quoc Truong, you are a great fruiterer and I'm the Fruit Nerd I am today because you allowed me to be. I hope I have made you proud. Although you're not the kind to say 'well done', I know you see where I am today and recognise that it is because you worked so hard for me to have the opportunities you didn't when you were younger. I am the storyteller I am today because every time I travel with you and listen as you describe your journey of war, hardship and, finally, a fruitful life in business, I absorb your emotion, truth and adversity.

To my family and the great team at Aus Asia Produce: Tu Le Truong, David Truong, Andy Quach, Long Ngoc To, Lam Phan and Tung Dang. Thank you all for supporting me on this journey. To my three cousins – fruiterers Raymond Chau, Raymond Truong and Roger Chang – thank you for being exceptional fruiterers in different ways and for always having my back whenever I am looking for fruit or needing to know what's happening on the market floor. Having family constantly walking the wholesale market floor is like having eyes over the fruit world, and we are truly fortunate to have each other. It makes waking up every morning at 2.30 am worth it.

To the Melbourne Market community, so many of you have shared your knowledge with me and I can't thank you enough for your generosity. Everyone who has encouraged and contributed to my Fruit Nerd journey has decades of fruit and vegetable industry experience. The collated wisdom would represent centuries of knowledge from across all fields of fresh produce. To all the crop physiologists, horticulturalists, ripeners, quality controllers, transport teams, cold storage teams, researchers, growers and consumers, thank you for sharing your knowledge, not just with me, but with the readers, who will benefit immensely from your experience and insight and become fruit nerds in their own right. Thank you for trusting me to communicate your specialist knowledge. Individually, we all hold small pieces of knowledge that form part of a bigger puzzle, and I am honoured to bring it all together to create a valuable and practical resource for all in this book.

To my Sonya Sun, thank you for supporting me on my crazy, nerdy fruit dream; I couldn't do it without you and wouldn't without your support. Thank you for your patience while I help others have better produce experiences. To my children, Oliver and Rayla Truong, your daily enjoyment and excitement about eating fruit and vegetables gives me so much joy. It is this excitement I see in you two that I hope to bring to others. To my mum, 'Siem', the love in every piece of cut fruit you gave me growing up is contained in this book. I only care so much for every orange segment and jackfruit seed because you showed me how to express love in this way – not only through words, but in actions, such as preparing a perfect plate of fruit. Now Sonya, Oliver and Rayla feel this same love you gave me.

To the Plum and Pan Macmillan team, thank you for taking on the mammoth task of creating a book the likes of which has never been seen before and making it come to life. Mary Small, thank you for taking on this challenge, being excited by our every step and believing we can make a difference. Clare Marshall, thank you for managing the whole book process from start to finish, ensuring its smooth production. Thank you to my manager, Dani Carey, for your sage advice and constant encouragement with every part of this journey.

Designer George Saad, thank you for translating my personality into friendly, approachable, exciting and useful pages. Thanks to editor Lucy Heaver, for ensuring that my sleep-deprived state didn't translate to the words. Photographer Mark Roper, thanks for putting up with my obsessive attention to detail to get the perfect shots ... and get the perfect shots you did! Stylist extraordinaire Kirsten Jenkins, thanks for adding your design flair to the dishes and making the produce shine. Chefs Caroline Griffiths and Claire Pietersen, thank you for helping me bring the recipes to life on the page.

Finally, to all the fruit and vegetables I have ever seen, heard, smelled, touched and tasted, thank you for giving me joy, surprise and delight!

Recipe index

Pan Macmillan acknowledges the Traditional Custodians of Country throughout Australia and their connections to lands, waters and communities. We pay our respect to Elders past and present and extend that respect to all Aboriginal and Torres Strait Islander peoples today. We honour more than sixty thousand years of storytelling, art and culture.

A Plum book
First published in 2023 by
Pan Macmillan Australia Pty Limited
Level 25, 1 Market Street,
Sydney, NSW 2000, Australia

Level 3, 112 Wellington Parade,
East Melbourne, VIC 3002, Australia

Text copyright © Thanh Truong 2023
Photographs Mark Roper copyright © Pan Macmillan 2023
Design George Saad copyright © Pan Macmillan 2023

The moral right of the author has been asserted.

Designed and typeset by George Saad & Brittney Griffiths
Edited by Lucy Heaver
Index by Helena Holmgren
Photography by Mark Roper
Food and prop styling by Kirsten Jenkins
Food preparation by Caroline Griffiths and Claire Pietersen
Colour reproduction by Splitting Image Colour Studio
Printed and bound in China by Imago Printing International Limited

A CIP catalogue record for this book is available from the National Library of Australia.

All rights reserved. No part of this book may be reproduced or transmitted by any person or entity (including Google, Amazon or similar organisations), in any form or means, electronic or mechanical, including photocopying, recording, scanning or by any information storage and retrieval system, without prior permission in writing from the publisher.

10 9 8 7 6 5 4 3 2 1